Lonely Planet

EPIC
ROAD TRIPS
of
EUROPE

Explore Europe's most thrilling driving adventures

CONTENTS

INTRODUCTION 06

SOUTHERN EUROPE 08
Mountain Roads of Mallorca (Spain) 10
A Culinary Circuit of Emilia-Romagna (Italy) 16
Driving Interest in Underrated Albania 22
Sardinia, North to South (Italy) 28
Cruising the Coastal Camino (Spain) 34
Naples and the Amalfi Coast (Italy) 40
The Treasures of Catalonia (Spain) 46
Around the Heel of Italy 52
Cruising Western Crete (Greece) 58
In Pursuit of the Targa Florio, Sicily (Italy) 64

WESTERN EUROPE
The Route Napoléon (France) 72

Joining the Lochs from Glasgow (Scotland) 78
The E-Grand Tour of Switzerland 84
Romancing the Road (Germany) 90
The Windswept Wild Atlantic Way (Ireland) 96
Portugal's National Route 2 102
A Corsican Grand Tour (France) 108
Oxford to Bath Via the Cotswolds (England) 114
A Day on the Belfast Loop (Northern Ireland) 120
Across Orkney in an EV campervan (Scotland) 126
The Name's Pass, Furka Pass (Switzerland) 132
Loire Valley Châteaux (France) 138
Finding Solitude in the Vale of Ewyas (Wales) 144
Rolling Through the Dolomites (Italy) 150
Around the Isle of Man TT Course 156
Southbound in Germany's East 162
Across the Top of Scotland 168

Easy   Harder   Epic

Through the Grapevine: Route des Vins d'Alsace (France) 174
Riding High on the Grossglockner Hochalpenstrasse (Austria) 180
Portugal's Atlantic Coast 186
On the Front Lines in Belgium and France 192
Shore to Summit from Geneva to Zermatt (Switzerland) 198
Top Marks for Britain's Longest Road 204
Along Wales' Coastal Way 210
Lapping the Nürburgring-Nordschleife (Germany) 216

NORTHERN EUROPE
Norway's Lofoten Islands 224
Legendary West Iceland 230
The West Coast of Jutland (Denmark) 236
Getting to Know the Sami (Finland, Norway, Sweden) 242
Kystriksveien, Norway's Coastal Highway 248

The Magic Circle (Iceland) 254
Winding Up on Norway's West Coast 260
Through the Wild Westfjords (Iceland) 266

EASTERN EUROPE
Slovakia's Storied Route 59 274
Croatia's Adriatic Highway 280
Bulgaria's Fortress Route 286
Roving the Baltic: Estonia to Lithuania 292
A Tour of Transylvania (Romania) 298
Montenegro's Canyons and Coastline 304
A Bohemian Beer Loop (Czech Republic) 310

INDEX 316
ACKNOWLEDGMENTS 320

© Nicola Fuerer | Switzerland Tourism

INTRODUCTION

On a misty November morning in 1896, the Emancipation Run departed from central London. A group of 33 early automobiles – flanked by 10,000 cyclists – set out for Brighton on the coast. At that primeval stage in the car's evolution, the 54-mile trip through southern England counted as a genuinely epic one. The run celebrated the passing of the Locomotives on Highways Act, that lifted a blanket 4mph speed limit. Finally acceptance had arrived that 'horseless carriages' be allowed to travel faster than the horses they would soon replace.

No one quite knew what the future held in store for these peculiar, pioneering contraptions. It wasn't even clear if they should run on petrol – many were steam powered, and a few, in a foretaste of technology to establish far later, were electric.

Today we find ourselves in another era of great change. Legislation across Europe in response to the climate crisis is coaxing a transition in cars from the use of fossil fuels and the internal combustion engine to batteries and electric motors.

This book gives fresh inspiration to get out there and explore Europe by road, recognising that sustainable choices are becoming more accessible than ever before. Whoever you are – young or more mature, a solo traveller or with a family to bring along – and whether you have just a weekend or a couple of weeks to spare, you'll find encouragement to revisit the unique freedom a road trip allows. A diverse mix of themes are covered in these pages, from travelling through wondrous landscapes to tasting delicious regional food and drink, and tracing fascinating local culture and history.

In the making of this book, we asked a global group of writers to suggest their favourite road trips in Europe, from which we gathered together the 50 shared here. Among them is Kerry Walker, who picked a route designed to prove just how simple it has become to drive an electric vehicle around Switzerland – which, like Norway, is at the forefront of building a charger infrastructure to support EVs. From the shores of Lake Zürich to the mountain highs of Sattel-Hochstuckli, her drive underlines how our

definition of 'epic' mingles cultured urban exploration with remote adventure, and slow travel with a quest for driving thrills.

Sara van Geloven's story celebrates the fantastic flexibility road tripping in a campervan can bring. Driving up the west coast of Jutland, Denmark, she spent nights parked alongside fjords and sprawling sand dunes, waking to watch surfers and fishers head to sea. Phoebe Smith, meanwhile, tells of driving a campervan – this one an EV – around Orkney, in the company of her baby son.

Anthony Ham describes driving through Arctic Sweden, Norway and Finland, where his car lent him the chance not just to gaze at wilderness landscapes, but to engage with Sami communities.

At times our writers' stories relate the fundamental excitement of driving, especially when a trip swerves a route's most congested seasons for travel. Matt Master tells of tackling the Nürburgring's Nordschleife in Germany, the world's greatest race track – one that any one of us, in any car, can drive at a cost of just a few euros. Henry Catchpole describes heading along Mallorca's glorious dead-end road to Sa Calobra, one he's also covered many times on two wheels. And Lonely Planet's co-founder Tony Wheeler writes about lapping the course of the Targo Florio road race in Sicily – a challenge also once savoured by the earliest motoring pioneers.

HOW TO USE THIS BOOK

The main stories in each regional chapter feature first-hand accounts of inspiring drives in that part of Europe. Each includes a factbox to start the planning of a trip – when is the best time of year, how to get there, where to stay. But beyond that, these stories should spark other ideas. We've started that process with the 'more like this' section following each story, which offers other ideas along a similar theme, not necessarily in the same country. In the contents pages all drives are colour coded according to difficulty, which takes into account not just how long, remote and challenging they are but the logistics and local conditions. The index collects different types of road trip for a variety of interests.

Clockwise from left: up-close access to coastal Denmark in a campervan; driving through the old port of La Maddalena, Sardinia; cruising the shores of Lake Lucerne, Switzerland, on a route ideal for electric vehicles

Opening spread, clockwise from left: switchbacks in the Italian Alps; camping in remote Norway; the Giant's Causeway, Northern Ireland; a tiny classic Fiat 500. Previous pages: Sattel, Switzerland

SOUTHERN EUROPE

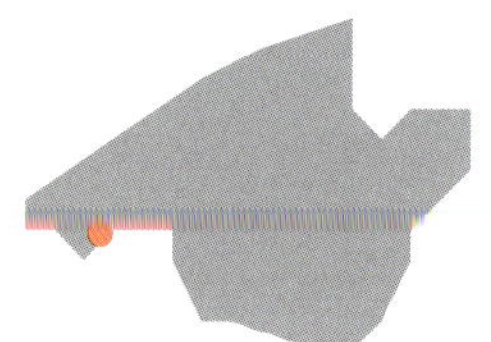

MOUNTAIN ROADS OF MALLORCA

Henry Catchpole savoured the driving challenge on incredible roads across the Balearic island of Mallorca, from the hedonistic southwest to the solitude of the north.

I always feel a twinge of sadness for the contestants on *Love Island*, the popular reality TV show. More or less incarcerated on idyllic Mallorca with no access to transport, no opportunity to get out and explore this marvellous island, they're forced to just sit by a pool, gazing at the distant mountains or along the coast, wondering what's out there.

If they could stage a jailbreak, then I imagine the contestants might take their gym-toned bodies to Magaluf, order a couple of margaritas and enjoy the delights of Nikki Beach. And why not? I'm a fan of contrasts, and the high rises and loud bars are the antithesis of the wild and rugged Unesco World Heritage Site that forms the gorgeous core of this drive. How much more do you appreciate the natural after the artificial? What's more, it seems rather fun to start a journey down in the southwest of the largest Balearic island, with the aim of heading to the most northerly outreach of the same lump of rock.

Perhaps Magaluf is a stretch too far. Maybe start as I did, up the coast in the capital, Palma, instead. I love getting a coffee at Arabay, sipping some speciality bean in this café located in the Old City. Then I wander downhill until I emerge from the maze of ancient streets and find myself squinting up at the overwhelming bulk of the Gothic cathedral. Spread out in front is the azure bay with its super yachts bobbing in the blue.

The road north from Palma is arrow straight for mile after mile across flat countryside. Windows down – roof down if you're lucky – the warm air gets cleaner as urban changes to rural. A lack of corners might sound dull, but there are plenty up ahead and I love the anticipation that builds as the Tramuntana Mountains

morph from a distant, indistinct mass into a collection of sharply defined ridges and peaks.

I'm always afraid I'll miss the turning and plunge into the view-obscuring tunnel on this road, but luckily there's a roundabout just beyond Bunyola to remind me. As the majority of the traffic carries straight on for the tunnel, I turn left and take the old road over the Coll de Sóller. Like dried spaghetti introduced to water, the unbending road suddenly softens and snakes up through 21 switchbacks before descending through 30 more. It's a 6.5 mile (10.5km) up-and-over journey compared to just two miles if you take the tunnel, but the views are rather better. And it's a nice appetiser for what's to come.

Sóller is the place to stock up on supplies and fill up with fuel for the next portion of the journey. I know I should recommend the seafood or the local soupy rice dish, *arroz brut*, but to be honest my tastes are baser. Chocolate-covered ring doughnuts are a must-have. These are not just topped, but fully encased in a hardened layer of cheap chocolate. Fresh from a supermarket are best, but I'm not above a petrol station packet.

Puig Major is the highest point on Mallorca (4741ft/1445m) and it's in that direction the road heads next. There's a real sense of climbing up into the Tramuntana range, and the feeling that you are leaving the rest of the world behind is exacerbated by the

> *"The Tramuntana Mountains morph from a distant, indistinct mass into a collection of sharply defined ridges and peaks"*

rough rock tunnel near the top. A last glance at the view back down to Sóller, then into the dark mouth of the tunnel like Alice entering the rabbit hole.

Emerging into the light again you're surrounded by pale peaks poking through the tree line. Aquamarine reservoirs are trapped in the valleys, suspended between the steep sides like small pools in a sagging, post-rainstorm tarpaulin. Then you reach the arches of an aqueduct. Do not pass under. Not yet. Instead turn left towards Sa Calobra. This dead-end road climbs, passes through a shallow cutting and then drops down through one of the most spectacular sequences of bends on the island. Don't believe me? It begins by circling around 270 degrees and diving back underneath itself. I always pause near here to look over the edge because the artistic way the tarmac falls down the landscape to the sea has the controlled fluidity of a painting by Miró (who lived on Mallorca). In fact, it is the work of an engineer born on the island, but we'll come back to him shortly.

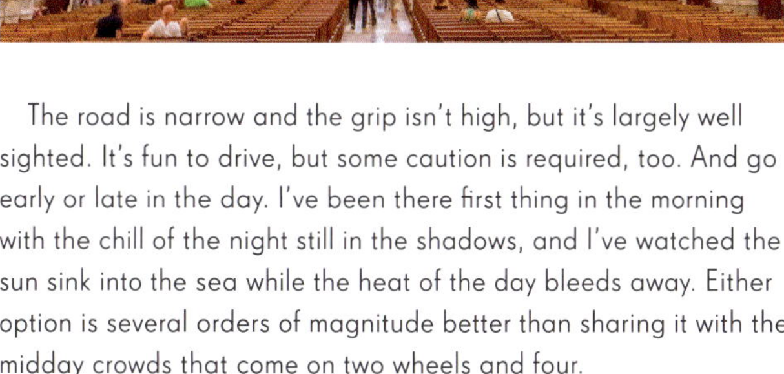

ANTONIO PARIETTI

Antonio Parietti (1899-1978) studied engineering in Madrid but returned to the island of his birth to create his masterpieces. The roads to Cap de Formentor and Sa Calobra were both finished in the early 1930s and were built purely in the interests of tourism. He designed them to have as few tunnels as possible, but nonetheless 31,000 cubic metres of rock were moved to get to Sa Calobra. Incredibly, it was built entirely by hand.

From left: the sinuous road to Sa Calobra; Port de Pollenca; fuel up with doughnuts in Sóller; the Cathedral of Santa Maria of Palma. Previous page: the Cap de Formentor lighthouse

The road is narrow and the grip isn't high, but it's largely well sighted. It's fun to drive, but some caution is required, too. And go early or late in the day. I've been there first thing in the morning with the chill of the night still in the shadows, and I've watched the sun sink into the sea while the heat of the day bleeds away. Either option is several orders of magnitude better than sharing it with the midday crowds that come on two wheels and four.

Back to the top and now you can go under the arches. Thread through the mountains and drop down to pretty Port de Pollença. Like Sa Calobra, the road from here to the Cap de Formentor lighthouse is the work of the man whose statue stands atop the first viewpoint – Antonio Parietti. Ever since I've known about him, I've always driven or cycled this road trying to see the landscape through his eyes. How did he have the vision to perch a road here? Was it purely for the vista that he chose to twist the route this way rather than that?

Beautifully surfaced and poetically picturesque, this coastal cul-de-sac is the equal of Parietti's masterpiece in the mountains. I remember parking up at the end one evening, looking out over cliffs as jagged as the cathedral's facade back in Palma. Then the lighthouse flashed into life – a simpler display but no less impressive than the light shows just starting a world away in the clubs of Magaluf.

DIRECTIONS

Start // Magaluf
End // Cap de Formentor
Distance // 96 miles (155km)

Getting there // Palma de Mallorca airport is the main entry point, with car rental options. If you want to bring your own car from the mainland, there are ferries from Barcelona to Palma.

When to go // Bad weather is a low risk, so the main consideration is the time of day that you drive these roads – they become busy with cyclists in the middle of the day. In recent summers the road to Cap de Formentor has actually been closed to cars between 10am and 7pm.

What to pack // A bicycle – explore the roads by car, then try tackling them under your own steam.

Further information // www.visitpalma.com
www.illesbalears.travel/en/mallorca

Opposite: the high altitude Ötztal Glacier Road, Austria, winds onwards towards the Rettenbach Glacier

MORE LIKE THIS
ROADS TO NOWHERE

PORT DE CABÚS, ANDORRA AND SPAIN

This stunning drive starts among the less than prepossessing architecture of La Massana – but that does at least give you the chance to stock up on some of Andorra's famous duty free shopping. Once out of town, you pass by the famous Vallnord Bikepark and then a huge sculpture by Dennis Oppenheim, *Storm in a Teacup*. It's from here that things get really interesting. The spectacular summit (7552ft/2302m) is inaccessible by car during the winter months, but in summer the precipitous final section of road scribes a thin grey scratch round the middle of a massive grassy bowl. Although the tarmac peters out at the top, right on the Andorra-Spain border, there is in fact a rough, stoney track that continues. This leads down into Spain and is the remnant of a path that was used by smugglers in years gone by. Duty free indeed.

Start // La Massana
End // Port de Cabús
Distance // 11 miles (17km)

LUZ ARDIDEN, FRANCE

This is a road you're only likely to visit after tackling the mighty Col du Tourmalet nearby, but it's well worth the effort. There are two ways up, but you want the one that goes via the small settlements of Sazos and Grust. The first portion of the ascent is lined with trees; the final section scales a dramatic mountain amphitheatre with stunning views across the Hautes-Pyrénées. Despite the remoteness, the road is well surfaced and has a white line down the middle all the way to the top – meaning you don't find yourself anxiously breathing in as you do on some Pyrenean roads. At the top is a ski resort, with all the architectural charm you'd expect of something opened in the mid-1970s. It's eerily silent in the summer and I love it. There's a sense of having snuck into school after hours. Just remember to bring a packed lunch.

Start // Luz-Saint-Sauveur
End // Luz Ardiden
Distance // 9 miles (15km)

ÖTZTAL GLACIER ROAD, AUSTRIA

A sign at the top of Ötztal Glacier Road says 'Highest road in the EU'. It's a claim Spain's Pico de Veleta road might contest, but technically that's only open to the public up to about 8200ft (2500m), so I think the Ötztal Glacier Road, at 9186ft (2800m), has a valid claim. The road was built in 1972 and is actually a toll road, so you'll need to show a lift pass or cough up €20.50. It's worth it though, as the views will take your breath away as surely as the altitude does. As the name suggests, it gives access from the Ötztal Valley to the Rettenbach Glacier, used for skiing, and there's also a road tunnel (definitely the highest in Europe) through to a second glacier, the Tiefenbach. James Bond found himself in these mountains in the film *Spectre* and you can access a 007 cinematic installation via a cable car from Sölden.

Start // Sölden
End // Rettenbach Glacier
Distance // 10 miles (16km)

A CULINARY CIRCUIT OF EMILIA-ROMAGNA

Following an ancient Roman road, Gabrielle Jaffe discovered how some of Italy's tastiest exports are made, from Parma ham and Parmesan to balsamic vinegar and olive oil.

There are generally two draws for travellers to the region of Emilia-Romagna: fast cars and slow food. Ferraris, Maseratis and Lamborghinis are all made locally – and there's an undeniable thrill in watching these sleek beauties drive by – but I'm here for the cuisine.

This northern region of Italy has known agricultural abundance since ancient times. The Roman Empire might have been forged through the sword, but its armies were fed from Emilia-Romagna's fields. And the road the Romans built through here, the Via Emilia, still connects a string of places today – Parma, Modena, Bologna – whose names represent some of the world's most sought-after foods.

I begin in Parma. From its ornately frescoed medieval cathedral to the sharply dressed locals, this city takes great care in its appearance. But perhaps the most elegant displays are in the delis, where Parma hams are hung as meticulously as the contents of an Armani store. At each cellar I visit, the air smells sweet with curing sugars of the meat, aged between 400 days and three years. 'The secret to good Italian food is taking your time,' a shopkeeper tells me.

I try *culatello*, a local cured meat, more highly prized than Parma ham, which sells for €130 a kilo. The name literally means 'little arse' because the cut comes from the pig's back leg. It's lesser known outside Italy, perhaps because of the unfortunate name, perhaps because it doesn't travel as well as Parma ham. Either way, it melts on the tongue with a sweetness that deserves greater recognition.

Leaving Parma, the Via Emilia – or rather its modern incarnation, Highway SS9 – is ruler straight. I share the road with Lycra-clad cyclists as well as sports cars, the flat-as-a-pancake terrain making for an easy ride for both. Fields filled with haystacks towering like castles attest to how fertile the countryside is.

It's only in this land of plenty that you could produce Parmesan. Each wheel of cheese is around 88lb (40kg). One hundred cows are needed to produce enough milk for just six wheels. I get a chance to see how these wonders are made at Fattoria Marchesini, a farm shop-B&B in Reggio Emilia. Milk, heated in copper vats, gives the room a comforting, rice pudding-like scent. Next door in the maturation room the finished cheese wheels are left to harden. Security cameras show how valuable they are, so valuable in fact that banks here take them as deposits. I sample the precious wares and buy a slab that's been aged for three years, its crumbly, umami-rich flavour lingering on my tongue as I drive to Modena, my next stop.

I park and wander the pedestrianised, cobblestone streets radiating out from the city's 12th-century, Unesco-listed cathedral, with its fairy-tale tower. But I'm here to worship at the city's temples to good food. Osteria Francescana, founded by Modena-born chef Massimo Bottura, is pick of the bunch, a three Michelin-starred restaurant that regularly tops the World's Best list. It gets booked up months in advance though, and I haven't been organised enough to nab a table here or at Bottura's more casual, less expensive Franceschetta58. Luckily, restaurant terraces occupy almost every street in central Modena and the locals seem to be on one long lunch break. I join them and eat incredibly well at Hosteria Giusti, a small-menu bistro hidden behind one of the oldest salami shops in Europe, and Gelateria Bloom, where the all-natural, seasonal ice creams range in flavour from traditional hazelnut to chocolate with thyme.

Before Bottura, Modena was already on the culinary map thanks to its speciality, balsamic vinegar. Pulling up at Antica Acetaia Villa Bianca, a gated estate ten minutes from the city centre, I'm surrounded by wooden pergolas weighed down with plump green Trebbiano grapes. Inside the white mansion, owner Emilio Biancardi shows me how grape must is fermented into vinegar. The evaporating liquid is decanted into smaller and smaller wooden casks every 12 months. After 25 years, 90% of the original volume has disappeared. What's left behind is sweet, tangy, syrup-thick, and a million miles from the supermarket-bought vinegars in my home cupboard.

PERFECT PORKER

To be officially recognized as Parma ham, prosciutto must be made from Large White, Landrace or Duroc pigs. These breeds were introduced after WWII, quickly becoming popular as they grow faster and bigger than local black pigs such as Nero di Parma. But some farmers are now crafting prosciutto from the former heritage breeds, claiming the meat is more flavoursome and closer to how local hams used to taste.

Clockwise from below: the Ghirlandina Tower rises above Modena; stalls on Via Pescherie Vecchie in the Quadrilatero, Bologna; tagliatelle al ragù. Previous page: vineyards line the hills of Castelvetro di Modena

© Francesco Riccardo Iacomino | Getty Images

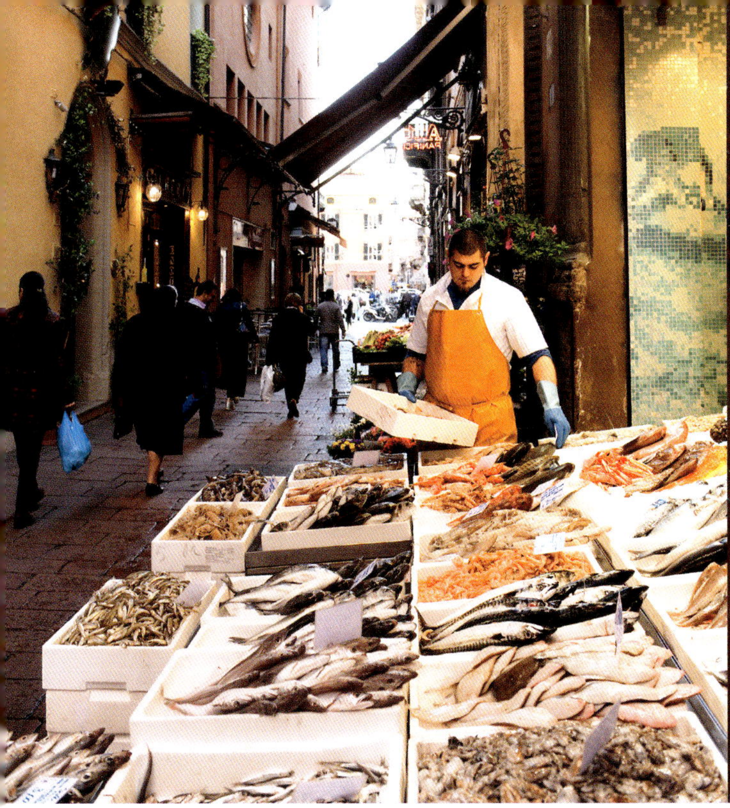

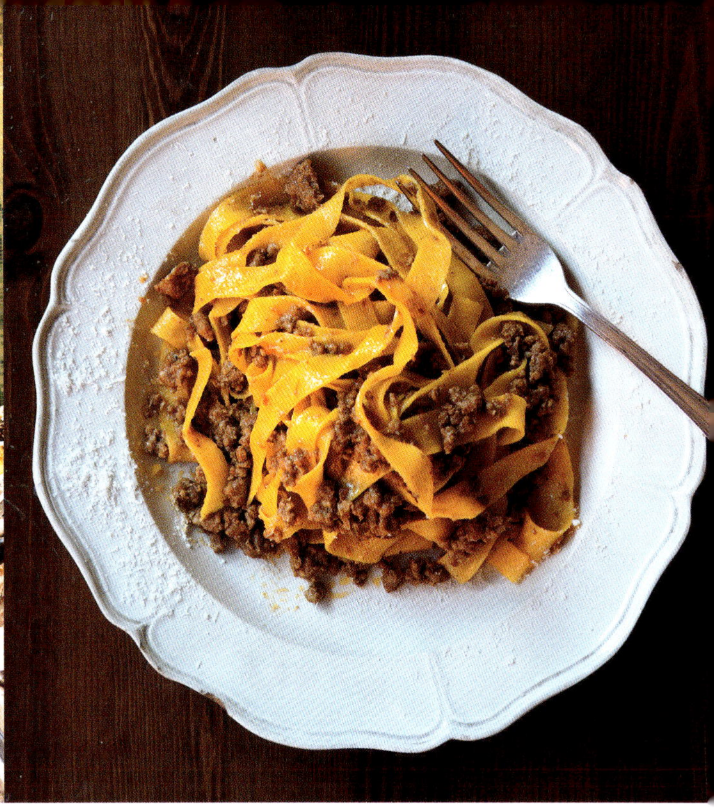

If there's one Italian dish we all think we know, it's spaghetti Bolognese. In its birthplace, Bologna – where the sauce is called *ragù* and it's served with tagliatelle pasta rather than spaghetti – I see how seriously the locals take cooking. As I amble among the market stalls of the Quadrilatero district, watching them inspect the produce is a masterclass in the importance of quality ingredients.

My market visit whets my appetite for a pasta lesson with a local in her own home, booked through Cesarine.com. We make ricotta and spinach tortellini, as plump as down pillows, as well as tagliatelle ladled with a real Bolognese *ragù*. Later, I work off my food stupor by climbing the 498 steps of Bologna's 12th-century Asinelli Tower.

Bologna is a dividing marker, between the culinary culture of Emilia to the west – built on pigs, cows and the Celtic traditions of northern Italy – and that of Romagna, which shares more in common with the sheep, goat and olive-based agriculture of southern Italy. I end my road trip in the latter, detouring from the Via Emilia to Brisighella, a medieval village southeast of Bologna. The route there grows hillier and is flanked by fields covered with vines and fruit orchards. Gnarled olive trees guard the hills beside Brisighella. From afar I spy the turrets of its 13th-century castle – the gypsum-veined rock it's built on glints like a natural beacon. At Terra di Brisighella, the local olive oil collective's shop, I learn that this rock is the secret behind their success. Olive trees shouldn't be able to flourish this far north but gypsum in the rock absorbs heat from the sun, providing vital warmth. The oil tastes like a distillation of all this Italian sunshine and I purchase a bottle. For now my suitcase – and my stomach – has reached its limit of culinary goodies. But I'll be back to explore more.

DIRECTIONS

Start // Parma

End // Brisighella

Distance // 99 miles (159km)

Getting there // Parma and Bologna have direct flights to various European destinations. Both are also connected by train to several cities in Italy.

When to go // Summer can be hot and humid and in August many restaurants close as locals escape to the coast. May/June and September/October are more pleasant weather-wise and are when many local food festivals are held. Time your visit for October and join the Sunday truffle fairs in Sant'Agata Feltria, a 90-minute drive south of Brisighella.

Where to stay // Some of the most atmospheric places to stay are agriturismo farm stays and restaurants with rooms in the countryside.

Further information // emiliaromagnaturismo.com

Opposite, clockwise from top: cypress trees mark a route through the hills south of Florence; 'Ananascosta' pizza, served at Pepe in Grani, Caiazzo; Arborio rice

MORE LIKE THIS
ITALY FOR FOOD LOVERS

TASTY TOUR OF TUSCANY

From bold reds to the meaty dishes they're paired with, Tuscan gastronomy can be as rich as the region's famous art. Begin this indulgent food crawl in capital Florence with *bistecca alla Fiorentina* – T-bone steak made from Chianina, a prized ancient breed. Then, if here in late autumn, head to San Miniato to hunt for white truffles or, at any time of year, sample pork from Cinta Senese, pigs reared locally since Etruscan times. Arrive in Bolgheri via the impressive Viale dei Cipressi – three miles of road lined with cypress trees that make a suitably grand entrance to the home of 'Super Tuscan' wines. Stay a while, not just for the excellent wine bars, but also to unwind at the nearby beaches, before finishing in Massa Marittima, a hilltop town whose atmospheric restaurants serve local specialties including wild boar stew.

Start // Florence
End // Massa Marittima
Distance // 124 miles (200km)

MILAN & THE RICE REGION

Beginning in Milan, try local specialities prepared *alla milanese*: veal; minestrone; risotto. Traditionally, the latter is made with beef marrow and gets its golden hue from saffron. As you drive southwest of the city, you'll see where the risotto's star ingredient comes from – the flooded paddies of the Lomellina area. Visit Vigevano (with its Renaissance town square), Mortara (with its frescoed 14th-century church) and Lomello (with its early Romanesque basilica) for their take on risotto and other Lomellina delicacies such as goose salami. Circle back via historic Pavia, where the cathedral was partly designed by Leonardo da Vinci and specialities include chicken soup with poached eggs and *torta paradiso*, a heavenly sponge cake often served with cream. On the way back to Milan, don't miss Certosa di Pavia, an ornate 14th-century monastery, still home to Cistercian monks and impressive artworks.

Start // Milan
End // Milan
Distance // 99 miles (159km)

ROME TO NAPLES

Rome and Naples bookend this backroads drive on which you can sample *la cucina povera* ('food of the poor'), some of Italy's tastiest. Start in Rome's working class Testaccio district, at Flavio al Velavevodetto, where simple dishes such as *cacio e pepe* (pasta with black pepper and pecorino cheese) are prepared to perfection. Leaving the capital, journey east past olive groves and vineyards and stop at Olevano Romano to join day-tripping Romans who come for the views and classics such as fried artichokes at Sora Marie e Arcangelo restaurant. There's more soul-stirring food and panoramas at Picinisco and Vairano Patenora (don't miss the ricotta ravioli at La Locanda di Arturo and grilled lamb at Sapori Miei). Between these hilltop towns take the detour to the Baroque Abbey of Montecassino. Grab a table at Pepe in Grani in Caiazzo for Italy's most celebrated pizza, before continuing to Naples to try its hole-in-the-wall versions.

Start // Rome
End // Naples
Distance // 205 miles (330km)

DRIVING INTEREST IN UNDERRATED ALBANIA

Putting the case for Albania as Europe's most underappreciated country, Oliver Smith took a beautiful, comprehensive top-to-tail road trip through the Adriatic nation's many delights.

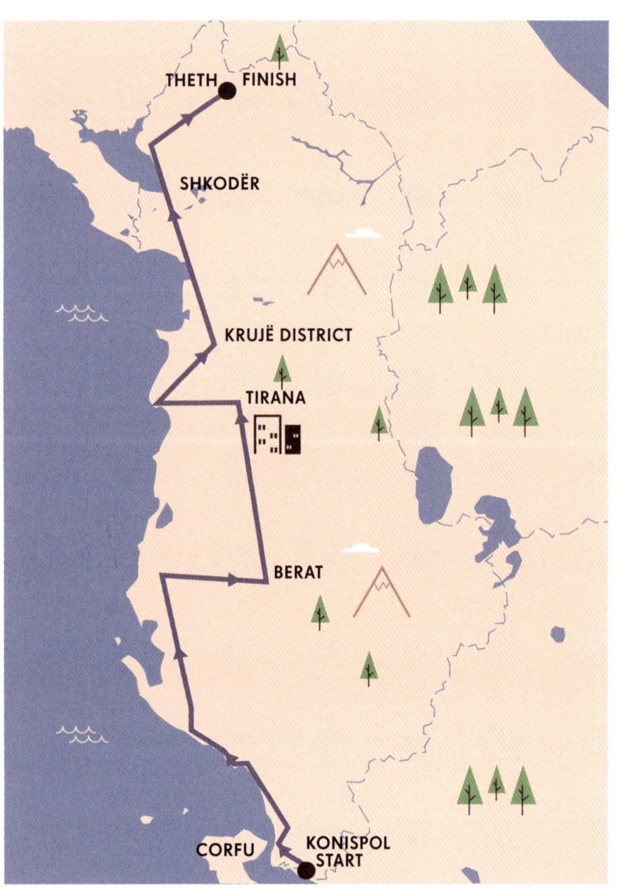

The Adriatic's coastline is hallowed ground for travellers. Come summer, thousands set sail for the archipelagos of Croatia, fill up the squares of Venice and relax on Corfu's sands. In the middle of all this action, though, is a nation featured in few holiday brochures, whose beaches and ruins are still miraculously unstomped by visitors – Albania. A road trip might seem adventurous but this wildly beautiful country rewards with eye-drawing karst mountains, proud Ottoman towns, empty coves and encounters with locals who are defined by their generosity and warmth.

My drive starts just across the border from Greece, from where it's a short drive to Butrint, an ancient city triumphantly sited on a wooded peninsula beside a lagoon. Shadowed by oak and ash are stones laid by Greek, Roman and Byzantine masons who toiled here centuries ago – something to ponder while lounging on the beach at Ksamil, a 10-minute drive away.

North of Ksamil stretches the Albanian Riviera, the road sometimes swerving with lethal abandon along the coastal cliffs. It's worth interjecting to say that Albania suffers from one of the continent's worst road safety records – the roadsides are strewn with stone memorials to deceased motorists and I notice more than one memorial which had, in grim irony, gone on to suffer a collision itself. If you dare take eyes away from the traffic, you might see tumbledown castles crowning the hilltops, Orthodox monasteries watching over the tides, ethnic Greek villages like Himara and, most exciting of all, a mysterious nuclear bunker that dates to the Cold War.

Brinkmanship and mutually assured destruction are relevant concepts when I drive the Llogara Pass – the grand finale to the

Riviera, where the road zigzags up a near vertical slope and traffic bundles down in the opposite direction. Thereafter, a much more composed day's driving leads through verdant valleys to historic Berat, a town that survived the sledgehammer upheavals of Albania's communist era. The night I arrive it's raining heavily. The cobbled alleys turn to temporary cascades. And the rain drums on the dome of an empty Ottoman mosque whose caretaker lets me in with a weighty iron key. That night I eat lamb kebabs and sink a cup of rich Turkish coffee. Here, and in other places in Albania, you often feel closer to the Bosphorus than the Adriatic.

Berat feels equally far from Tirana. Approached on traffic-clogged highways from the south, the Albanian capital is a brutalist place, with tower blocks stacked in neat grids. It is, however, the best spot to measure the heartbeat of the nation and get to grips with its recent past. The murals of Skanderbeg Square give a flavour of communist years, when Albania was a pariah state at loggerheads with the West, the Eastern Bloc, Yugoslavia, and pretty much everyone else after a feud with its only ally, China. Stranger still is the Pyramid, an edifice rumoured to have been built as the mausoleum for former dictator Enver Hoxha, the eccentric leader who turned Albania into the world's first atheist state, banned beards, executed his ministers

and had a penchant for British comedian Norman Wisdom.

The wisest course of action after a day or two in Tirana is to head back to the Adriatic. I detour along a multi-lane highway to Durrës. A salty port with ferry connections to Italy, the city offers wide sandy beaches backed by pizzerias and cafés. It has a deeper kinship to the Italian peninsula, too – there's a stout Venetian tower and a Roman amphitheatre where I spend happy hours watching stray cats sunbathing where gladiators once fought in bloody combat.

It goes without saying that Albania is a country caught in cultural crosscurrents – a home to both Muslims and Christians, sandwiched between the Slavic, Romance and Hellenic worlds, coveted at different times by the generals of Rome, Istanbul, Sarajevo and Athens. The unifying figure at the heart of Albanian identity is Skanderbeg – a 15th-century lord who fought off the Ottoman Empire and whose near-mythical castle rises at Kruja, a short drive north of Durrës. I stop to scale its hulking towers, atop which the double-headed eagle of the Albanian flag ripples in the sea breeze. Half the nation seems to fall away beneath the battlements.

From here the coastal plain unravels northward in the direction of Lake Shkodra, an inland sea which marks Albania's northern border with Montenegro. Shkodra's shore makes a fine place to recuperate

BUNKER BUNKER PARTIES

Scattered around Albania are an estimated 750,000 concrete pillboxes erected on the orders of despot Enver Hoxha, who was terrified his country would be invaded by foreign enemies. The classic joke goes that there are more bunkers than there were guns or soldiers to fire them. Since the end of communism, they have proved too robust to remove meaning you can make long car journeys more lively with a game of 'spot the bunker'.

Clockwise from left: skirting lakes in Butrint National Park; the historic city of Berat; a 6th century CE mosaic in the Butrint Baptistery. Previous page: descending from the Qafae Pëjes pass towards Theth

after weeks on the road. I spend a lazy morning swimming in the reedy shallows, an afternoon dozing in a lakeside hammock while fish plop nearby, and an evening listening to the call to prayer while the sun infuses the waters with gilded light.

Shkodra would offer a fitting end to an Albanian road trip were it not for the lure of the Accursed Mountains – the highest peaks in the Balkan Peninsula, whose glowering summits rise where Albania, Kosovo and Montenegro meet. Many travellers visit the mountains by bus, owing to the terrifying road from Shkodra that switchbacks to the mountain village of Theth. If you're at peace with your creator (and with your insurer) you can go it alone in your own car – contouring up above the shadowy forests, driving higher than soaring eagles as the car crests the alpine passes and your ears go pop.

Theth itself has become a popular hiking hub, but the surrounding countryside offers a rustic vision of bygone Europe – rickety farmsteads, meadows full of butterflies, trails trodden by shepherds and their flocks – all enclosed by a circle of karst mountains. It was only in the 20th century that roads of any kind reached this hidden nook of the continent, and only in recent times that solid tarmac has started to make its approach towards Theth over the passes. For now, at least, there could be no better place to reach the end of my road.

DIRECTIONS

Start // Butrint
End // Theth
Distance // 360 miles (580km)

Getting there // The nearest international airport to Butrint is Corfu – regular car-carrying ferries link the Greek island to the Albanian port of Saranda. If you're renting a car in Greece, be sure to check that the company covers driving in Albania. Alternatively, Tirana airport is the main international hub within Albania and has car rental options aplenty: it's centrally poised for the drive south to start this drive.

When to go // Albania can be visited year round. Note that the Accursed Mountains can be cut off during winter snows.

Where to stay // Lake Shkodra Resort makes for an excellent finishing line near Shkodra. Look out for various homestays in the storied Ottoman mansions of Berat.

Driving Interest in Underrated Albania

MORE LIKE THIS
ROAD TRIPS ALONG THE ADRIATIC

A CIRCUIT OF ISTRIA, CROATIA

Istria may officially be part of Croatia but a rich cultural and linguistic stew simmers on this sun-blessed peninsula. A road trip promises a slice of La Dolce Vita, with ethnic Italian communities resident along its coastal towns. The prettiest town is Rovinj, where the tower of St Euphemia's Church is a dead ringer for the bell tower in St Mark's Square, Venice. Continue south along the shore, beside blue bays shaded by Aleppo pines, and you'll soon reach Pula, whose landmark is a Roman amphitheatre where you can channel Russell Crowe. The town is also a gateway to the archipelago of the Brijuni National Park. Trace Istria's east coast to the port of Rijeka before veering inland to return to your starting point at Rovinj, passing wooded countryside and picturesque hilltop towns like Buzet and Motovun.

Start // Rovinj
End // Rovinj
Distance // 186 miles (300km)

VENICE TO RIMINI, ITALY

Venice justifiably hogs the limelight on the Italian Adriatic, but drive south and you'll find other serene and stately towns. Beyond the lagoons and marshes of the Veneto lies Ravenna, a powerful city long before Venice ruled the waves. Once a capital of the Western Roman Empire, it later became a Byzantine foothold in Italy – the golden mosaics in the Basilica di San Vitale count as a shining pinnacle of art in Europe's Dark Ages. Continue south to the spirited resort of Rimini, the sometime home of Federico Fellini, set on a vast, suitably cinematic swathe of sand. Returning to Venice via an inland route, you can tick off more of Italy's cultural titans. The gastronomic capital of Bologna beckons along the arrow-straight Roman road from Rimini, followed by the fortress at Ferrara and the venerable university town of Padua, Venice's neighbour.

Start // Venice
End // Venice
Distance // 298 miles (480km)

TRIESTE TO PIRAN, ITALY & SLOVENIA

Once the seaport of the Austro-Hungarian Empire, undervalued Trieste sits in Italy's northeastern corner, enclosed almost wholly by Slovenia. Its appeal lies in wandering grandiose boulevards, riding clattering trams and exploring the dreamlike Miramare Castle nearby – but it's also the starting point for a scenic jaunt south along the Slovenian Riviera. The first stop is Muggia, an affable Italian fishing village capped by a 14th-century castle. Over the border, the Slovenian port of Koper initially seems unappealing, but beyond the container ships you'll find a labyrinthine centre graced by elegant Venetian architecture. Pushing further south still, passing forested headlands and pebbly beaches, Slovenia's tiny shoreline offers a showstopping finale in Piran, a heartbreakingly beautiful town set on a spit of land.

Start // Trieste
End // Piran
Distance // 31 miles (50km)

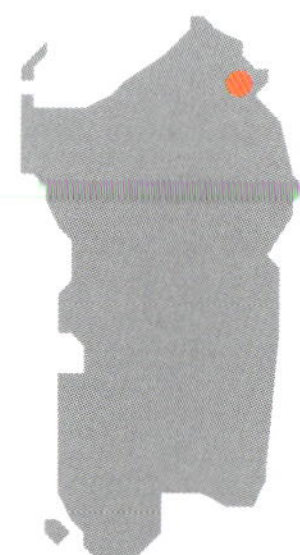

SARDINIA, NORTH TO SOUTH

A top-to-bottom trip across Sardinia – taking in jet-set haunts, mountain villages and Neolithic ruins along the way – helped Alexis Averbuck fall in love with this Mediterranean island.

Sardinia captures all that I'm so drawn to about island travel: rich local cultures; deep (and, in this case, mysterious) history; glorious terrain; and beaches that live on in my mind long after I've left them. I love islands, but it was not until later in life that I came across this great beauty.

From Olbia, a thriving town on the northeast coast, I've twice traversed the length of Sardinia, zigzagging from wonder to wonder until reaching Cagliari, the capital, in the south, with its handsome architecture and spirited cultural life.

One of the reasons Olbia makes such a good place to start an island road trip is its proximity to the famed Costa Smeralda. The road tracing the 'Emerald Coast' follows promontories abutting eye-popping turquoise bays. Linger on the white sands, wade out into the water and you'll soon understand what attracted the likes of the Agha Khan and other high rollers here in the 1960s.

Where the road curves across the northern coast, I depart the luxury of Costa Smeralda's seafront mansions and head for small-scale port towns like Palau and Santa Teresa Gallura.

From Palau, a quick ferry hop brings me to the windswept islets in the Arcipelago di La Maddalena. It's easy to take a small boat to a hidden cove here, but I simply continue the drive along narrow tracks to the home of Italian unification hero Giuseppe Garibaldi, on tiny Isola Caprera. As I push further into the forested island, wild mouflon play hide-and-seek on stone outcroppings and wild boar forage in the woods.

Back on Sardinia proper, Santa Teresa Gallura is a sherbet-coloured grid of summer houses, close to craggy Capo Testa where simple trails allow for exploration of enormous wind-created stone sculptures while waves pound the shore below.

As I follow the route inland from there, wild lavender lines the roadside and the aromatic scent of mountain thyme wafts in through the window. I pass Bronze Age settlements with their mighty towered *nuraghe* or *tombe dei giganti* (giants' tombs) – megalithic mass

graves sealed off by stone stele that are best seen on foot. Each village I encounter has its own long history, as well as local crafts, food and traditions. Here on my earlier road trip, driving through the

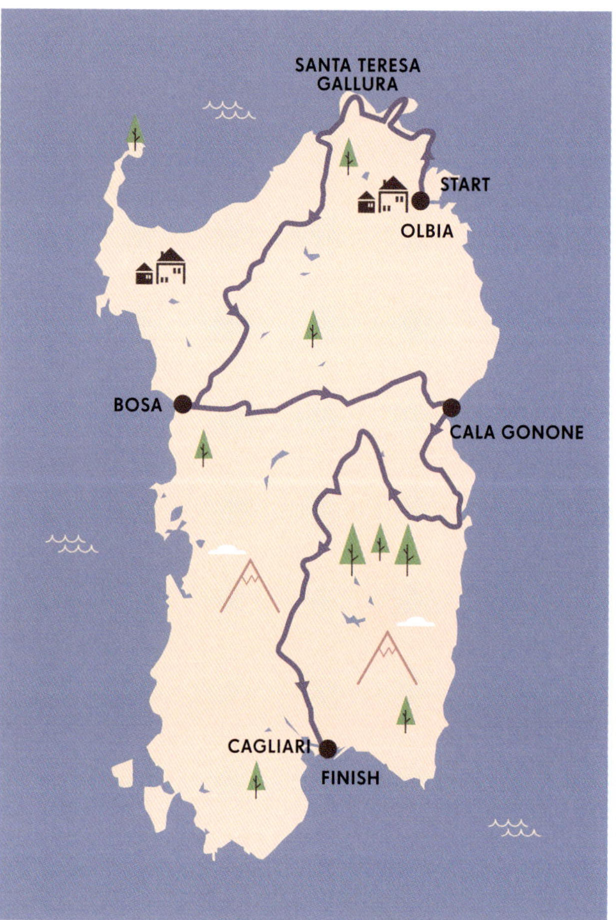

high plains with my sister, we had visited the home of a local tapestry artist who walked with us to houses where she and other women operate enormous hand looms, creating kaleidoscopic carpets of ruby-red, coal-black, terracotta and myriad other colours.

I now dart back across the island, climbing past deep gorges at Valle di Lanaittu and its many hiking trails, to Cala Gonone and the vast cliff-rimmed shores of the Golfo di Orosei. There, you can boat to distant beaches backed by sheer escarpments and striated formations not accessible from the road, and then, back in the car, take on one of Sardinia's most extravagantly scenic and famous sections of road: the SS125.

This two-lane spiral of tarmac hugs cliff edges and offers alternating glimpses of shining blue seas and deep chasms and gorges. As it twists, motorcyclists who have travelled from all around the world to drive this stretch, rocket past. I stop at the main café on the road for a deep breath, a coffee and a small badge to affix to my gear, showing that I, too, have driven this famed strip.

Time comes to head inland again, to the mythic Monti del Gennargentu and the storied town of Mamoiada. The Barbagia mountainous area of eastern Sardinia is rough and rocky terrain, with hidden valleys opening up to stark, mist-wreathed mountains, each the historic domain of a particular village. This is the land of clan warfare and hard-scrabble survival, continued over centuries – the painted town of Orgosolo displays elaborate graffiti on almost every building, telling tales of the vendettas and fiery politics of the ages.

I reach Mamoiada's small but intriguing museum, which focuses on the culture and rituals of the local masked dancers here. During

FOOD AND LONGEVITY

Sardinia is a famous 'Blue Zone', with a preponderance of centenarians and long-lived people. What's their secret? Family and friends, lots of walking, a nip of red wine and keeping their speciality suckling pig, or *porcheddu*, for special occasions. Sardinians frequently drink goat's milk and eat sheep's milk *pecorino* cheese made locally, but focus their diet on whole grains and the rich local vegetables and fruits you will see grown all along this drive.

Clockwise from above: the lighthouse at Capo Testa, Santa Teresa Gallura; a dish of spaghetti alle vongole (clams are widely farmed in Sardinia); La Maddalena. Previous page: the Temo river winds through the town of Bosa

the annual carnival, throughout the village and region, men wearing shaggy animal hides and masks chase a 'scapegoat' in dance through the streets, the craggy features of their intimidating face coverings mimicking something in the rocky landscape – foreboding and fortitude alike.

One night, I stay in a high mountain inn, surrounded by low shrubs, the tinkle of goat bells sounding as the evening mist rolls in. The lady of the house, a farmer who has worked the land for generations, teaches me how to make *fregola* pasta by hand. We gently roll and work the dough into even, miniscule balls for the delicious meal to come, which includes cheese made from her own goats' milk. I sit with her husband as she serves us both, and we eke out a pidgin conversation, using hand gestures and Italian to bridge the local Sardinian dialect. Each area of the island has its own dialect of Sardo, Sardinia's first language, depending on who occupied it – the Spanish, the Venetians, the Genoese – though the original inhabitants and their language, the Bronze Age settlers now known as the Nuragic civilisation, are still a largely mysterious people, having left no written records.

I descend from the mountains to the Unesco World Heritage Site of Nuraghe Su Nuraxi, a tower of black stone surrounded by the ruins of an encampment of huts. The size of the boulders in the structure are like enormous black molars, stacked one upon the next to create this powerful fortress that has lasted since around 1500 BCE.

My route drops further, through pastureland and fields to a modern highway – a reality jolt after my detour from life as we know it in the 21st century. I motor on into Cagliari and its ornate walled Castello neighbourhood, set on a hilltop overlooking the harbour. Climbing narrow lanes, I stop at a restaurant that serves delicacies from all over this special island – a culinary reflection of Sardinia's diversity and bounty.

"Wild lavender lines the roadside and the aromatic scent of mountain thyme wafts in through the window"

DIRECTIONS

Start // Olbia
End // Cagliari
Distance // 435 miles (700km)
Getting there // There are international airports in both Olbia and Cagliari, meaning that this drive can be done in either direction or as a loop.
Car rental // Most rental outfits, whether local companies or the international chains, will allow for one-way rentals, especially if you arrange this in advance.
When to go // The spring and autumn shoulder seasons (April/May and September/October) are best for weather and to avoid summer crowds.
Tip // While many people on the island can speak a smattering of English, the more rural you get the more useful some basic Italian phrases will be. Plus, it's nice to show you're trying.

MORE LIKE THIS
COASTAL CULTURE

BRITTANY, FRANCE

Bretagne, or Brittany to anglophones, offers
an embarrassment of riches, from ancient
stone monuments to wonderful food and
drink. Picking up a car in Rennes is the easy
way to drive this loop, following the coast
from the charming walled town of Vannes
– which tumbles down a hill to its harbour
on the Golfe du Morbihan – to Carnac
and the world's greatest concentration of
megalithic sites, dating to between 5000
and 3500 BCE. Continue to the far reaches
of the Finistère region near Crozon,
sampling crepes, buckwheat *galettes*
and local seafood as you go. Make sure
to indulge in copious amounts of *kouign
amann* – butter-laden sweet pastries. In
fact, butter is a Breton speciality, so wrap
up your road trip in gorgeous St-Malo,
where some local restaurants even offer
tasting menus of the butters of the region.
Start // **Rennes**
End // **St-Malo**
Distance // **345 miles (555km)**

SNÆFELLSNES PENINSULA, ICELAND

A jewel box of volcanoes, whale-watching
and seafood chowders, this ravishing spur
of land juts out into the Atlantic on Iceland's
western shore and brings together all you
could want from this remarkable island
nation. The drive starts in Stykkishólmur, a
small human incursion into all the natural
splendour, which offers flavoursome cuisine
at local beer houses and restaurants. From
here it's a wonderland of coastal hamlets
interspersed between lava fields and settings
from the legendary Icelandic Sagas until
your road trip is crowned by the majestic
Snæfellsjökull National Park. Set around
an eponymous glacier, the area was given
a starring role in Jules Verne's *Journey to
the Centre of the Earth*. Take a break from
driving and organise a guide to take you up
the glacier slopes. The peninsula's southern
coast is dotted with horse-riding facilities and
hot springs – ideal for a gentle trot along
broad beaches followed by a hot soak before
your day, and drive, is through.
Start // **Stykkishólmur**
End // **Vegamót**
Distance // **103 miles (165km)**

TINOS, GREECE

A Greek island dream, gentle Tinos rises
from the sea with hillsides leading to central
valleys, terraced by the agriculture which
provides its hallmark local cuisine. Between
sampling delicious artichokes, cheeses and
sausages, you can tour tiny villages that
display the results of a long history of marble
quarrying and carving here. You'll leave
from the main village, Hora, which is home
to the Church of Panagia Evangelistria – its
healing icon has made it a pilgrimage site
for Greek Orthodox believers the world over.
As you meander out of town, head north
to Volax for its peculiar granite boulders
and Tarambados where you'll find paths
to unusual dovecotes in the fields. Famous
Greek sculptor Yannoulis Chalepas was from
Pyrgos, in the island's northwest interior,
which is also home to a small museum on
the marble history of the island. From there,
descend to Panormos, a windswept bay with
seafood tavernas, perfect for lunch after a
swim at its beautiful beach.
Start // **Hora**
End // **Panormos**
Distance // **25 miles (40km)**

CRUISING THE COASTAL CAMINO

Orla Thomas rode a route traditionally taken by those seeking religious enlightenment, Spain's northerly Camino de Santiago, with pit stops for tapas, beaches and historic hotels.

Christians devote weeks to walking the various iterations of the Camino de Santiago. Choosing the Northern Way, they cross 'Green Spain' wearing sturdy boots and lugging backpacks. Spend time in the region and you might spot an exhausted *peregrino* having a rest in a field or a roadside picnic. All are united in their goal — to reach the tomb of St James in the city of Santiago de Compostela.

However, those lacking spiritual motivation and/or a generous annual leave entitlement might like to follow my lead and cheat, as the Camino del Norte suits road-trippers equally well. Beginning in the Basque resort town of San Sebastián, the route skirts the Cantabrian and Asturian coastlines before arriving in the Galician capital. Covering around 500 miles (800km), this is a drive to savour, so plan on overnight stops, and lazy, tasty meals that make a mockery of a sandwich stuffed down in transit.

There's no better place for food than San Sebastián. Driving my rental car into town, the windscreen frames the Bay of Biscay and the surrounding hills, hyper-green, even in summer. These fertile lands have helped garner the city a dazzling 18 Michelin stars — more per square metre even than Paris — which attract gastronomic pilgrims to sample not only its world-class restaurants but also its take on tapas, *pintxos*.

The Basque word for 'spike', in its simplest form a *pintxo* is a single portion of food speared onto a piece of bread. The narrow streets of San Sebastián's Old Town are lined with bars offering them, and I head first to Casa Vallés for a Gilda: an anchovy, *guindilla* pepper and olive sandwich, said to be the original *pintxo*. Next it's on to Ganbara, sampling grilled mushrooms and a glass of *txakoli*, a lightly sparkling white wine. Holding the bottle aloft, the bartender dramatically pours into an oversized tumbler, stopping at an abstemious inch. Locals know the trick to a *pintxo*-crawl is pacing yourself.

With that in mind, I stay a couple of nights, squeezing in the miniature steak at Bar Gandarias and Nestor's famously good *tortilla*, as well as a nine-course tasting menu at three Michelin-starred Akelarre. When I get back behind the wheel, I feel a twinge of regret about my low-effort approach to the Camino, and vow to forgo next stop Bilbao's bars for its cathedral to art, the Guggenheim Museum. The building's deconstructed approach to architecture reminds me of modern art pioneer Pablo Picasso, and its light-filled galleries are filled with work by those who followed in his wake.

The drive to Santillana del Mar takes barely an hour and a half, but it's as though the clock has been wound back centuries. Ditching my car at the town's entrance, I set out across the cobbles to explore what philosopher Jean-Paul Sartre called 'the prettiest village in Spain'. Pale brick houses line perfectly preserved medieval streets, their wooden balconies brimming with flowers. At its heart are a Romanesque church, Renaissance palaces and Baroque mansions, one of which is now part of the state-owned Paradores hotel group. I skip its fine-dining restaurant in favour of a courtyard table at La Villa and a bowl of mountain stew.

Hearty *fabada Asturiana* is a dish of beans and meat rarely off the menu in Cangas de Onís, to the west, but stay overnight if you want to try the local cider, aerated by a long-distance pour. Both are fuel for those using the town as a base for the magnificent Picos de Europa mountains. Rolling past the town's famous arched bridge, I glimpse the Río Sella snaking below, then head up to the Covadonga lakes, stopping at their namesake town en route. Absurdly picturesque, the spires of its 19th-century basilica look more like a romantic castle, rising against a backdrop of peaks. The road winds up again until its pay-off time for the effort – Lago de Enol, its surface a mirror of the blue skies overhead, and Lago de la Ercina, which I have all to myself.

Moving on to Asturias' coast, I hope to find uncrowded beaches and am rewarded by Playa de Silencio, a suitably empty arc of sand backed by a natural amphitheatre. The last stretch is by foot, and at journey's end I plunge into the cool water. Afterwards, my mind turns to a seafood dinner in nearby Cudillero, a good-looking fishing village clustered with pastel-coloured houses. I stay in a rustic hotel tucked just behind the port, waking to a dawn chorus of gulls.

Back on the road, I make a brief diversion to the Galician beach, Praia As Catedrais – so named because its rock towers, arches and chambers evoke ecclesiastical architecture – before heading on to the real deal in Santiago. On arrival, I find myself in no hurry to seek out the city's main sight, its cathedral, instead exploring souvenir shops selling St James figurines and several side-street cafés. I stop for coffee and a slice of Tarta de Santiago, an almond cake stencilled with an icing sugar crucifix, and later for a glass of queimada, the local firewater, said to ward off evil spirits.

Fortified, I make my way to the main square, Praza do Obradoiro, watching as pilgrims take the last steps of their long journey. Some fall to their knees at the sight of the cathedral, tears streaming down their faces as they tilt them to the heavens. A group wear matching t-shirts for their finale, smiling beatifically for photos. Unusually for Spain's municipal plazas there are no cafés here, but that doesn't stop people coming to drink in the magical atmosphere. They sit on the sun-warmed stones and congregate on the steps – some in quiet contemplation, others with a beer in hand. I am reminded of a 13th-century quote, found in a guidebook to my route: 'The door is open to all – not only to Catholics but also to pagans, Jews, heretics and vagabonds.' Straddling the latter two categories, I feel like I belong.

MENÚ DEL DÍA

The fixed-price three-course lunch has been a cornerstone of Spanish culinary and social life since it was introduced in the 1960s. Until 2010 restaurants were legally obliged to offer one, ensuring citizens had access to a reasonably priced meal during their working day. Many establishments continue to fly the flag for the *menú del día* – expect soup or salad to start, meat or fish to follow, plus *postre, pan y bebida* (pudding, bread and a drink).

Opposite from top: fabada Asturiana (bean stew); the Praia As Catedrais, 'Beach of Cathedrals'. Previous page: assending into the Picos de Europa

DIRECTIONS

Start // San Sebastián
End // Santiago de Compostela
Distance // 500 miles (800km)

Getting there // San Sebastián has the closest airport, but the French city of Biarritz is just over an hour away by shuttle bus. There's ample car rental at both airports. Trains connect San Sebastián to several cities in the rest of Spain and France.

When to go // The north is cooler than the rest of the country, even in the height of summer, making it a popular holiday destination for Spaniards. Visit in June or September for the best chance of dodging both crowds and the region's notorious rainfall.

What to pack // Swimwear and shorts for when it's sunny; a waterproof jacket for when it's not.

Further information // www.spain.info/en

*Opposite: full comportas ready to be
carried to a bodega during the grape
harvest in La Rioja, Spain*

MORE LIKE THIS
FOOD AND DRINK DETOURS
IN NORTHERN SPAIN

LA RIOJA

Rioja is a by-word for quality red wine. With
more than 500 wineries across a relatively
compact region, you don't have to travel
far to try the signature drop. Begin your
education in the honied-stone town of
Briones, unfairly quaint and home to the
Vivanco Museum of Wine Culture. Drive
on through rolling vines – at their fulsome
best in September and October – to
Marqués de Riscal, a historic winery with a
spectacular Frank Gehry-designed visitor
centre that also houses a posh hotel. Book
a room to make the most of the sommelier's
selection at its Michelin-starred restaurant,
or a wine tour if you're pressed for time or
cash. Next, roll back the centuries as you
cruise into Laguardia, a medieval fortress
town that's equally well-fortified with
traditional wine cellars. It's a short hop to
regional capital, Logroño, whose *pintxos*
rival even San Sebastián's.

Start// Briones
End// Logroño
Distance// 30 miles (45km)

GALICIA

Spain's northwesternmost region is the
place to try some niche speciality foods,
from *pulpo a la gallega* (octopus with
olive oil and paprika) to *tetilla*, a cow's
milk cheese shaped like a breast. Begin
in the Rías Baixas, four coastal inlets
peppered with sandy shores and great
seafood restaurants, and home to the
Albariño wine region, of which Cambados
is capital. After some beach time at Praia
A Lanzada, Galicia's best, follow the
coast to Combarro, where historic raised
stone granaries sit among atmospheric
taverns. Next, stop in lovely Pontevedra
before heading south to Vigo, famed for
'oyster street', where an early morning
market serves the super-fresh delicacies
for breakfast. For night-time fun it's inland
to Ourense, where a maze-like old quarter
hosts a lively tapas scene.

Start// Cambados
End// Ourense
Distance// 107 miles (172km)

ASTURIAS

Responsible for producing 80% of Spain's
sidra (*cider*), Asturians are also mad for
their regional speciality. Join them for a
bottle or two in the capital, Oviedo –
specifically on el bulevar de la sidra, whose
bartenders have mastered the traditional,
and theatrical, above-the-head pouring
technique that gives the drink its bubbles.
Stay at least a night before driving north to
the fun port of Gijón, which has its own fair
share of rustic *sidrerías* – plus beaches. The
coast is even prettier between Ribadesella
and Llanes, with many of its sandy coves
backed by casual seafood restaurants. Next,
head inland for the mountains and Asturias'
other culinary ace, Cabrales cheese. This
extremely pungent blue cheese is produced
exclusively in the foothills of the Picos de
Europa mountains. You can visit the 'Cheese
Cave' in Arenas before finishing up with
lunch at El Molín de Mingo, a secluded
restaurant surrounded by forest.

Start// Oviedo
End// Peruyes
Distance// 120 miles (190 km)

NAPLES AND THE AMALFI COAST

Picking the perfect time to visit some of Italy's most popular destinations meant Etain O'Carroll had Roman ruins, cliffside villages and coastal views almost to herself.

There's something profoundly pleasing about travelling south in late October if you live in northern Europe. Swapping low clouds, raincoats and reluctant acceptance that winter is coming for clear blue skies, swaying palm trees and one more week squeezed out of your flip flops is like scoring a last-minute goal in an international final.

Everything provides a heightened sense of awareness: colours seem more vibrant; food tastes better; and every breaking wave feels like a thing to be treasured. A trip at this time of year is worth ten times that of an August break, and it comes without the crowds.

Because crowds are a problem on the Amalfi Coast. This legendary stretch of shore deserves every drop of its celebrity, but the views of turquoise seas, ribbon-like cliffs and cascading villages are often blocked by queues of traffic, and the villages themselves can be overrun. And so, as I drive down narrow winding roads looping around hairpin bends, every empty parking spot feels like a pat on the back, confirmation of what good sense I had to travel off-season.

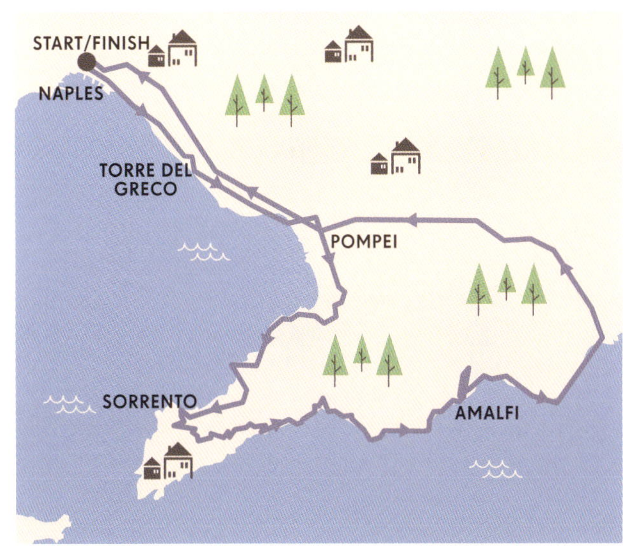

I had arrived in Naples a couple of nights before and found my way to a small apartment in the tangle of central back streets. Although for first time visitors Naples' Centro Storico (historic centre) with its frescoed ruins, flamboyant palaces and museums stuffed with priceless wonders is the place to go, my heart lies in the side streets.

The chaotic traffic, honking horns and loud conversations can be an assault on the senses, but there's also a raw energy to it all that's reflected in edgy street art, boisterous bars, artists' studios, artisan workshops, colourful street markets and tiny pizzerias that serve a slice that lingers in the memory for years.

Leaving Naples, I've barely got comfortable before I stop at Herculaneum, an ancient city buried during the same cataclysmic eruption as Pompeii in AD 79. Here, it was a mudslide – rather than volcanic ash and pumice – that devoured the streets, and the detail of life preserved is extraordinary. Legible price lists are frescoed on walls, wooden doors and beds survive along with interiors decorated with elaborate floor mosaics. The site is also far smaller than Pompeii, making it easy to get around, especially if you've got older or younger family members to accommodate.

Pompeii, of course, is the main draw south of Naples, and no matter how many times I visit, I'm left in awe all over again. This once prosperous port town sits under the taunting gaze of Vesuvius, the volcano which turned it into an open-air museum piece. As you stroll stone streets rutted by ancient wagon wheels to temples, bathhouses and villas, the sophistication of the city means it's hard to comprehend just how old everything is. I mean,

"As I drive narrow winding roads looping around hairpin bends, every empty parking spot feels like a pat on the back"

who would have thought people enjoyed underfloor heating over 2000 years ago?

Back in the car, driving along the winding coast road, I round a bend and get my first view of Sorrento. I heave a sigh of contented relief.

A resort town with a warren of little streets flanked by mansions and chapels, gift shops and restaurants, Sorrento is beautiful at this time of year. There's a certain delight in wandering streets so obviously geared up for tourists when there are only a handful of us about, and in the evening light, the sun setting over the sea, I'm more than happy just to sit on a quiet terrace and soak it all up.

Sorrento is also a jumping off point for trips to glamorous Capri, but instead I head south along increasingly narrow roads to find a quiet cove and a deserted beach. There are lots of them along the southern coastline at this time of year. Places accessed by a long series of steps, deep green pines parting to reveal a view of multiple headlands disappearing into the distance.

Trips to the beach are tempered by sublime walks and drives along the Amalfi Coast, a region every bit as gorgeous as the photos suggest. Designated a Unesco World Heritage Site as an

LIQUID GOLD

While limoncello, lemon soap and brightly painted ceramics are the most obvious local souvenirs, the smart choice is *colatura di alici*, an extract of fermented anchovies known locally as liquid gold. A speciality of Cetara, legend has it that a group of Cistercian monks adapted the classical Roman recipe for *garum*, layering anchovy fillets and salt in barrels for three years to produce this flavour-packed amber sauce with a serious punch of umami.

From left: pizza served 'wallet style' at Pizzeria Bellini, Naples; the port of Sorrento; fresh lemonade in Positano, and a view across the village. Previous page: entering Minori

outstanding example of a Mediterranean landscape, the drama of its scenery is matched by a need to concentrate.

The coastal road demands the full attention of both driver and passenger – so don't volunteer to be the driver if you can avoid it. Hairpin bends wind around cliffs that plunge into the water, terraced vineyards tumble down steep hills, and towns cling to the lower slopes like a colourful Slinky making its way to the sparkling sea.

From the romance of Positano with its maze of streets to the cultural heavyweight of Ravello, the coastline offers enough interest for a lifetime of exploration. Wander Ravello's gardens following in the footsteps of writers, musicians and filmmakers. Visit the former naval power of Amalfi. Or, better still, ditch the car and get out on one of the many walking trails that edge their way along the cliffs. The most well-known routes, the Sentiero degli Dei and Maestra dei Villaggi, make it possible to walk from Positano all the way to Amalfi.

Rising early in the morning and making my way on foot through pine trees and chestnut forests, the view changing at every turn, I try not to gloat. I soak up the vistas and the scent of pine, thyme and rosemary as I pass ruined farmhouses, vineyards and lemon groves. Each morning I go a little further or take another path. The sea glitters below and a deep-seated sense of contentment rises within me.

The crowds are long gone, the sea is still warm enough to swim in, and the coastline is swathed in a dusky haze. The night before I drive back to Naples and, from there, home, I slip down to the beach at dusk for one last swim, and one last ounce of summer before the return to winter.

DIRECTIONS

Start // Naples
End // Naples
Distance // 112 miles (180km)
Getting there // Up to 30 trains run daily between Naples and Rome; Naples International Airport offers flights across Europe. Car rental is available at Naples train station and Naples International Airport.
When to go // April or October for sun and fewer crowds.
Where to eat // In a region renowned for its stellar restaurants, you'll be spoiled for choice, but Da Adolfo, five minutes from Positano by boat, is a low-key beach shack with a legendary reputation. Look out for the boat with the red fish flag.
What to take // Camera, sunglasses and a soft-top convertible car if you can get one.

*Opposite from top: the
Romanesque bridge in Besalú,
Catalonia; the Temple of
Aphrodite in Corinth, Greece*

MORE LIKE THIS
ANCIENT RUINS
AND COASTAL VIEWS

THE PELOPONNESE, GREECE

History and legend collide on this
mountainous peninsula where you'll find
classical temples, Mycenaean palaces,
Byzantine cities and Venetian fortresses.
Combined with dramatic peaks and deep
gorges that give way to turquoise seas and
deserted beaches, it makes a glorious spot
for a road trip. In the northeast corner of
the peninsula sits Ancient Corinth, a mostly
Roman city, home to Jason of the Argonauts,
stealer of the Golden Fleece. From here,
you can take a route that combines historic,
fortified cities with beaches and some of
Greece's most interesting wineries. Head
for the sanctuary of Zeus at Nemea, hilltop
Mycenae or coastal Epidavros with its
4th-century-BC theatre, one of the best
preserved ancient Greek structures in the
country. Then loop by the mountaintop
Byzantine city of Mystras, ancient Olympia,
home to the original games, and the
Lousios Gorge where you'll find the cliffside
Prodromou Monastery.

Start // Ancient Corinth
End // Nemea
Distance // 395 miles (635km)

THE COSTA BRAVA, SPAIN

Mixing Greek and Roman ruins with
medieval towns, the eccentricities of
Salvador Dalí and a wild and rugged coast,
Spain's Costa Brava makes a fascinating,
eclectic destination for a road trip. Begin
by exploring Girona's hilly medieval core
with its web of alleys and Romanesque,
Gothic and Baroque churches. From here
it's an easy trip to Besalú, its strikingly
well-preserved medieval streets fanning
out around the handsome 11th-century Pont
Fortificat (Fortified Bridge). Heading east to
Figueres things get decidedly more bizarre at
the Dalí Theatre-Museum, a fittingly trippy
tribute to the local hero and Surrealist artist.
Dalí spent his later life nearby in Port Lligat
near Cadaqués, a whitewashed village with
a pretty harbour and bohemian vibe. South
along the coast are the extensive ruins of
the Greek city Empúries and its later Roman
neighbour, while inland is Castell de Púbol, a
14th-century castle that was Dalí's gift to his
wife and muse, Gala.

Start // Girona
End // Girona
Distance // 118 miles (190km)

HVAR, CROATIA

Fought over by the Illyrians, Greeks,
Romans, Byzantines and Venetians, Hvar
has long been a sought-after destination.
Medieval walls topped by an imposing
Spanish fortress enclose the Old Town,
whose marble streets are lined with
elaborate Gothic and Renaissance
palaces. In high summer, Hvar attracts a
party-hard international jet set, but outside
the peak it's a magical place that acts as
the perfect gateway to crystalline waters
and quiet villages. Head for Stari Grad
on the north coast, a quieter town set on a
horseshoe bay, to visit Stari Grad Plain, a
Unesco Cultural Landscape whose stone
walls and terraces of olives and grapes
were laid out by the ancient Greeks. Drive
backcountry roads through a patchwork of
lavender and rosemary to discover isolated
beaches and hidden coves, colourful former
fishing villages such as Vrboska or Jelsa,
and some of Croatia's best wineries.

Start // Hvar Town
End // Jelsa
Distance // 22 miles (35km)

THE TREASURES OF CATALONIA

Regis St Louis navigated between Pyrenean peaks, rugged coastline and surreal festivals of teetering human towers on a road trip through the northeast corner of Spain.

Regardless of your feelings on separatism, it's hard to deny that Catalonia is a place with a distinct character. Here, in the Iberian Peninsula's northeast corner, Pyrenean peaks frame windswept valleys and fertile vineyards, while the coastline is strewn with hidden coves and cliff-backed shores. Roman ruins and thousand-year-old churches hide amid stone villages, and Surrealist masterpieces lurk in wondrously bizarre art spaces.

The region is also home to a captivating city that has been turning heads for centuries. No, not that one. I'm talking about Girona, a riverside city northeast of its bigger, better known cousin, Barcelona. Like the Catalan capital, Girona is home to Modernista mansions, an atmospheric medieval quarter and celebrated restaurants headed by imaginative chefs. It's also a place with a decidedly Catalan soul, which makes it a fine starting point for a meandering road trip through the region, focusing both on Catalonia's natural wonders and its incredible cultural heritage.

Before setting off, I spend an afternoon strolling Girona's old Jewish quarter, peeking into the Gothic cathedral and admiring the view from the medieval walls. Down by the river, an 11-piece band of flutes, oboes and trumpets plays lilting rhythms on a tiny stage. Before them, a group of elderly but high-stepping dancers hold each other's hands aloft while performing the meticulous steps of the sardana, a folkloric dance that's been around since the Renaissance. Like the Catalan language, the dance was banned under the Franco regime, which ironically helped transform it into an emblem of Catalan identity.

Next morning, I drive the slow, scenic route over the Gavarres Massif. I pull over at the Santuari dels Àngels, a tiny chapel at the summit of Puig Alt with a view over dense forest to the distant foothills of the Pyrenees. Inside, I try to imagine where Surrealist artist Salvador Dalí and his bride Gala stood when they tied the knot (for the second time) in 1958.

The Costa Brava follows a jagged line, as if the map were drawn by the shakiest of hands. Narrow, sun-dappled roads descend to boulder-fringed coves, sparkling bays bobbing with sailboats and wave-battered headlands perched above glistening beachfronts. I stop for lunch in the cobblestone centre of Cadaqués, then stroll to the neighbouring village of Port Lligat to peer at the seaside cottage where Dalí and Gala resided. Naturally, the roof is topped with a giant egg.

Dalí's imprint seems omnipresent in this corner of Catalonia, just as this landscape appears everywhere in Dalí's work. On a

walking track near the wave-battered Cap de Creus – mainland Spain's easternmost point – I spy striking rock formations that inspired the artist, including one horseman-shaped boulder that figured prominently in a painting entitled *The Great Masturbator*. The following morning, I drive inland for more Dalí. I've visited the Dalí Theatre-Museum in Figueres several times, but I never tire of exploring the cinematic showrooms bristling with ingenuity and whimsy. Standing before *Taxi Plujós* (Rainy Taxi), I slip a coin into the slot and watch a rain shower spray the vine-covered mannequins seated inside a 1930s Cadillac.

Heading west takes me into the Pyrenees, along sinuous mountain roads with views over green valleys and the odd stone village. The next day I abandon the car to hike amid alpine lakes, trickling mountain streams and chiselled summits in the vast Parc Nacional d'Aigüestortes i Estany de Sant Maurici, Catalonia's majestic (and only) national park. Steep mountains surround nearby Vall de Boí, and its weathered granite churches bestow an air of mystery on the tiny villages encircling them. I had long wanted to explore this corner of Catalonia after seeing the extraordinary Romanesque frescoes rescued from these forgotten buildings in the early 1920s and displayed in Barcelona's MNAC (National Catalan Art Museum). Today, nine churches, all built between the 11th and 12th centuries, comprise the densest concentration of Romanesque architecture in Europe. Despite their renown, I have Sant Climent de Taüll entirely to myself as I walk along the austere northern apse beneath frescoes painted some 800 years ago, and climb its six-storey, Byzantine-style bell tower.

A WALK IN THE PARK

The Parc Nacional d'Aigüestortes i Estany de Sant Maurici has dozens of excellent trails, from half-day walks around the beautiful Sant Maurici Lake to the multi-day trek along the 34-mile (55km) Carros de Foc circuit, overnighting at mountain refuges along the way. For an intense but rewarding one-day outing, make the Sant-Maurici-Boí traverse, a 14-mile (22km) sequence of lakes, waterfalls, green valleys, rocky peaks and inspiring vistas.

Clockwise from above: a castell builds during the Festas de Santa Tecla in Tarragona; semi-wild horses in the Pyrenees; Tarragona's Roman Pont del Diable. Previous page: Aigua Blava, a cove on the Costa Brava

The view takes in the surrounding mountains, sentinels protecting these Catalan treasures from discovery.

The final leg of my road trip takes me into Tarragona, a city on the Costa Daurada famed for its Roman ruins. This time, I'm not here to visit the well-preserved amphitheatre or Roman circus. Instead, I've come to catch September's Festes de Santa Tecla, a 10-day extravaganza of street parades, religious processions and open-air performances. Brave kids, wearing long sleeves, wide-brimmed hats and protective goggles, line the narrow streets for the nightly *correfocs* – the aptly named 'fire runs' in which devilishly attired troops carrying dragons, sphinxes and other mythical creatures bombard spectators with exploding firecrackers.

During the day, I join a dense crowd on the main plaza and watch as four teams take turns building *castells*, human towers that sometimes rise eight 'storeys' high. I hold my breath as a small child, no older than six, scampers up the quivering legs and trunks of her compatriots and straddles the shoulders of the person at the top. She raises her hand, indicating the tower is complete, and the crowd, many with tears in their eyes, cheer wildly. This unusual tradition of risk-sharing cooperation culminating in soaring achievement (or brutal failure should the tower collapse) was born near Tarragona over 300 years ago, and remains a deeply beloved one in parts of Catalonia.

A feeling of euphoria tinged with sadness hangs in the air on the final night of Santa Tecla. There is no respite from the percussive fireworks and minstrel music crisscrossing town. Though I tire of dodging explosions and stumbling through smoke-filled intersections, the enthusiasm is contagious and I can't imagine being anyplace else. That's the magic of Catalonia, and the reason I contemplate my departure the next morning with a heavy heart. I haven't left and yet I am already aching to return.

"Dali's imprint seems omnipresent in this corner of Catalonia, just as this landscape appears everywhere in Dali's work"

DIRECTIONS

Start // Girona
End // Tarragona
Distance // 447 miles (720km)
Getting there // Girona-Costa Brava Airport, located 9 miles (15km) southwest of Girona, has flights from various European destinations. The airport also has major car rental companies.
When to go // June through October are the best months as ice and snow can close mountain roads in winter. For warm but busy beach days, try July or August, and for pleasant weather and Tarragona's biggest festival, visit in September.
Where to stay // Expect atmospheric guesthouses and hotels at towns along the route.
Further information // Tourism offices in Girona, Cadaqués, Figueres, Boí and Tarragona provide helpful information.
Tip // Bring good shoes/boots for the trails along the Costa Brava and in the Parc Nacional d'Aigüestortes i Estany de Sant Maurici.

*Opposite: the Isola di San Giulio lies
within Lago d'Orta in Piedmont, Italy*

MORE LIKE THIS
ENCOUNTERING AUTONOMOUS CULTURES

WALLONIA, BELGIUM

Tucked into the south of Belgium, Wallonia is a largely French-speaking region of rolling green countryside, medieval castles and picturesque villages. Starting in Brussels, you'll leave the big city behind as you motor west to the sleepy village of Lessines, birthplace of beloved Walloon artist René Magritte. Aside from offering strolls in the footsteps of the great Surrealist master, Lessines also hides a fascinating medieval hospital complex dating from the 13th century. Further up the road, you can climb Belgium's oldest belfry and gaze out over Tournai's striking Grand Place and towering cathedral. Meandering south, country lanes lead to Mons and Binche, famous for their wild festivals. Before looping back to Brussels, stop in Chimay for Trappist ales, wander the corridors of Namur's castle, and tread the Waterloo battlefields where Napoleon suffered inglorious, final defeat.

Start // Brussels
End // Brussels
Distance // 242 miles (390km)

PIEDMONT, ITALY

Once part of the mighty Kingdom of Sardinia, Piedmont sets itself apart from the rest of Italy with its Parisian-influenced capital Turin, the regal *palazzi* dotting the countryside and its native language (Piedmontese) still spoken by some two million residents. The sizable, landlocked region has snow-capped mountains and lakes of the deepest blue, best experienced on a multi-day road trip. Not far southeast of Turin, you'll enter the rolling hills and valleys surrounding Barolo and other tiny wine-loving villages. Turning north, you'll pass through the gastronomic powerhouse of Alba (famed for its truffles) before reaching lovely Lago d'Orta and the even more dramatic Lago Maggiore, where steep, wooded hillsides descend right to the edge of the lake. Narrow, twisting roads take you up to eagle's nest heights in the Parco Nazionale della Val Grande, a wooded wilderness in the Italian Alps and a fine place to ponder Piedmont's abundant natural beauty before returning to Turin.

Start // Turin
End // Turin
Distance // 330 miles (530km)

MENORCA, SPAIN

Spain's easternmost Balearic Island stretches just 30 miles (48km) from east to west, but you can spend days exploring its beaches, archaeological sites and villages. Start off in the harbourside city of Maó (Mahón), then make your way north across a lunar landscape to Cap de Favàritx, stopping at the freshwater lagoon of S'Albufera along the way. Further north, the attractive fishing village of Fornells lies near fine sandy beaches; for many, the town's waterfront seafood restaurants make it an obligatory lunchtime stop. Menorca's cliff-edged northernmost point, the Cap de Cavalleria, is reached by a drive across a rocky, otherworldly landscape that unfolds beyond gently rolling hills. Heading inland, 1174ft (357m) high Monte Toro affords awesome views of the entire island on clear days. End your road trip in the west coast settlement of Ciutadella, its evocative old quarter dotted with gracious squares and grand noble houses.

Start // Maó (Mahón)
End // Ciutadella
Distance // 81 miles (130km)

AROUND THE HEEL OF ITALY

Fuelled by the region's delicious local food, Brett Atkinson explored whitewashed hill towns, historic cities and remote coastal roads on this Italian itinerary around Puglia.

've been here before, in full backpacker mode a few decades ago, viewing the southern Italian city of Bari fleetingly before catching a ferry towards a silvery Adriatic horizon and the Greek island of Corfu. Shifts in borders and geopolitics have now added Croatia, Montenegro and Albania to the destinations reached from Bari – but instead of segueing immediately from a train journey from Rome onto an overnight ferry, this time I'm embarking on a road trip around Italy's southeastern tip.

Bari Vecchia (Old Bari) anticipates the shared themes of history and food infusing this journey. Byzantine, Romanesque and Norman architectural influences all abound, and I bookend exploring tree-shaded plazas, an imposing castle and the incense-scented Basilica di San Nicola with feasts of *panzerotti* (deep-fried pastries stuffed with cheese and tomato) from old bakeries, and creamy sea urchins and oysters at Bari's harbourfront market. It's a local tradition to team the freshest of seafood with a frosty Peroni beer, so I clink bottles with Bari fishermen to toast my upcoming road trip.

Heading southeast from Bari through an amber, green and gold patchwork of farms, vineyards and villages, my little rental Lancia swiftly covers the distance to Alberobello. A few unpainted and tumbledown examples of the region's unique *trulli* feature along the final stretch into town, and from the elevated lookout of the Piazza del Popolo, I take in views of these signature slate-roofed beehive-shaped structures. Energised by an overflowing ice cream, it's just a short pistachio-powered stroll downhill to get pleasantly lost in Alberobello's thousand-plus *trulli* huddled together in the Rione Monti neighbourhood.

Travelling east from Alberobello through the Valle d'Itria, I detour along winding country roads trimmed by squat drystone walls and almond orchards through a landscape dotted with scores more *trulli*, many now transformed into accommodation and restaurants. The hill town of Locorotondo is revealed on the near horizon and,

after parking at the base of the Old Town, I follow a leisurely path uphill through narrow lanes enlivened by window boxes of crimson geraniums. Locorotondo is often rated as one of Italy's most beautiful towns, and, on this warm afternoon, the accolades are well-deserved. Shaded squares are lined with gleaming cafés and wine bars, including laid-back Controra where I team a taste of citrusy Verdeca wine with views across the olive groves and vineyards of the valley.

Further east in Ostuni, it's time to abandon my strategy of walking uphill to the historic centres of Puglian hill towns, and instead jump aboard an Ape Calessino, a quirky equivalent of a Thai tuk tuk that's a popular form of transport in Italy. Soundtracked by a commentary that's 50 percent English, 50 percent Italian, and 100 percent unbridled enthusiasm, my 45-minute 'Giro di Ostuni' efficiently takes in all the town's historic highlights before my guide drops me in the

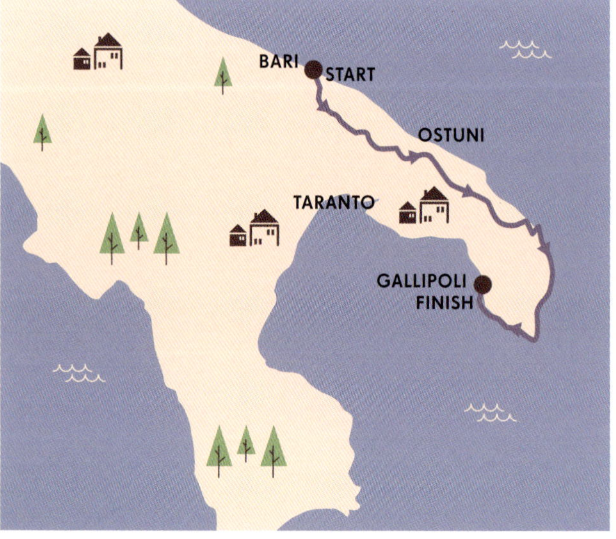

© Cristi Popescu | Shutterstock

"It's a local tradition to team the freshest of seafood with a frosty Peroni beer, so I clink bottles with Bari fishermen to toast my upcoming road trip"

main square as dusk is beginning to fall. In Italy, that's conveniently known as *aperitivo* time.

Leaving Ostuni the next day, I continue southeast to Lecce on quieter roads via San Vito del Normanni and Mesagne – avoiding the busy four-lane highway near Brindisi – travelling from the relatively verdant Valle d'Itria to the Salento region, hot and dry, and dotted with sparse groves of centuries-old olive trees. In contrast to Salento's elemental landscapes, the architecture of Lecce is over the top and exuberant. Entering through its grand gates, I explore the city's honey-coloured Old Town, crammed with more than 100 churches and heritage townhouses, and awash with the ornate 17th-century architectural style known as *barocco leccese* (Lecce Baroque). Piazzas that glow in southern Italian sunlight are further enhanced after dark by shapeshifting moonlit shadows. Bar-hopping near the extraordinary stonework of the Basilica di Santa Croce, I'm caught up in wedding celebrations overflowing from a nearby trattoria. A throng of Lecce's best-dressed families fills the narrow thoroughfare, and glasses of local wine are raised with congratulations offered in a variety of languages.

South from Lecce, I begin a clockwise spin around the 'heel' of Italy's 'boot', the southeastern extremity of the mainland. Once part of the extended Greek empire, the impact of Hellenistic civilisation lingers in coastal towns like Otranto and Gallipoli. Detour options include the Grotto of the Poets, a perfect saltwater swimming hole fed by the sea. On a weekday morning, it's not too busy, and I carefully scramble down a rough-hewn stone staircase to its clear waters. On the cliffs above, the grotto's resident *gelato* vendor maintains a persuasive sales pitch. I can definitely recommend the tangy lemon flavour.

Refreshed and refuelled, I arrive in Otranto and explore its cathedral before negotiating the town's harbourfront precinct, where echoes of the Greek, Roman and Ottoman eras overlap. From here, a diversion south continues along the quietest coastal roads of the journey. A few Vespa scooters and a couple of improbably small classic Fiat 500s join me on the narrow and winding drive south to Capo Santa Maria di Leuca, on Italy's stiletto-like southeast tip. Along the way I stop for another chance to explore this remote Adriatic coastline. Just north of the spa town of Castro, a series of switchbacks lead to the Grotta Zinzulusa. As I continue by foot down a rocky walkway to this huge coastal cavern, swells rolling in all the way from Albania make a flotilla of fishing boats bob and sway.

Driving on to Capo Santa Maria di Leuca, the 'end of the road' aura is enhanced by a towering lighthouse and an ancient clifftop temple site that's now an 18th-century basilica. From the cape, more coastal meanderings transport me north to Gallipoli on the western side of Italy's heel. Located on a compact promontory, the name of the whitewashed town translates to 'Beautiful City' in ancient Greek, and who am I to disagree? Red prawns are the local seafood speciality here, and one of Gallipoli's waterfront restaurants proves the ideal spot to celebrate completion of my trip around one of Italy's less discovered but richly rewarding regions.

CUCINA POVERA

Southern Italy's *cucina povera* (literally 'food of the poor') is well represented in Puglia, with restaurants serving traditional dishes that evolved because of the economic hardship suffered by the south over the centuries. Pasta is made without eggs, there's an intense focus on local and seasonal vegetables, and seafood is eaten more frequently than meat. Classic dishes include the Bari speciality of *riso, patate e cozze*, a baked dish of rice, potatoes and mussels.

Opposite, clockwise from top left: sea urchins; Ape Calessinos tour Ostuni; trulli in Alberobello. Previous page: the Grotto of the Poets in Rocha Vecchia

DIRECTIONS

Start // Bari
End // Gallipoli
Distance // 198 miles (320km)
Getting there // Bari's Karol Wojtyła Airport has domestic flights from Rome and Milan, and year-round and seasonal charter flights from many European cities. The train station is served by services from across Italy.
When to go // May or September, for a combination of good weather and fewer crowds than in the summer peak.
Where to stay // Masseria Trapana (www.trapana.com) offers luxury accommodation on a working farm near Lecce.
Where to eat // Osteria Ricanatti dishes up innovative Puglian dishes and Salento wines in Ostuni. Make sure to seek out the *pasticciotti* (custard-filled pastries) in Lecce.
Further information // www.viaggiareinpuglia.it

Opposite, clockwise from top: Vieste in Gargano National Park, Italy; market day in Sarlat-la-Canéda, France; the grand staircase in Caltagirone, Sicily

MORE LIKE THIS
BACKROADS OF SOUTHERN EUROPE

DORDOGNE RIVER VALLEY, FRANCE

Plot a meandering journey along the Dordogne River Valley, toasting the upcoming drive the evening before you depart with a glass of local Monbazillac wine in Bergerac. Head east along the river to Lalinde, stopping to explore the English heritage of the town's historic bastide (fortified town), or negotiating walking trails along the river's traditional towpaths. Every Thursday morning, there's an excellent food market crammed with local treats. Follow the river's northern bank around a gentle loop, stopping for sky-high views at Trémolat and to spot canoeists and kayakers during the summer. Further upstream, La Roque-Gageac's cliffside location and the mighty châteaux at Beynac and Castelnaud-la-Chapelle are some of the Dordogne's most memorable sights. End this riverside adventure amid the traffic-free cobblestoned squares and lanes of Sarlat-la-Canéda, one of southwestern France's best preserved medieval towns.

Start // Bergerac
End // Sarlat-la-Canéda
Distance // 62 miles (100km)

GARGANO PENINSULA, ITALY

This circular drive, north from Bari to the Gargano Peninsula, starts with the dramatic seafront cathedral at Trani before continuing along winding roads high above the ocean to a spectacular area of cliffs, forests and coastal grottos refreshed by the Adriatic. The promontory town of Vieste is a compact and walkable blend of Naples and Dubrovnik – and the departure point for boat trips up and down the coast. From nearby Peschici, a hilltop walled town of whitewashed houses, journey to Isole Tremiti's remote three-island archipelago before cruising back to the Italian mainland to dine at clifftop seafood restaurants housed amid Gargano's *trabucchi* (traditional fishing platforms). Hike or mountain bike in the Foresta Umbra (Forest of Shadows) before returning to Bari via the mountaintop pilgrimage town of Monte Sant'Angelo and the Unesco World Heritage-listed 13th-century fortress at Castel del Monte.

Start // Bari
End // Bari
Distance // 273 miles (440km)

HILL TOWNS OF CENTRAL SICILY, ITALY

Explore the rugged heartland of central Sicily on a road trip combining mountaintop towns with the echoes of earlier history. Begin in Caltagirone, high on a hill and famed for its ceramic studios and the monumental staircase of the Scalinata di Santa Maria del Monte. En route north to the lanes and plazas of Piazza Armerina, detour to the extraordinary Villa Romana del Casale. Built as a sumptuous country retreat in the 3rd century CE, the sprawling site features some of the world's finest Roman wall and floor mosaics. Earlier Greek history lingers at nearby Morgantina, as this journey continues to the imposing hill town of Enna – the geographic centre of Sicily, and the perfect location to take in the region's monumental landscapes. Just to the north, more compact Calascibetta is also dramatic, and crowned by the Chiesa Madre, the village's landmark 14th-century cathedral.

Start // Caltagirone
End // Calascibetta
Distance // 66 miles (107km)

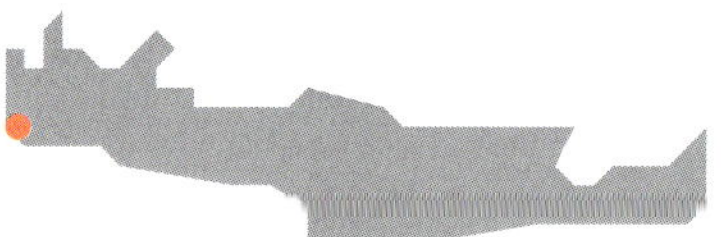

CRUISING WESTERN CRETE

To see the best of western Crete's history, geography and contemporary life, Alexis Averbuck drove across Greece's largest island, stopping at tavernas, beaches and gorges on the way.

Crete stands alone in Greece. A sprawling island with a culture and a terrain all its own, it is a place of myth and magic. My drive from the hectic capital out to Crete's serene western half – via sable beaches, forested gorges and intimate villages – endeavours to seek examples of the best this storied land has to offer.

I begin in Iraklio (Heraklion), the capital, and combine picking up a rental car with a visit to the archaeological museum, where I examine gorgeous finds preserved from areas on my route ahead. The city wraps around the coast and as I leave its traffic thrum behind, I head through the surrounding countryside to the vast palace complex of Knossos. This elaborate remnant of the ancient Minoan civilisation is still shrouded in mystery – not much is definitively known about the sophisticated group of people who were the early inhabitants of Crete. An unhurried wander through the structures, sculptures and murals is a playground for my imagination.

As I later drive the northern coast road, I ponder how the Minoans once ruled this land – and then consider the conflicts of a different time, between the Greeks and Ottoman occupiers, as I reach the monastery at Arkadi. Sitting on a golden plain, the monastery's most eye-catching element is its 16th-century Venetian church, with a Renaissance facade marked by eight slender Corinthian columns and topped with an ornate triple-bell tower. I dive inside and find its hushed, ornate interior a reverent contrast to a very different time in the monastery's life, when in 1866 hundreds of Cretan people sheltered here under siege by two thousand Ottoman soldiers. Rather than surrender, the Cretans set fire to their gunpowder stores, killing everyone, Turks included – everyone except for one girl who lived to a ripe old age in a village nearby.

I think of yet another era in the island's past as I approach Rethymno and spy its 15th-century Venetian fortress. The town's narrow lanes open up to a sparkling seafront, ideal for a lunch

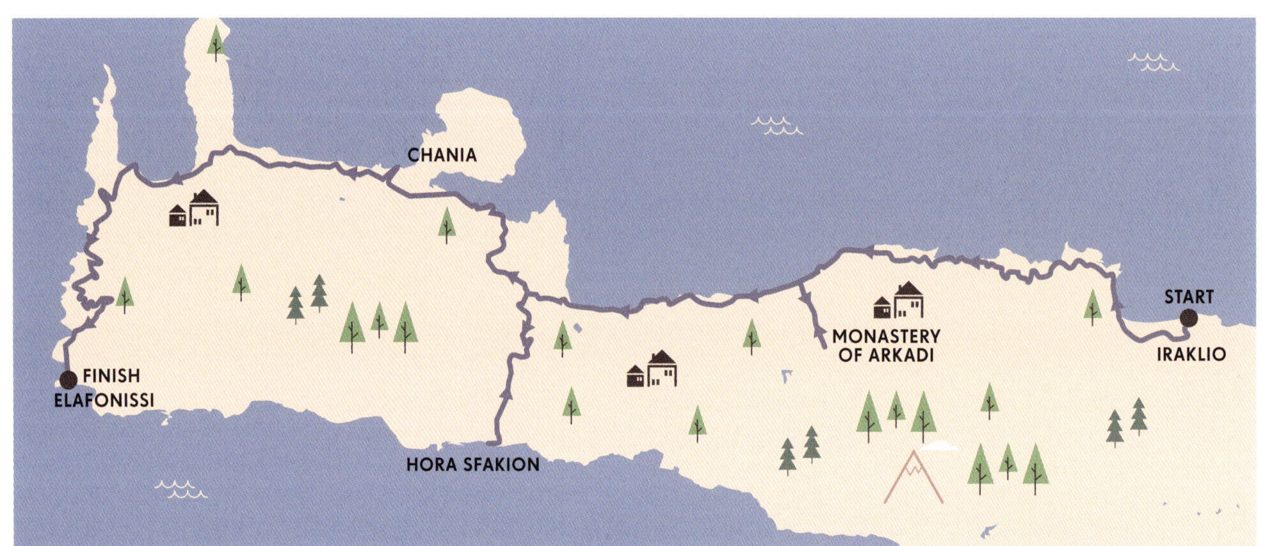

of local seafood before motoring on along the north coast and cutting inland to head over the mountains toward Hora Sfakion.

As the interior road undulates, it cuts along the edges of small villages teetering on hillsides or tucked into river valleys. Each has its own history and culinary traditions, meaning a stop is well worthwhile to explore the local markets, sampling cheeses made from local sheep and goat's milk, or to collect pastries – delicate layers of filo and honey – for a sweet morning treat the next day. Vineyards line the roads beyond, which prove perfect for stretching my legs and sipping a small glass before continuing.

I also stop for a Greek coffee in one of the village *kafeneia* (cafés) and speak with an elderly gentleman who sits in the town square watching the world go by. It's still early in the season so I am one of the first foreigners he's seen this year, and he has plenty to say. In Crete, local life has a colour and flare easily missed if you hurry.

As I drive on into the late afternoon, golden light falling soft on the pastures, I visit Askyfou, site of battles during the 1821 Cretan Revolt. The sunset shines up over the mountain pass and the road starts to feel remote as I drop down towards the south coast.

Increasingly the road signs become dented by bullet traces as I approach Hora Sfakion, the main village of the Sfakia region, famous for its rebellions against the Ottomans. The town was also a main evacuation point for Allied forces during WWII. Now, though, it's an amiable harbour spot, dotted with seafood tavernas, and also the jumping off point for regular boats that shuttle between the villages lining the 37 miles (60km) of coast as far as Paleochora to the west. Inaccessible by car, these waterfront hamlets, such as Loutro, are

BOUGATSA TOU IORDANIS

When in Hania take the time to make a pilgrimage to Bougatsa tou Iordanis. Not much more than a simple storefront, it nonetheless serves up some of the world's best *bougatsa*, a flaky, sweet-cheesy Cretan treat that is cooked fresh in great slabs here and sliced up while you wait. The owners offer nothing more than platters of *bougatsa* and piping hot coffee – and that's all you'll need.

Clockwise from above: variations on Greek salad, staple of a taverna lunch; Rethymno; Hania's port; ruins of the Palace of Knossos. Previous page: snaking into the White Mountains

© Matt Munro | Lonely Planet

worth a pause for a swim and lunch, or to find the southern ends of the several gorges that cut through the mountains to this coast. The most famous of these canyons is Samaria Gorge, which descends to the village of Agia Roumeli. It makes for wonderful walking, so I've brought my boots and stride into the canyon as far as my energy will take me that day, leaving enough for the return to the coast.

After the wild side of Crete, I drive back over the mountains for a dose of Greek port life in Hania. This is one of my preferred spots to overnight, a university town with a gorgeous harbour that fills with promenading students and locals every evening. People gossip, push prams and stop for coffees and cocktails all around the quay, which edges the pastel-coloured buildings, domed church and the boats bobbing in the harbour.

Hania's back streets are a joy, too, with bougainvillea spilling across pedestrianised lanes and some of the best eating that Greece has to offer. It's always tough to choose a restaurant – am I in the mood for seafood or straight-up Cretan fare? The latter ranges from olive oil and *dakos* salad (tomatoes and cheese over barley rusks) to homemade cheese pies and rich *gamopilafo* (lamb or goat accompanied by rice cooked in its broth). Whichever I pick, I plan to chase my choice with a bracing *tsikoudia* (raki or brandy).

What trip to a Greek island is complete without a moment on the beach? The next day I wind this road trip up with a detour to two of my favourites. First, Falasarna, with its honeyed sands, broad and clean, and the Mediterranean waves crashing ashore. Then, further south, Elafonissi – my dream beach, best enjoyed outside of peak hours. I wander its coral-tinted sands and, once the tide has receded, trace my way out to an offshore islet, now connected by a land bridge. It's the perfect place to contemplate, with feet pushing into soft sand, on the geographical and historical span of this grand drive.

"Vineyards line the roads beyond – perfect for stretching my legs and sipping a small glass before continuing"

DIRECTIONS

Start // Iraklio (Heraklion)
End // Elafonissi
Distance // 208 miles (335km)
Getting there // Fly or take a ferry to Iraklio or Hania. Each has car rental options from local and international companies.

Hiking the gorges // You can also reach Crete's magnificent coastal gorges from the inland, northern side. For example, start hiking the length of Samaria Gorge at Omolos, accessible by bus from Hani (or use the services of a local tour operator to drop you and pick you up).

Further information // Western Crete Information (www.west-crete.com) and Hania information (www.chania.com) are both useful sources. For more information on Knossos, visit the website of the British Archaeological School at Athens at www.bsa.ac.uk.

Cruising Western Crete

Opposite from top: meandering towards the village of Halki on Naxos; white volcanic rocks at Sarakiniko beach, Milos

MORE LIKE THIS
GREEK ISLAND DRIVES

NAXOS

Majestic mountains and a lone, ruined gate from an ancient Temple of Apollo welcome you as your ferry arrives in Naxos harbour. Grab a rental car and amble along the sweep of the shore then cut inland to the Temple to Demeter. The goddess of the harvest and protector of farmers is honoured here not so much by a grand structure – although the harmonious ruins remain extremely evocative and beautiful in their own right – but by the spectacle of the setting in open pastures and orchards, surrounded by the island's peaks. From here, you can head north to visit some of the enormous, fallen, marble *kouroi* (statues of youths) which are dotted around the countryside. Wrap up the day with a swim and a seafront taverna meal at Apollonas, on the island's northeast coast.

Start // Hora (Naxos)
End // Apollonas
Distance // 22 miles (35km)

KEFALLONIA

To understand why Kefallonia is known throughout Greece for its raw beauty and independent spirit, take a driving adventure starting from the little port of Pesada. Head north, towards the mountains, to find Agiou Gerasimou Monastery and its subterranean cavern in a high central valley, surrounded by vineyards. Stop off at the Cooperative of Robola Producers for a wine tasting, then take country lanes further north to the coast at famed Myrtos Beach, its sweep of blonde sand and cobalt waters living up to its reputation as one of Greece's most magnificent. Finish your day in quaint Fiskardo, one of the few survivors of the hugely destructive 1953 earthquake. The small crescent of natural harbour is rimmed by swaying sailboats and exceptional restaurants housed in vividly-coloured townhouses.

Start // Pesada
End // Fiskardo
Distance // 44 miles (71km)

MILOS

Milos is an island of beaches, from white smooth stone escarpments to molten red sand, all of which reward exploration. Begin in the buzzing harbour of Adamas and then make several spokes out on your drives. One spoke takes you along the northern coast and the white-stone beach at Sarakiniko, then on to Pollonia, a chic resort town. Another spoke brings you to the soft sands of Kyriaki Beach and its rose, grey and rust-striped hills. Nearby Paleohori bubbles with hot springs that make the sands warm, too. The final spoke is the short hop to Klima, a unique line of *syrmata* (traditional fishers' encampments) tucked into a cliff. From here, it's a short drive north for a sunset viewed from the churchyard in Plaka and a wander in its Cycladic-cubist streets, followed by your choice of excellent restaurants.

Start // Adamas
End // Plaka
Distance // 35 miles (56km)

IN PURSUIT OF THE TARGA FLORIO, SICILY

Motor racing started on public roads before moving to specialised race tracks. Tony Wheeler found that no early road circuit conjures up the magic better than Italy's ultimate test.

The photograph was taken in 1970 and I had no trouble tracking down its location in Campofelice. The coastal town is an easy drive east of Palermo, on the north coast of Sicily. Campofelice di Roccella has a long beach, an important church, a 14th-century castle, and nearby there are the Greek ruins of Himera, but it's what's happening in the street on that Sunday in May that has clearly entranced a large contingent of the local population. Under the building balconies, which I found so easy to identify, the citizens of Campofelice are lining the pavements, leaning out into the street, waving ecstatically, clearly cheering loudly for a local Palermo schoolteacher.

The schoolteacher is Nino Vaccarella and he is hurtling towards them, obviously travelling at something approaching warp speed, in a bright-red 600 horsepower Ferrari 512S – and he is in the lead of the Targa Florio. He didn't go on to win the Targa Florio that year, but he did the following year and again in 1975, when he clinched his third Targa victory. That 1970 photograph summed up what made the Sicilian sports car race so utterly irresistible: the setting, the enthusiasm and the sheer absurdity of it. You simply do not let people stand in the street, totally unprotected, when racing cars are hurtling past.

From 1906 to 1977, however, the world's oldest sport cars race did exactly that. At first the race was a complete circuit of Sicily, and over the years assorted other routes were tried, but from 1951 the race used the Circuito Piccolo delle Madonie. The Madonie is one of Sicily's principal mountain ranges, and since *piccolo* is Italian for 'little' this was the small racing track in the mountains. The short one, the little track with more than 700 corners. You went around it 11 times if you were going to win the Targa Florio. And although the long straight that stretches along the

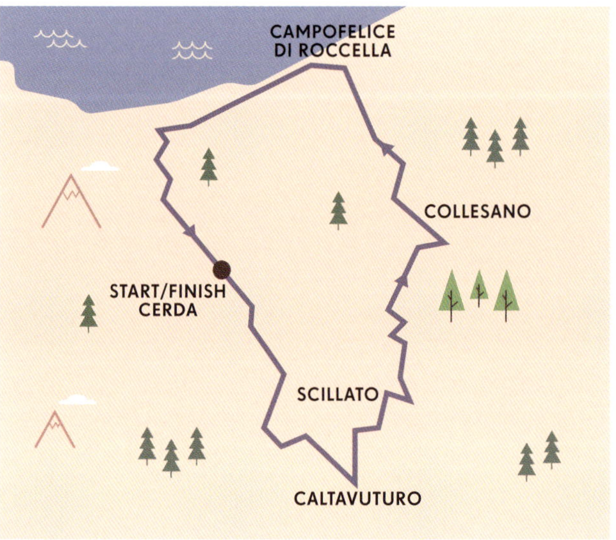

coast towards Palermo might have given Signor Vaccarella the opportunity to push his Ferrari to its maximum speed, all those twisting corners as the circuit climbed up into the hills meant that the fastest anyone ever got around the circuit was an average of just under 80mph (129km/h).

Nino Vaccarella turned up at historic motoring events well into his old age to demonstrate the fire-breathing racing monsters of his heyday. Although he did drive in a handful of Formula 1 Grand Prix races, sports cars were his speciality, when he could get away from his day job: teaching accounting. He won all sorts of races, including the Le Mans 24-Hour-Race, but it was the Targa Florio where he was always the popular favourite. When he crashed his Ferrari into a wall and out of the race in 1966, 'Viva Nino' was graffitied on the wall he hit.

From Campofelice, where I tracked down that evocative motor racing photograph, it's about 6 miles (10km) along the coast to where the track turns sharp left and starts to climb – and twist and turn – from sea level towards the town of Cerda at 272 metres. Cerda was the start and finish point of the Targa Florio; on such a narrow winding track it was impossible to start the cars together so, like the Mountain Circuit Tourist Trophy (TT) motorcycle track on the Isle of Man, the cars started one by one, 15 seconds apart. The starting order was often a confusing jumble, but even if they didn't all start together there would soon be plenty of racing on the road. The pit counter still stands beside the old starting line, and manufacturers still like to bring their latest creations down to the track to try them out. The

SICILIAN PIT STOPS

Casale Drinzi, which is just a short stroll out of Collesano, features an acclaimed Slow Food restaurant that serves hearty Madonie mountain specialities on the menu and pizzas at night. If you've imbibed too much Sicilian wine there are also B&B rooms available. With Casale Drinzi's food, wine, architecture, old churches, history and beautiful Sicilian mountain scenery, motor racing almost comes as something of a surprise bonus.

Clockwise from above: the town of Collesano; central Palermo; Mondello beach. Previous page: Luigi Tarramazzo's Ferrari 250 GTO takes a bend in the 1964 Targa Florio

impossibly beautiful countryside with its photogenically perfect driving roads certainly helps.

If the road wasn't already torturous enough, from Cerda it really beings to corkscrew as it hairpins its way up to Caltavuturo, the 'Fortress of Vultures,' at 635 metres altitude. From the coast the track has been running south, but now the route turns north and starts the descent back towards the coast, dropping down through Scillato and Collesano at 468 metres before the final breakneck plunge down towards the sea. Collesano has Greek and Arab historic connections, the remains of a Norman castle and an assortment of interesting churches. It also boasts the official Targa Florio Museum, which features a model of every race winner.

Targa simply means 'plate' and the plate in question was presented as a prize by Vincenzo Florio, a wealthy Sicilian businessperson, wine merchant and fast car enthusiast. The name lives on in the Targa Tasmania, an annual race around the Australian island state, and in every Porsche 911 Targa to cruise Rodeo Drive in Los Angeles or the King's Rd in London's Chelsea. Porsche was a Targa Florio specialist; it won the race 11 times, although that's only once more than Alfa Romeo.

In the Targa Florio's racing days, drivers would often practise when the road was open to everyday traffic, and dodging wayward donkeys was part of the fun. But with so many corners to memorise, regular racing practice time was clearly inadequate. The Circuito Piccolo delle Madonie is still a wonderful road to drive, although you're obviously not going to do it in anything like the sub-34 minute lap record. Two hours and seven minutes is the suggestion from Google Maps, an average speed of just over 20mph (35km/h). Given the 700 corners, the twists, the turns, the climbs, the descents... that's probably quite fast enough.

"In the Targa Florio's racing days, drivers would practise when the road was open to traffic – donkeys included"

DIRECTIONS

Start/End // Cerda, Sicily

Distance // 45 miles (72km) and – apart from 5 miles (8km) along the coast, good for 200mph (322km/h) when the roads were closed – it's all either corkscrewing uphill or twisting and turning down.

Getting there // Palermo, the capital of Sicily, which welcomes frequent flights from all over Europe and plenty of ferry services from other Italian ports, is just 31 miles (50km) to the west.

When to drive // Avoid summer crowds or go very early: venturing out at dawn for a pre-breakfast Targa lap is recommended.

What to drive // A Porsche or an Alfa Romeo are totally appropriate, but in Italy, for anything requiring some speed, a Ferrari can't be beaten.

Where to stay // Lots of excellent little hotels along the coast or in the mountain villages.

*Opposite: a 1922 Fiat 501 S on a
re-run of the Mille Miglia rally*

MORE LIKE THIS
RACING CIRCUITS

COL DE TURINI, FRANCE

Often listed as one of the most dangerous roads in the world, the Col de Turini is nothing of the kind – if you are careful. But not everyone is careful, especially the drivers of the Monte Carlo Rally, whose rally cars have knocked the ends off the typical French stone balustrades that guard the drop to the valley. Thirty-four hairpins take you up 1604 metres to the top of the pass, where three hotels wait to help you calm your pulse. The Hôtel Les Trois Vallées has walls full of photos from the Monte Carlo Rally; while there is a warning that the road may close in winter, this doesn't seem to apply to rallyists whose cars are often depicted up to the windows in snow. Unfortunately, you'll have little chance to enjoy the outstanding scenery along this section of the D2566, because if you don't pay constant attention to the road it will justify its reputation in the most unfortunate manner.

Start // Sospel
End // Col de Turini
Distance // 15 miles (25km)

SPA-FRANCORCHAMPS, BELGIUM

The wooded hills of the Ardennes conceal perhaps the best-loved of all classic Formula 1 circuits. On a select few days each year, you can book to drive the 4.4 mile (7km) track – including that Everest of corners, Eau Rouge. But even when that's not possible, you may still tap into the legend on surrounding roads, including ones that made up part of the longer circuit used until 1970. From the village of Francorchamps, head south to Burnenville and continue round to join the N68. After a long straight, you'll pass the Masta Kink – in its day more awesome even than Eau Rouge. The old route back turning right just before Stavelot is now a dead-end road, so why not see more of the countryside with an extended drive? Continue through Stavelot, then take the N633 and N606 north as they curl through river valleys and cut through forest, before looping back through the town of Spa (yes, the one that coined the word).

Start // Francorchamps
End // Francorchamps
Distance // 31 miles (50km)

MILLE MIGLIA, ITALY

Starting in Brescia in northern Italy and heading south to Rome and then back to Brescia, the Mille Miglia covered 1000 miles. Miles, real miles, not those newfangled kilometres. It ran between 1927 and 1957, attracted up to 5 million spectators and was finally halted because far too many people – spectators more than drivers – had been killed. The classic Mille Miglia win was by British driver Stirling Moss in a Mercedes-Benz 300 SLR in 1955. His co-driver Denis Jenkinson – later famous as motor racing journalist 'Jenks' – read out instructions like a human version of a modern satnav from an 18ft roll of paper. Their average speed of just under 100 mph (161km/h) was never beaten. Today the Mille Miglia survives as an annual rally for cars from 1957 or earlier that have a connection with the original race.

Start/End // Brescia
Distance // 1000 miles (1609km)

9
BF 6821

WESTERN EUROPE

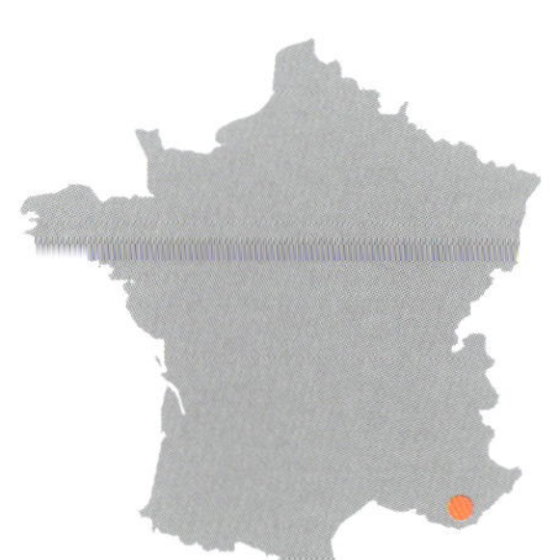

THE ROUTE NAPOLÉON

Road-markers blazoned with eagles and stone busts topped with bicorne hats signal a mountainous route through southeast France, where Rory Goulding followed Napoleon Bonaparte's last but one adventure.

The most famous figure ever to set foot in Cannes did not tread the red-carpeted steps at its film festival, but he did camp out just yards away. On the wall of a church, under a stone eagle with wings outstretched, a message is spelled out: 'HERE on the dunes beside the former chapel of Notre Dame de Bon Voyage, NAPOLEON, returned from the island of Elba, set up camp for the night of 1–2 March 1815 before dashing to Paris by the perilous Alpine road.'

It's this adventure that I've come to the French Riviera to retrace, following a road now celebrated as the Route Napoléon. It's a drive of around six hours to the Alpine city of Grenoble, but it took Napoleon and his men seven days to cover that distance, going at great haste.

His aim in taking the difficult road through the mountains was to win back the throne he had been exiled from the year before, but avoiding the more obvious route to Paris up the Rhône valley, with its garrison towns thought to be loyal to the new French king Louis XVIII. Cannes was a small fishing village when Napoleon and his thousand men spent their first night back on French soil there, having landed earlier that day in neighbouring Golfe-Juan. I follow the villa-covered coast from Cannes to this more low-key slice of the Riviera. Standing at the sign that announces the official start of the Route Napoléon, I watch a Citroën 2CV trundle past: a perfect pairing of Gallic icons.

It should be a signal to leave the warmth of the coast behind, but I don't speed away just yet. I stop in the towns of Vallauris and Mougins on the trail of another legend gone into exile, Pablo Picasso, and – further inland – breathe in the heady scents of the gardens around Grasse, 'perfume capital of the world'.

But after two days of dalliance, it's time to get serious. The Route Napoléon takes on an epic quality for the first time as it leaves Grasse, and zigzags into the mountains. Not in tidy hairpin bends, but in big, impatient strokes. No longer lost amid Riviera development, the road is now an obvious line on the map. After half an hour, the playful glitz of the coast seems an age away, replaced by a landscape of rock, oak forest and sparse villages. I stop at the entrance to Escragnolles to retrace the emperor's steps along a rare surviving stretch of the original stone road, watched by enormous goats.

The road has its moments of virtuoso engineering up in the mountains, such as the arch-like cut through the rock just beyond Taulanne. But they all seem tame in comparison to the Route des Crêtes – the biggest detour I take from Napoleon's path. From Castellane, I follow the blue-green Verdon River downstream as the cliffs on either side rise ever higher. The Gorges du Verdon is Europe's answer to the Grand Canyon, and the winding road hugs its north rim closely. From a viewpoint, I watch rock climbers begin their descent down a limestone wall almost half a mile above the valley floor.

Returning to Castellane to rejoin the Route Napoléon, the scenery continues to invite Wild West comparisons. After my unorthodox departure to see the gorges, I atone by sticking more closely to imperial footsteps than the signposted route does. Past Barrême, where the army spent their third night, I leave the N85 and take the narrower D20 up to the Col du Corobin. Few cars pass this way; it's a while before I meet another vehicle – a support van for cyclists.

Napoleon had to emerge from the mountains to tackle the suspected royalist choke-point of Sisteron – at the spot where the Durance River forces through a spine of rock, a citadel stands guard at the old northern gateway of Provence. He entered without a fight and moved on quickly. In the province of the Dauphiné to the north he expected a surer welcome.

Between Sisteron and Gap, the road crosses a broad, flat bowl of fruit orchards seemingly ringed by mountains on all sides. Napoleon made his swiftest passage here, and likewise I am back on the autoroute for the first time since day one. But on leaving Gap, a sign announces a layby for putting on snow-chains. The houses begin to take on an Alpine look, not in the Provençal way, but in the ski-poles and fondue sense. There was snow on the road when Napoleon travelled it, and he must have been glad of warm lodgings in the village of Corps for his last night before the crucial test at Grenoble.

Napoleon was 12 miles (19km) from the city when the king's soldiers at last stood in his path, before the village of Laffrey, where a horseback statue of a familiar figure in a bicorne hat now stands. The ex-emperor walked up to the opposing line of rifles, opened his waistcoat and challenged anyone to shoot him – whereupon the king's soldiers went over to Napoleon en masse.

His entry into Grenoble was triumphant, and at his lodgings in an inn, he had to make constant trips to the window to satisfy the crowds with a wave. My last few miles lead through suburbs that have grown since 1815, so in an effort to end the trip with some visual drama, I take a cable-car up to the mountaintop Bastille fortress. Joggers who have made the same arduous ascent stop for a breather on a terrace that surveys all of the city. I join them.

Grenoble was not the end of Napoleon's own journey. Between his return to Paris, defeat at Waterloo and death in exile on St Helena, there are other end-points to choose from. Nor was the Route Napoléon the hardest expedition he had faced, after his campaigns in Egypt and Russia. But there's an appealing simplicity in following these seven days, when Napoleon's challenge was to win back the country he had once dominated.

IMPERIAL IMAGE

Towns and villages along Napoleon's path have found creative ways to honour/cash in on his memory. These range from the somewhat undignified (depicting him on signs grilling sausages at a campsite or on a bike in a jarring combo of bicorne hat and polka-dot Tour de France jersey) to a more tasteful silhouette advertising Courvoisier cognac. In Volonne, a sign records the spot where tradition says that Napoleon paused to answer a call of nature.

Opposite, clockwise from top left: the Gorges du Verdon; Cannes' Plage du Midi; gondolas ascend to the Bastille of Grenoble. Previous page: the Durance River in Sisteron

DIRECTIONS

Start // Golfe-Juan
End // Grenoble
Distance // 204 miles (328km); the detour from Castellane to the Route des Crêtes and back adds another 44 miles (70km).
Getting there // Nice-Côte d'Azur Airport is the closest to the southern end of the route. Although Grenoble at the northern end has its own airport, many flights there run only in the winter ski season. Lyon-Saint Exupéry Airport, 56 miles (90km) from Grenoble, makes a good alternative. France's excellent railways allow easy access to the start and end points.
Further information // The best overall site for information is www.route-napoleon.com. The website is in French only, but look out for 'dépliant Anern' at the bottom to find a PDF of a useful brochure also in English, with route descriptions for the Alps, Haute-Provence and Côte d'Azur.

*Opposite: a stretch of the Military
Road in Northumberland, England,
running parallel to Hadrian's Wall*

MORE LIKE THIS
IN HISTORIC FOOTSTEPS

BERTHA BENZ MEMORIAL ROUTE, GERMANY

In the cult of the automobile, what pilgrimage route could be more sacred than this: the first long-distance car journey in history. In August 1888, Bertha Benz, wife of inventor Karl, secretly took his Patent-Motorwagen, which had barely been driven outside the factory in Mannheim, and set off for Pforzheim with her two sons, ostensibly to visit her parents but also to prove the practical use of this hitherto poorly-selling new contraption. Challenges included having to improvise repairs with her hairpin and garter, and finding somewhere to refuel. The town pharmacy in Wiesloch where she bought Ligroin (a detergent and early type of fuel) is now honoured as the world's first petrol station. A signposted figure-of-eight route from Mannheim to Pforzheim and back follows Bertha Benz's journey where practical.

Start // Mannheim
End // Mannheim
Distance // 121 miles (194km)

CAMINO DEL CID, SPAIN

Rodrigo Díaz de Vivar, the 11th-century knight better known as El Cid, rode to campaigns on his legendary warhorse Babieca. The modern Camino del Cid goes further, with options for hikers, cyclists and drivers. The itineraries all cut across northeast Spain, visiting historic sites connected with the medieval hero, who fought with both Christian and Muslim armies, immortalised in the 1961 epic starring Charlton Heston and Sophia Loren. The slightly meandering route runs from El Cid's supposed birthplace north of the cathedral city of Burgos, to the southernmost reach of the domains he briefly carved out in Orihuela, taking a recommended fortnight. Even if you choose to speed up the pace, you'll enjoy a stirring parade of castle towns such as Albarracín and Xàtiva, Moorish heritage including the date palm grove at Elche, and gastronomic discoveries, not least in the city of Valencia.

Start // Vivar del Cid
End // Orihuela
Distance // 858 miles (1380km)

B6318 MILITARY ROAD, ENGLAND & SCOTLAND

The B6318 has two claims to fame. The niche-interest one is that it's the longest B-road in Britain. The more historical is that for much of its route, it parallels Hadrian's Wall, or even runs on the foundations of this one-time northern border of the Roman Empire, ordered by the emperor Hadrian in AD 122. More than 16 centuries later, in the aftermath of the Jacobite Rebellion, General George Wade built one of his many 'military roads', unfortunately cannibalising some of the original wall. To be faithful to the road-numbering, if not the end-points of the wall, start in Langholm just north of the Anglo-Scottish border and continue east on a narrow, zigzagging track through a region once known ominously as the Debatable Lands. The B6318 joins the wall at Gilsland, and in its Northumbrian stretch it follows the kind of ruler-straight, hills-be-damned course that a Roman would have been proud of.

Start // Langholm
End // Heddon-on-the-Wall
Distance // 62 miles (100km)

JOINING THE LOCHS FROM GLASGOW

From Scotland's largest city, Glasgow, Adam Weymouth set out on a quest to find seafood from the source, outdoor swimming, craggy summits and majestic castles.

went to university in Glasgow, and despite living in a flat in the heart of the West End, I never felt hemmed in, as I always had in London. I could see mountains from the bedroom window, and just a 30-minute ride away on my bike I could be up in the hills – and then back home in time for a gig. I loved this lively, edgy city that was only a stone's throw from the beauty of Scotland's Southern Highlands. A favourite way to make the most of this proximity was on a drive to Inveraray, on a route that never strayed more than a few hours from my student home, yet, by the time I arrived at the icy waters of Loch Lomond, always felt a world away.

I've lost count of the number of times I've travelled the A82, the prosaic name for a poetic road. While at university I would hitch up it almost every weekend – standing with my thumb out at the petrol station at the end of Great Western Rd always spelt the beginning of adventure. And every time it would come as a shock to me how suddenly the city fell away. The road leading out of Glasgow is much like any other, a mishmash of shops and suburbia, car showrooms

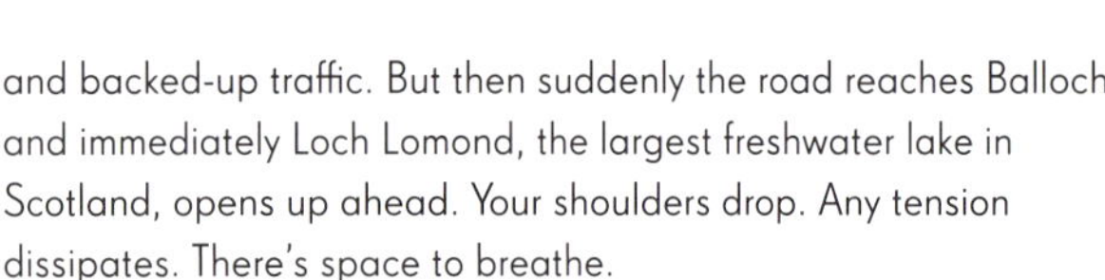

and backed-up traffic. But then suddenly the road reaches Balloch and immediately Loch Lomond, the largest freshwater lake in Scotland, opens up ahead. Your shoulders drop. Any tension dissipates. There's space to breathe.

It's no wonder that Loch Lomond is where Glaswegians go to relax and indulge in some outdoor fun. And in my post student life, and with my own car, I had more time to explore its varied corners. A short detour from Balloch, up the loch's eastern edge, lies the little village of Balmaha, where a five-minute ferry ride drops me on Inchcailloch, one of many islands scattered across Loch Lomond's southern end. Even though it's a glorious day in early May, it's midweek and early, so I can wander through the oaks with the whole place to myself. I can hear nothing but birds. And the tiny biting midges are, thankfully, not flying yet. A half hour walk to the far side of the island brings me to one of the few sandy beaches on the loch, and the single yacht anchored there doesn't deter me from stripping off and plunging into the water. The cold arrives as a fiery slap across the body and I swim hard to warm up, my whoops of glee breaking the morning stillness. All thoughts of the city are now forgotten, washed off.

Drying off on the beach I gaze up at Ben Lomond, Scotland's most southerly Munro (Munros, of which there are 282, are Scottish peaks over 3000ft/914m). In my student days, as part of an art project, I walked from my house to the top of Ben Lomond – 'flat to summit', I

> ## "The road reaches Loch Lomond and your shoulders drop. Any tension dissipates. There's space to breathe"

cleverly called it. Even that only took two days. I have climbed Ben Lomond several times since: from the car park a little further up this road, a few steep hours taking me to the peak and extraordinary views across the loch and back over the city. I slept up there once, and woke to deer and a pink sunrise. It might be one of Scotland's most climbed peaks, but it's no less special for that. Today, though, there's no time. The road calls.

Back in the car, I drive back through Balloch and follow the A82 up the western side of the loch, keeping one eye on the road and one on the lookout for ospreys, hunting over the water. Once extinct in Britain, these magnificent raptors returned to Scotland in the 1950s and there are now more than 200 breeding pairs. It's not uncommon to see them in this area.

I leave Loch Lomond at Tarbet, and in a little over a mile I am already at the head of Loch Long. The Arrochar Alps begin here, the land bunching up into a small cluster of mountains between the upper reaches of Loch Long and Loch Goil. I have seen them brushed with snow in summer, and in winter they can be as austere

ECCENTRIC POLO

Inveraray Castle is still owned by the Duke of Argyll, currently Torquhil Ian Campbell, who once became known for captaining Scotland to their wins in the 2004 and 2005 World Elephant Polo Association World Championships. This unconventional activity was played with four elephants per side, and polo sticks up to 10 feet long. It had a following of eccentrics, but allegations of animal cruelty led to its removal from the *Guinness Book of World Records*.

From left: Dumbarton Castle before the River Clyde; seafood served fresh from the source at Loch Fyne; open water swimming on Loch Lomond; Inveraray Castle; the village of Balmaha from the West Highland Way. Previous page: the A82 viewed looking north along Loch Lomond

and beautiful as anything in mainland Europe. The Cobbler is the best known of them, supposedly resembling a shoemaker at work, although I never could see it myself. The drive itself is spectacular, too, rising up through Glen Croe in the shadow of Beinn Ìme to the pass at the exquisitely named Rest and Be Thankful, a reminder of quite what a journey this would have been for travellers in times past.

The road descends to Cairndow and the third loch of my route, Loch Fyne, known for seafood, oysters in particular, and the eponymous UK-wide chain of restaurants. It all began here, at the Loch Fyne Oyster Bar. The family-owned Fyne Ales, made just round the corner up a little track, are equally excellent. They too are found all over Scotland now, but there's nothing like going to the source. I stop in for a cold beer in the shaded courtyard. Tempting as it would be to linger over another, I get back behind the wheel and head west, making Inveraray for sunset.

The weather still holds and the long light of a late spring evening spills across the buildings on Inveraray's harbour front. This place is a beautiful spot, a grand Georgian town conceived by the Duke of Argyll in the mid-18th century, designed to complement his newly rebuilt castle. It still feels grand, all whitewashed houses and wide streets. I do what I always do here and get a fish supper from the chip shop on the high street, taking it down to the water's edge. The first of the swallows have returned, dipping over the loch. I lie on the grass. It's just a few hours back to Glasgow, and I'm not in any rush.

DIRECTIONS

Start // Glasgow
End // Inveraray
Distance // 64 miles (103 km)

Getting there // The most luxurious way to get to the start of this route in Glasgow is on the recently refurbished Caledonian Sleeper from London.

When to go // The drive is beautiful at any time of year, although Rest and Be Thankful can close after heavy snows: check trafficscotland.org for up-to-date information.

What to pack // The long summer days are beautiful, but the midges (biting insects) can be awful from June to September so don't forget the repellent – or even a bug hat.

Where to stay // The Drovers Inn, a ten-mile detour at the top of Loch Lomond, is a fascinating pub full of stuffed animals and local history, with live music at weekends.

*Opposite from top: the lakeside city
of Ohrid, North Macedonia; Lake
Saimaa, in the Finnish Lakeland*

MORE LIKE THIS
LAKESIDE DRIVES

ANNECY, FRANCE

Lake Annecy found fame in Paul Cézanne's
Le Lac d'Annecy painting, a post-
Impressionist masterpiece that captures all
the beauty, grandeur and violence of the
landscape here. But nothing beats seeking
out that drama yourself. It takes just a lazy
day's driving to travel its circumference,
along glimmering blue water with
snowcapped Alps behind. Base yourself
in Annecy and explore the gorgeous Old
Town and lively markets before setting off.
Impressive Château Menthon is well worth
visiting, and has guided tours throughout
the summer months. Stop at Talloires for
lunch – it has a fine selection of restaurants
and good swimming beaches – and then,
if you've still got the energy, hike one of the
many trails that wind up to the peaks that
surround the lake. Finish back in Annecy for
a sunset drink with panoramic views across
the water at the Hotel Belvédère.

Start // Annecy
End // Annecy
Distance // 25 miles (40km)

FINNISH LAKELAND

A quarter of the Finnish Lakeland region
is water – there are at least 55,000 lakes
here, making it the largest lake district in
Europe. To drive in this area is to lose all
distinction between the water and the road.
From Varkaus, it's less than an hour's drive
to the Järvisydän spa, offering every type of
soaking and sweating you can imagine. It's
not all about relaxing though – as you drive
across this watery landscape there is ample
opportunity for swimming and canoeing,
fishing and boat trips, or, in winter, skating
and snowshoeing. Finland's 'Right to Roam'
means that camping is permitted just about
anywhere, but the hotels might still tempt
you. The Ollinmäki Wine Farm, just outside
Anttola, has villas, fabulous food, homemade wine and nearby lakes for a final
road trip dip.

Start // Varkaus
End // Anttola
Distance // 86 miles (138km)

LAKE OHRID TO LAKE PRESPA, NORTH MACEDONIA

Lake Ohrid is one of the oldest and
deepest lakes in the world, straddling the
border between North Macedonia and
Albania. Despite its Unesco status and
being home to a multitude of endemic
species, it remains remarkably unvisited.
Begin in the ancient, picturesque city
of Ohrid, continuously occupied since
Neolithic times. Its Grecian theatre,
recently rediscovered and restored,
hosts an arts festival each summer. As
you drive south you pass fortresses and
monasteries, teetering dramatically above
the water. Leave Lake Ohrid on a series of
switchbacks climbing up through Galičica
National Park, where at the road's highest
point a trail leading farther up offers a view
across both lakes. Descend to the tranquil
Lake Prespa in time for dinner, stopping
at one of the many small restaurants in
Oteshevo that serve fish landed straight
from the lake.

Start // Ohrid
End // Oteshevo
Distance // 34 miles (55km)

THE E-GRAND TOUR OF SWITZERLAND

Swinging from cultured cities to natural wonders, Kerry Walker's eco-minded Swiss drive delivered abbeys, medieval castles, legendary lakes and yodel-worthy Alpine views.

When it comes to bridging the gap between the urban and the outdoors, nowhere nails it quite like Switzerland. I muse this point as I wind down my car window on the shores of Lake Zürich, in the hush of early morning. The water spreads out like a deep-blue silk sheet, with late-spring light promising to render every photo a masterpiece.

I'm on a stretch of the 'Grand Tour of Switzerland', a 1000 mile (1600km) route that shows off this proud little Alpine nation's most flattering angles. Devised with stereotypical Swiss efficiency, the entire well-signposted drive whisks you effortlessly from chic cities to Unesco World Heritage Sites, great lakes to glaciers, mountain passes to castles. The Alps often pop into view. The scenery is always distractingly lovely. And the drive is wholly sustainable, entirely doable by electric vehicle, with plenty of charging stations along the way. But it's too big for one trip so, with a week on my hands, I decide to take on the 196 mile (315km) leg that links Zürich to Bern.

I spend just a day in the former, where outstanding art galleries, architect Le Corbusier's boldly coloured designs and the edgily post-industrial Zürich-West neighbourhood notch things up a gear culturally. Zürich is a city that never seems to miss a beat, from cool waterside bars on the banks of the Limmat to its alley-woven Old Town. But it's the Romanesque Grossmünster that really grabs me. Legend has it that Holy Roman emperor Charlemagne founded the twin-spired church when his horse tripped over the graves of the city's patron saints, Felix and Regula. Now the interior shines with the kaleidoscopic brilliance of Augusto Giacometti's stained-glass windows. It's hard to drag myself away, but the road south beckons.

I don't get far, because who could resist Rapperswil? The mellow town at the tail end of Lake Zürich is straight from the pages of a bedtime story. It's outrageously pretty, with a turreted castle presiding over white gabled houses that stagger down vine-streaked slopes to the lakeshore. The Glarus Alps are etched on the horizon, some

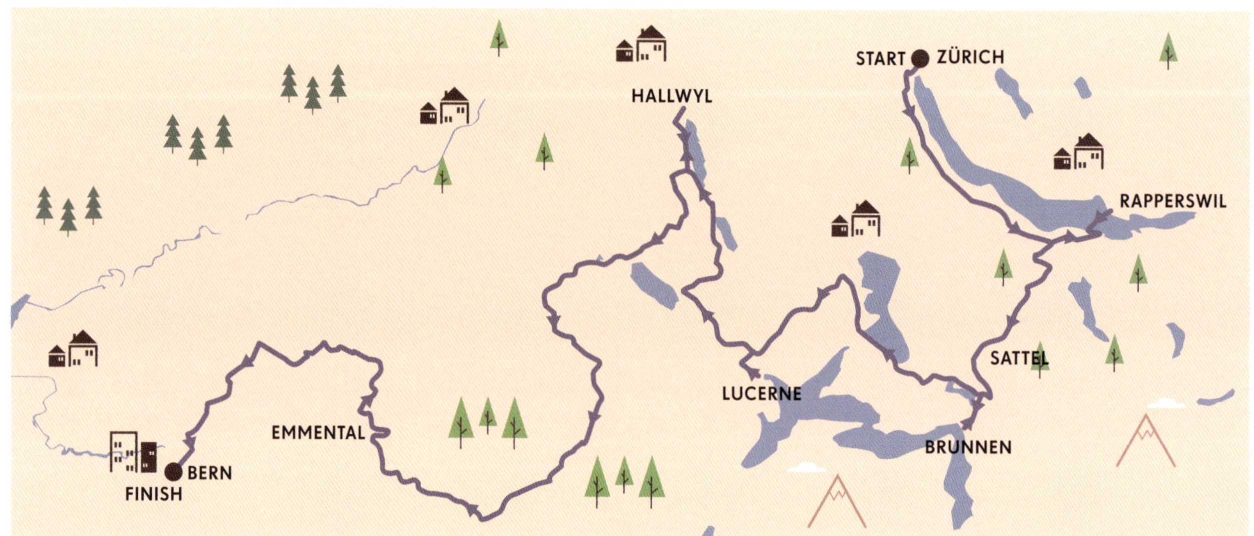

peaks still lightly dusted with snow. Deer roam in the castle grounds and, I'm told, 16,000 varieties of rose bring a riot of scent and colour to the nearby gardens of the Capuchin monastery in summer. In half an hour's drive from Zürich, I've gone from hip to Heidi in a flash. But that's the beauty of Switzerland.

Moving from one lake to the next, the road dips south to Einsiedeln on the shores of Sihlsee. Though small on the map, this town looms large in the national consciousness, with a huge Benedictine abbey that has drawn pilgrims for centuries. This is Switzerland's answer to Lourdes. In AD 964, the Bishop of Constance tried to consecrate the original monastery but was halted by a heavenly voice, declaring: 'Desist. God Himself has consecrated this building.' Or so the story goes. A papal order later recognised this as a genuine miracle. I step into the Klosterkirche and don't know where to look first. The church is Baroque in overdrive, fussy with frescoes, cherubs and stucco – as intricate and delicate as a Fabergé egg. True pilgrims direct their focus and prayers to the Black Madonna near the entrance.

Continuing, the mountains rise higher en route to Sattel, sitting astride placid, sapphire-blue lake Ägerisee. I ride the revolving cable car up to Sattel-Hochstuckli, where the air is pine-fresh, the first wildflowers are sprinkling the slopes and there's an arresting view of the jagged Schwyzer Alps. From the Skywalk suspension bridge, dangling giddily above the Lauitobel Gorge, the treetops feel close enough to reach out and touch.

Back at ground level, my drive south swings to Brunnen, clasped between craggy forested peaks on the shores of fjord-like lakes Lucerne and Uri. Turner raved about the romance of this view,

MOUNTAINS OF MYTH

Lake Lucerne's mythical twin peaks make a scenic day trip. Take the world's steepest cog railway up to Mt Pilatus, said to be haunted by Pontius Pilate's ghost. Wagner raved about its still-astonishing Alpine panorama and Queen Victoria trotted up on horseback. If a pretty sunrise or sunset grabs you, make your way up Mt Rigi too. The peak fascinated Turner, who painted it in three different lights to reflect its changing moods.

Clockwise from above: Lake Lucerne, viewed from Brunnen; the route traces the banks of Lake Lucerne; the medieval town of Murten, by the lake of the same name. Previous page: skirting cliffs by Lake Thun

immortalised in his painting *The Bay of Uri*, from Brunnen. It's lovely, undoubtedly, and even more so from the water, so I board a ferry to chug across Lake Uri for a better look at Switzerland's geographical and spiritual heartland. We cruise past the meadow of Rütli, birthplace of the Swiss nation, where the Oath of Eternal Allegiance was signed in 1291, and on to the Tellskapelle, a tiny speck of a chapel embedded in woods. Lore has it that apple-shooting, rebel-yelling folk hero William Tell leapt from the boat of his Habsburg captors to safety here more than 700 years ago.

At the opposite end of the lake, I wander along the promenade in Lucerne as the sun sets. The little city punches above its weight culturally, with a covered medieval bridge, Jean Nouvel-designed KKL arts centre and the Sammlung Rosengart, which holds a prized private collection of Picassos. Ambling past the Belle Époque hotels lining the lake, the same views that captivated Goethe, Queen Victoria and Wagner in the 19th century hold me in their thrall.

The final days of my electrically propelled road trip are a feast of culture, nature and food. I revel in the beauty of Hallwyl and its moated castle, plonked in the middle of the River Aabach. I spend quiet, happy moments hiking in the mountains and moors of Entlebuch Biosphere Reserve, pausing to picnic beside glass-clear streams. I slow tour through Emmental, land of holey cheese, working my way through meadows grazed by doe-eyed, bell-swinging cows, and sampling cheese at the show dairy in Affoltern.

The Swiss capital Bern is my final stop, with its elegant arcades, flag-festooned Old Town, Einstein legacy and Renzo Piano-designed Zentrum Paul Klee. Needing a pick-me-up after the drive, I decide to take a swim in the Aare River. Like many Swiss rivers, it is startlingly turquoise, having sprung up in the glaciers that ice the country's highest mountains. It's a clear reminder that even when you are right in the heart of a city in Switzerland, nature is only ever a step away.

> *"The drive whisks you effortlessly from chic cities to Unesco Sites, great lakes to glaciers, mountain passes to castles"*

DIRECTIONS

Start // Zürich
End // Bern
Distance // 196 miles (315km)
Getting there // Zürich has fast, efficient train connections linking up to major European cities, and an international airport, served by airlines including SWISS and easyJet.
Electric car rental // Companies including Sixt and Europcar rent out electric vehicles, including the latest Tesla models. To find charging stations en route, check the clickable map of the E-Grand Tour of Switzerland on the My Switzerland website www.myswitzerland.com.
When to go // This depends on your Grand Tour route, but if you're aiming high, May/June through to September is the best time, dodging snow and ice on Alpine passes.
Further information // grandtour.myswitzerland.com is the definitive go-to for comprehensive route details, maps, planning information, bookings and more.

The E-Grand Tour of Switzerland

Opposite: looping switchbacks of the St Gotthard Pass, in the Swiss Alps, seen from the Tremola viewpoint

MORE LIKE THIS
GRAND TOUR DRIVES

LUGANO TO ZERMATT

This phenomenal drive takes you into southern Switzerland's Alpine heart. Kick off in lakeside Lugano, with a generous pinch of dolce vita and a shot of culture at the progressive LAC arts centre. From here, swing north to mountain-rimmed Locarno, with its botanical gardens and palazzo-filled Renaissance Old Town, and Unesco World Heritage-listed Bellinzona, with its hat-trick of medieval fortresses. The language flicks from Italian to German as you power north into the Alps proper and Airolo at the foot of the looping St Gotthard Pass. Andermatt is all about big wilderness and lofty peaks, while just west, the heart-quickening, hairpin bend-riddled Furka Pass leads you up and over into the glacier-encrusted mountains of Valais. Bettmeralp and the epic Aletsch Glacier, and Brig with its whimsical Stockalper Palace, are but the drumroll for Zermatt, where the mighty fang of the Matterhorn elicits gasps of wonder.

Start // Lugano
End // Zermatt
Distance // 165 miles (265km)

APPENZELL TO ST MORITZ

This road trip begins in a deeply traditional, little-explored corner of northeast Switzerland, Appenzell, where dairy country rolls to rugged mountains and folksy, fresco-adorned towns. From Appenzell, swing south to Säntis for views embracing six countries, then head west to Toggenburg and the seven wavy limestone peaks of the Churfirsten. Up next is Werdenberg, a tiny speck of a medieval hamlet, with a sprinkling of timber chalets. Close by is Vaduz, Liechtenstein's princely, castle-topped capital on the banks of the Rhine. Inching further south brings you to Maienfeld, of pinot wine and Heidi fame. Things take a more dramatic Alpine turn as the road meanders southeast to the gorge-spanning Salginatobel Bridge and ski-and-hike hub Davos, where Thomas Mann penned *The Magic Mountain*. Dally a while in lovely Engadine villages like Guarda and Zernez, fringing the lonely, wild magic of the Swiss National Park, as you cruise south to St Moritz, where sky-high mountains promise big adventures.

Start // Appenzell
End // St Moritz
Distance // 124 miles (200km)

GENEVA TO NEUCHÂTEL

Lakes, vineyards, castles and canyons – this route spotlights the country's off-the-radar northwest, where Switzerland snuggles up to France in a dense blanket of fir forest. Starting with galleries and gardens in Geneva, the drive cruises along the same-name lake to castle-crowned, vine-rimmed Nyon. From here, head north to the Jura Vaudois Nature Park for hikes with dress-circle views of the lake and tastings of Gruyère cheese at rural huts. On the shores of Lac de Joux, the watchmaking village of Le Sentier is a well-timed stop en route to Vallorbe, richly honeycombed with Switzerland's biggest (and most impressive) limestone caves. Lac de Neuchâtel and its surrounds enchant, particularly the thermal waters of Yverdon-les-Bains, the lushly rolling Val-de-Travers (birthplace of absinthe) and the great crescent-moon canyon of Creux du Van. Cultured Neuchâtel is a fitting climax, with a lavishly turreted medieval château fulfilling every childhood fantasy.

Start // Geneva
End // Neuchâtel
Distance // 100 miles (160km)

ROMANCING THE ROAD

Love was soon in the air as Andrea Schulte-Peevers drove along Germany's fabled Romantic Road, enjoying storybook villages, lyrical landscapes and mighty castles on her trip.

The moon is high when the heavy oak door of an ancient wine tavern clanks shut behind me. Palate still abuzz with the mineral crispness from a glass of classic Silvaner, I embark on an aimless amble through cobbled lanes worn smooth by centuries of horses' hooves and shoe leather. Twinkling gas lanterns illuminate half-timbered houses where red geraniums billow from flower boxes. The turreted town hall watches over a silent market square in all its Gothic grandeur.

I'm in Rothenburg ob der Tauber, the unofficial capital of the Romantic Road, a scenic 285-mile (460km) ribbon of cultural, natural and historical riches meandering from the vineyards of Würzburg to Füssen in the foothills of the Bavarian Alps. By day, hordes of day-tripping tourists give this gingerbread town the air of a medieval theme park. But at night, wrapped into stillness, Rothenburg does justice to the Romantic Road's name.

Created in 1950 as a marketing ploy to polish Germany's post-WWII image, the Romantic Road is a string of highways and byways weaving through a matrix of vine-covered hillsides, sun-dappled pastures, river valleys, meadows smothered in wildflowers and Hansel-and-Gretel forests. It's a deliciously easy drive that connects storied villages, castles, churches, monuments, abbeys and palaces.

It was American soldiers stationed in post-war Germany who were first smitten by this mix of delights, while today the Romantic Road pulls in travellers from China to Chile in their millions. Yet, despite all that, it's worth falling for the sales pitch. I certainly did.

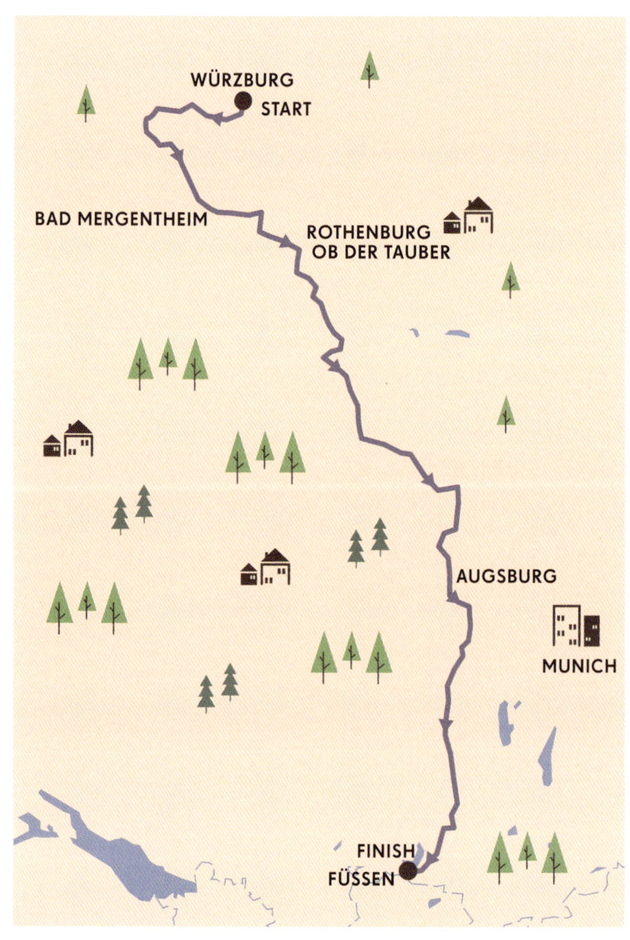

I pick a balmy Tuesday in May to launch my adventure and kick off an ambitious sightseeing schedule with a bang: Würzburg's Unesco-listed Residenz, an erstwhile prince-bishop's palace famous for its zigzagging grand staircase lidded by the world's largest ceiling fresco. The city is also the hub of the Franconian wine region, renowned for its whites, especially the crisp and slightly citrusy Silvaner. I resist the temptation – for now – to sample more local vintages, and hit the road.

Vineyards mix it up with fields of wheat and barley as I steer towards the Taubertal, a valley carved by the usually placid Tauber River. My first stop is bucolic Bad Mergentheim, a spa town famous for its underground springs and a humongous palace that served as the base for the Teutonic Knights, a Europe-wide military religious order founded in 1190. Down the road, clumps of blooming lilacs perfume the air in tidy Weikersheim, where I'm charmed by a coterie of cheeky gnomes, part of the sculpture ensemble scattered around the Baroque garden of tangerine-roofed Schloss Weikersheim. In Creglingen, I almost drive past the blink-and-you-miss-it Herrgottskirche chapel, whose Marienaltar – carved in dizzying detail by medieval master sculptor Tilman Riemenschneider – might even coax atheists into raptures.

The sun has started to drop towards the horizon, tinting the landscape with shades of crimson and ochres. Soon I see Rothenburg ob der Tauber, my stop for the night, looming above the Tauber Valley – there are few places in Germany with such a perfectly cinematic medieval look.

The next morning, a veil of mist lies over the ramparts as I take a last spin around the town before driving to Dinkelsbühl, which has a similar olde-worlde vibe but is less overrun. On a guided tour I learn how local children saved the town from destruction during the Thirty Years' War, pleading with Swedish troops to pass it by. Tall tale or not, the legend is still celebrated every July with a festival.

Back on the road, I plunge on to Nördlingen, another beautiful medieval settlement cradled by a fortified wall. This town, though, has the distinction of sitting smack within a massive crater gouged by a meteor some 15 million years ago. A short trail takes me to a platform overlooking the quarry where astronauts from NASA and the European Space Agency have conducted field-training sessions since the 1970s. Back in town, I tackle the 350 steps of the St Georgskirche church tower to take in the full panorama of Nördlingen's near-perfectly circular shape and hilly surrounds.

Cruising beyond, I encounter few roadside attractions until the silhouette of Harburg Castle pops up. The mighty 12th-century fortress is so well preserved, I expect to bump into a knight in shining armour, a fair lady at his arm, as I explore the grounds.

My day winds down in Augsburg, founded 2000 years ago as a Roman military camp under Emperor Augustus, although it's more famously associated with a medieval tycoon named Jakob Fugger. Not only did this banker and merchant lend money to emperors and popes, he also masterminded the world's oldest social housing complex, the Fuggerei. For 500 years, its residents

ROYAL DREAMS

Neuschwanstein is Germany's most famous palace, but King Ludwig II's favourite retreat was petite Schloss Linderhof, a worthy 30 mile (45km) detour from Füssen. Dripping in ornate finery, it's where the eccentric monarch indulged his quirkiest fantasies. Picture him rowing a conch-shaped boat around a stalactite-studded grotto, lounging like a pasha on a peacock throne or dining with imaginary friends at a 'magic' table cranked up from the kitchen below.

From left: colourful medieval buildings in Nördlingen; Schloss Weikersheim; King Ludwig II's best known folly, Neuschwanstein; the Rococo interior of the Wieskirche, Steingade. Previous page: the Old Bridge spans the Main River in Würzburg

have paid the equivalent of 1 Reichsgulden (about 88 US cents) per year for their small but functional abodes. A show flat and museum provide insights into the history of the Fuggerei and the everyday lives of its inhabitants through the ages.

The final stretch of the Romantic Road first has me cruising serenely past fields and forests, meadows and wetlands with the Lech River never far away. I skirt Landsberg am Lech, an ancient and pretty riverside town that has the misfortune of having entered history books as the place where Adolf Hitler penned *Mein Kampf* in prison after the failed 1923 Munich Beer Hall Putsch.

By now, the Bavarian Alps have whipped into view, all muscular glory carved by glaciers and the elements – and still flaunting a tiara of snow at this time of year. I break my journey at the Wieskirche, a Unesco World Heritage Site and place of pilgrimage, whose elegant but modest white exterior belies the full-on symphony of Rococo exuberance that lies within.

My drive comes to an end in Füssen. This is where the Romantic Road reaches its climax at Neuschwanstein, the archetypal fairy-tale castle dreamed up by Bavarian King Ludwig II and the primary inspiration for Disney's Sleeping Beauty Castle. Ludwig himself found inspiration in the operas of Richard Wagner. As I find myself entranced by this dreamy snowy-white composition of towers and turrets, an apt quote attributed to Romantic literary lion Johann Wolfgang von Goethe drops into my head: 'Architecture,' he said, 'is like frozen music'.

DIRECTIONS

Start // Würzburg
End // Füssen
Distance // 285 miles (460km)
Getting there // The nearest international airports are in Frankfurt, northwest of Würzburg, and in Munich, northeast of Füssen.
When to go // Travel midweek in May, June, September and October to avoid major crowds.
Timing // Budget at least one overnight stop, preferably two, to do this sight-intensive route justice.
Where to stay // Hotel Sonne in Füssen has suitably romantic rooms and art in the public areas.
Further information // Check out the official Romantic Road website at www.romantischestrasse.de for trip planning information (in English).

Romancing the Road

MORE LIKE THIS
GERMAN HISTORIC DRIVES

DEUTSCHE MÄRCHENSTRASSE

Once upon a time there were two brothers who published a compendium of fanciful stories that captivate people around the world to this day: *Grimms' Fairy Tales*. The German Fairy Tale Route not only strings together waystations in the lives of Jacob and Wilhelm Grimm but also takes in dozens of sites that inspired the fables, legends and sagas they collected. Snoop around the cottage where Snow White hung out with the Seven Dwarfs; spend the night in Sleeping Beauty's rose-draped castle; traipse around Mother Hulda's mountain. The route kicks off in the Grimms' birthplace of Hanau, just east of Frankfurt, and weaves past half-timbered villages, bewitching castles and enchanted forests before wrapping up at a statue featuring a donkey, a dog, a cat and a rooster – aka the Town Musicians of Bremen. No matter if you drive all of it or just a short stretch, expect the Fairy Tale Road to charm you.

Start // Hanau
End // Bremen
Distance // 373 miles (600km)

DEUTSCHE BURGENSTRASSE

Even if you're not a royal groupie or, at least, a *Harry Potter* fan, let's agree that castles and palaces exude an undeniable mystique. Perhaps it's the tales of intrigue, love, power and betrayal lurking behind those thick walls that fuel our fascination with the past. Maybe it's the jumble of turrets, towers, ramparts and drawbridges that spur our imagination. Or it could be the commanding hilltop locations or lush interiors drenched in gold and jewels. All of the above is what you encounter along Germany's Castle Road, your route to the Middle Ages. Take two days or better two weeks to follow in the footsteps of queens and knights as you travel through the picturesque hamlets, romantic towns and undulating landscapes of this fabled route linking Mannheim and Bayreuth. Top stops: the fortresses in Heidelberg, Nuremberg and Veste Coburg.

Start // Mannheim
End // Bayreuth
Distance // 485 miles (780km

STRASSE DER ROMANIK

The eastern German state of Saxony-Anhalt is famous for its saints' ransom of abbeys, churches, cathedrals and castles, built during the early Middle Ages in an architectural style called Romanesque (Romanik in German). Almost 90 of them are linked by the Romanesque Road which careens around the region roughly in a figure of eight shape. Most people don't aspire to see them all, preferring to cherry-pick their favourites. Places that will likely make you step on the brakes include: the exalted cathedral in Magdeburg, which contains the tomb of Otto I, the first Holy Roman Emperor; Quedlinburg, with one of Germany's oldest half-timbered houses; and Naumburg, where you can admire a statue of 'medieval supermodel' Uta von Ballenstedt. The latter two have been recognized as Unesco World Heritage Sites.

Start // Magdeburg
End // Magdeburg
Distance // 620 miles (1000km)

THE WINDSWEPT WILD ATLANTIC WAY

Untamed and utterly divine, Ireland's west coast is a dramatic procession of deserted beaches and towering cliffs, where Etain O'Carroll found traditional music and ancient castles abound.

A 'savage beauty' said Oscar Wilde and it's certainly true. Ireland's west coast is battered by Atlantic rollers, strewn with jagged cliffs and littered with wide beaches and sandy coves. It's a place where inky lakes shelter between mountains, sinewy stone walls clamber across hillsides and trees are frequently bent double by the wind. The roads here are narrow and winding, grass often grows along a hump in their middle and a herd of sheep can easily scupper all plans.

It's the part of Ireland I love most. I grew up only an hour from the coast but now that I live abroad I rarely get to spend much time here. Trips home are a whirlwind of family gatherings and, despite my best intentions, a stay on the coast never quite seems to happen. But then the contorted back roads, deserted beaches and turquoise coves of my childhood got rebranded as the Wild Atlantic Way: a 1600-mile (2600km) route that traces all the twists, turns and crenulations of Ireland's rugged west coast. I fell for it, hook, line and sinker.

Why take a day trip when I could investigate every little side road and dead end route that I never had time to take? I could wander aimlessly on a set course and just let the incredible landscape unfold along the way.

The route commences on the Inishowen Peninsula in Donegal, which is a remote and rugged place that's also Ireland's most northerly point and an area peppered with traditional thatched cottages, ancient ruins and enormous numbers of birds. Donegal is wild and mountainous and I start out on my journey by meandering down coastal roads past gloriously deserted beaches. I climb the thick walls of the Grianán of Aileách,

© Andrea Ricordi | soopx

a 2000-year-old circular stone fort perched on a 244 metre-high barren hillside, sit mesmerised by the views of Mount Errigal and marvel at the Slieve League cliffs, which plunge 600 metres down into the ocean below.

Heading south, the familiar, flat-topped monolith of Benbulben soon appears, every bit as beautiful as I remember it. From Streedagh Beach the view is sublime, back to Slieve League and south to mountain tops littered with prehistoric graves. I'm tempted to climb to Queen Maeve's grave but speed off instead to Enniscrone and unwind with a hot and slippery dip in an Edwardian seaweed bath. I forge on, aware there's a long way to go and little time to linger. I pass the Céide Fields, the world's most extensive Stone Age monument, holler in the wind on the beach at Belmullet and feel the sorrow of the past in Achill's abandoned famine villages.

Impetuous weather and tortuous roads remind me that it's a harsh place to live but it's all forgotten in a blur of colourful good cheer and rousing traditional music in Georgian Westport. I climb Croagh Patrick, Ireland's holiest mountain, and am treated to a clear view of the islands of Clew Bay. I stop for a bowl of steaming Killary Harbour mussels at the head of the moody inlet, see salmon being smoked on the pier at Ballyconneely and watch the sun set over turquoise waters from the idyllic white sands of Dog's Bay.

Vibrant, bohemian Galway soon gives way to the limestone fields of the Burren, the precipitous Cliffs of Moher and the reels and jigs that are a feature of Doolin's pubs. The driving is easy; the challenge is not getting waylaid along the way.

I make my way to places I've only ever heard of on the shipping forecast, where colourful lighthouses pilot ships to safety. In a downpour I remind myself why I set out to do this at all, to reach places just like this, that I would never have bothered to visit otherwise, where dead end roads question my commitment but reward me with incredible views.

I take a ferry across the Shannon Estuary and enter the 'kingdom' of Kerry. I drive Slea Head and round furrowed headlands to see brilliant beaches embraced by rocky cliffs. The Blasket Islands look beguiling but I struggle to see beyond the tales of unrelenting hardship recounted by author and islander Peig Sayers, which are a staple on the Irish school curriculum. I revel in Dingle's traditional pub-cum-hardware shops before blowing away the cobwebs on the sweeping expanse of Inch Beach.

Then it's on to the Ring of Kerry to wind my way around Ireland's highest peaks, Macgillycuddy's Reeks, and past the jagged Skelligs where a 6th-century monastery doubled as Luke Skywalker's secret hideaway in *The Force Awakens*. As I head south from Kenmare the traffic eases away as I make my way along the wonderfully remote Beara Peninsula. Vividly painted fishing villages and farming communities dot the mountainsides, sheep wander everywhere, some even transported to their island home by cable car.

The scenery calms as I make my way through prosperous West Cork and I can feel my journey is almost at an end. I soak up the sun in remote Barleycove before making the final push through picturesque villages with quaint names and bobbing yachts, trendy shops and organic farmers' markets to the narrow, winding streets of Kinsale, where gourmet restaurants tempt me to celebrate the end of this epic journey.

I don't really feel like celebrating, though. Instead of scratching an itch, this invigorating journey has succeeded in opening up a legion of longing. I want to go back again, to do all the things I missed this time around: to hop on ferries to outlying islands, kayak around headlands, hike up mountains, scramble over castle ruins, visit oyster beds and spend however long it takes to learn to surf.

Yes, the rain poured and the wind whipped at my skin at times, but it's only when you've given up on the downpour ever stopping that you appreciate the magic of the clouds parting and the sun lighting up the hillsides. It's only then you realise that there's nowhere quite so beautiful.

FRUIT OF THE SEA

Great seafood is one of the consummate joys of driving the Wild Atlantic Way with everything from slick restaurants to cosy pubs and roadside trailers serving succulent lobster, oysters, mussels and salmon straight from the sea. You can forage for seafood with a local guide, visit smoke houses and mussel farms, tour oyster beds or join in a food festival to see how the landscape and customs influence the fine foods the region produces today.

Opposite: the still waters of Derryclare Lough in Connemara. Previous page: Fanad Head lighthouse, close to Inishowen Peninsula

DIRECTIONS

Start // Inishowen
End // Kinsale
Distance // 1600 miles (2600km)
Getting there // Just across the river from Inishowen, Derry has a small airport but Belfast, 95 miles (150km) away, has more choice. Kinsale is 12 miles (20km) from Cork Airport.
When to drive // April to October when it's marginally less inclined to rain.
What to take // Raincoats, wellies, hiking boots, umbrellas, wet suits, an ark; whatever it takes to withstand the changeable weather.
Car hire // At Derry and Belfast airports in Northern Ireland but returning to Cork Airport will incur a hefty fee. It's better to hire and return to the same spot in the Republic.
More info // www.thewildatlanticway.com

Opposite: fishing boats at harbour in
Saint-Jean-de-Luz, southwest France

MORE LIKE THIS
IN SEARCH OF SEAFOOD

SOUTHWEST COAST, FRANCE

The Bay of Biscay is a source of thrills for surfers and often dismay for seasick ferry passengers, but its French shore also offers up prized ingredients and produce such as Arcachon oysters and *fleur de sel* from the salt marshes of the Île de Ré. This island's pale-hued fishing ports are a fitting lead-in for a drive that continues over a bridge to mainland La Rochelle (home to triple-starred seafood restaurant Christopher Coutanceau), and then to Royan and the ferry south across the Gironde estuary. The Côte d'Argent begins on the far side: 145 miles (233km) of sand broken only by a few river outlets and Arcachon Bay. Roads run inland of the dunes (including Europe's largest, Dune du Pilat) through the pine forests of the Landes. Finish in the Basque Country, by the smiling harbour of Saint-Jean-de-Luz, with a bowl of *ttoro*, the local fish soup.

Start // Les Portes-en-Ré
End // Saint-Jean-de-Luz
Distance // 283 miles (455km)

CORNISH FISHING PORTS, ENGLAND

From crab shacks to celebrity chefs' restaurants, Cornwall's harbour towns and villages have never laid on such a varied seafood feast as now. Though quaysides with boats a-bobbing can be found on both coasts, it's the north shore that has the biggest names, including Michelin stars in Port Isaac and Padstow. An exploration of the county's old fishing ports could well start at Boscastle, its impossibly tight inlet a demonstration of how Cornish fishermen worked around the contorted geography here. A drive south (sticking close to the coast where possible, on often narrow roads) includes Tintagel and its castle, the sands of Polzeath and Harlyn, sea stacks at Bedruthan Steps, and bigger-town attractions at Newquay and St Ives. To finish, cut south across Cornwall's toe past Penzance and Newlyn, to reach Mousehole and its dinky half-moon harbour.

Start // Boscastle
End // Mousehole
Distance // 97 miles (156km)

ARCHIPELAGO TRAIL, FINLAND

In the Archipelago Sea, the Finnish mainland appears to dissolve into the Baltic, with tens of thousands of islands and skerries – most uninhabited, some barely big enough to fit a painted cabin and a jetty clamped to the rocks. Year-round settlements are served by car ferries (mostly free of charge), and from mid-May to the end of August when all are running, you can drive a circular route southwest from the city of Turku right out into the archipelago. Much of the area is Swedish-speaking, and everywhere shares a love of locally sourced seafood. Alongside salmon and Baltic herring (prepared in a hundred and one ways), the sea's brackish waters allow for species such as pike, zander and vendace. The parts of the Archipelago Trail spent aboard ship are times to whet your appetite for the next stretch of road through quiet islands such as Houtskär and Iniö.

Start // Turku
End // Turku
Distance // 155 miles (250km)

PORTUGAL'S NATIONAL ROUTE 2

From the border with Spain in the north, Ann Abel travelled past mountains, vineyards and farmland to the beaches of Portugal's south, along the country's heartland road, National Route 2.

I feel it as I drove along the curves that hug the steep vineyards of the Douro Valley, slowing down for the tight twists. I feel it again as I cruise through the hills, cork forests, wheat fields and wide-open landscapes of the Alentejo, speeding up for the arrow-straight sections where it is just me and the clouds overhead. And I even feel it in the final stretch, the gentle downhill through scrubby countryside as mountains give way to sea in the Algarve, waiting for a glimmer of the ocean to appear in the distance. I feel I have made a good choice, choosing to live in this country.

Ever since I moved from the United States to Portugal in 2017, I've come to realise that Portugal is small yet incredibly diverse. Travel 30 miles in any direction and you're likely to encounter something remarkable – and quite different from something equally remarkable 30 miles the other way.

Still, I was surprised to learn that the longest national highway in Europe lies in my little adopted country. Portugal's National Route 2 (Rota da Estrada Nacional 2, or N2) runs for 459 miles (738.5km) from the border with Galicia in Spain to Portugal's southern Atlantic coast. You could do the whole trip in a long day's travel. But that would be a waste. A road that takes in four mountain ranges, 11 rivers, 29 municipalities, countless medieval hamlets, grand monuments, beautiful vineyards and rugged vistas along the way deserves at least a week, probably two. So what if that means just an hour or two in the car each day? Not every road trip is only about the road.

For some reason – probably due to the focus on ending up at a beach – almost everyone follows the N2 from north to south. And, with the beach in mind myself, I do too. That means starting in Chaves, in the Trás-os-Montes region, where the 'KM 0' distance marker is by an old Roman bridge over the Tâmega River. A pleasant starting point, certainly, but the drive really comes alive for me around 60 miles (100km) south when the road crosses into the Alto Douro Wine Region, a Unesco World Heritage Site (one of four along the drive) and the oldest demarcated wine region in the world. Heading south from Peso da Régua, a functional riverside town, I notice the

road bending more and more as it follows the curves formed by the Douro River and its tributaries. The steep hills around here are terraced with vineyards, all of which have big signs showing the names of the wineries.

"Portugal is small yet incredibly diverse. Travel 30 miles in any direction and you're likely to encounter something remarkable"

Later on, I pass through Lamego, a pretty wine-country town that retains traces of its grandeur from the 18th century, when it was a significant producer of the fortified wine that later became known as Port. I leave the car to explore the town with its glorious churches and a monumental hilltop Baroque shrine. Back on the road, I make a detour from the N2 to a nearby winery hotel where I sleep inside a giant barrique (wine barrel) transformed into a luxury room.

The road continues on another 37 miles (60km) or so to Viseu, one of the grandest cities of Portugal's Centro region. Along the way, it passes through the small village of Bigorne, notable as the route's highest point (a fairly modest 3280ft/1000m), and Castro Daire, a small town with lovely azulejo tile murals and enticing views of vineyard terraces and mountains. I pause again to explore Viseu on foot, a place known for its many well-preserved medieval structures.

From there, I push south, past more vineyards. Less steep and less terraced than those in the Douro Valley, these hug gentler slopes, and the road is more winding than curving, allowing me to enjoy the views of the Caramulo Mountains and, since it is a clear day, continental Portugal's highest range, the Serra da Estrela, rising to 6539ft (1993m) in the distance.

Soon the landscape and, especially, the architecture change again where the N2 passes near the schist villages of Portugal's interior, which look more like medieval Hobbit towns than the sun-drenched, whitewashed villages more commonly associated with the country. Truth be told, the central section of the route is not the most exciting, although it goes through bucolic farmland and

RIVER BEACH LIFE

Along with its world-famous Atlantic beaches, Portugal also takes pride in its river beaches. There are many good ones along or near the central section of the N2, such as Reconquinho, Canaveias, and Peneda. Unlike the coastal sands, which are often hectic with international tourists, these river beaches see mostly Portuguese visitors. They tend to have good infrastructure, including sundecks, changing rooms and cafés.

Clockwise from left: azulejo tiles decorate a stairway at the Sanctuary of Our Lady of Remedios, Lamego; a Roman bridge in the city of Chaves; wine tasting at a quinta; the Mondego River. Previous page: dramatic terraced vineyards of the Douro Valley

charming villages, and offers the chance to cool off at one of the many river beaches in the region.

Around 90 miles (150km) later, I enter the Alentejo, Portugal's breadbasket, a place where the pace of life slows notably. Some have compared it to Tuscany, but taking in the sprawling landscapes, beneath the dramatic clouds and brilliant sun, I think also of the vastness of the African savanna, albeit with different vegetation. In summer, the wheat fields are ripe for harvest; in spring they're a mass of yellow wildflowers; and in the rainy winter, they're a vivid green.

I park in Montemor-o-Novo, a centrepiece of the region, to see the ruins of the castle and walled citadel, which date from the 13th and 17th centuries. Then it is back in the car for a soothing few hours crossing empty landscapes, sometimes passing through those famous whitewashed villages, their houses trimmed in yellow or blue.

There's a good 125 miles (200km) of travel along the N2 before it passes from the Alentejo into Portugal's southernmost province, the Algarve. I know I've reached the latter when I arrive in São Brás de Alportel, a hill town that was prosperous during the heyday of the cork industry and has retained some of that splendour. The town is also home to Casa Memoria EN2, a museum dedicated to the early 20th century building of the road I've just driven.

The last 9 miles (15km) take me to Faro, capital of the Algarve, where the final distance marker, near the centre of town, is covered with stickers from the motorcycle clubs that have completed the route. I drop off the car, and finally answer the call of the beach that I'd heard back at 'KM 0'.

DIRECTIONS

Start // Chaves
End // Faro
Distance // 459 miles (738.5km)
Getting there // The closest international airport to the starting point in Chaves is Porto, about 90 miles (150km) west along the A7 motorway. Faro, at the route's southern end, also has international flights.
Accommodation // There's a good range of accommodation, from inexpensive campsites to upmarket palaces, on the route. If five-star luxury is important, be willing to detour from the road and book ahead.
When to go // April or May for the wildflowers, or June, July or September for the river beaches. Avoid August, which is hot and crowded everywhere in Portugal, and winter, as it can be rainy.

Opposite from top: switchbacks into the Furka Pass, among the driving challenges on Switzerland's North–South Route; the Autopista AP-7 and the A7 track parallel to the Mediterranean in Andalucía, Spain

MORE LIKE THIS
CROSS COUNTRY DRIVES

THE A7, SPAIN

Also called the Autovía del Mediterráneo, the A7 follows nearly the entire Mediterranean coast of Spain and holds the record as the longest national motorway (a limited-access, high-speed road that is more substantial than a highway) in Europe. It's also one of the newest, as the final sections were completed only in 2015. It starts near the French border and ends near the Strait of Gibraltar. Altogether, you'll drive some 930 miles (1500km) on this free alternative to the toll-access-only Autopista AP-7. You'll head quite close to Barcelona, and directly through Valencia, but the highlight is the final stretch, along the Costa del Sol from Almería through Málaga and on to Algeciras, where the road runs very close to the sea. Parts of this route are still an old national road, with curves that encourage you to slow down and savour the scenery you're passing through.

Start // La Jonquera
End // Algeciras
Distance // 930 miles (1500km)

THE A89, FRANCE

Though its nickname, La Transeuropéenne, might sound boastful, this autoroute across central France is one day expected to be part of a link between the Atlantic and Eastern Europe. It's also known as the 'route of presidents', as it takes you past the homes of Jacques Chirac and Valéry Giscard d'Estaing, and also as the 'empty route', because you'll encounter no major cities between Bordeaux and Clermont-Ferrand, some 230 miles (370km). Several of the bridges that the road passes beneath are marked not with numbered signs but with cut-outs of running boar and leaping deer, to show that they are animal crossings. In general, the modern road was designed to be well integrated with the countryside and so includes crossings for smaller animals, even water crossings for otters and toads. Expect to see some striking modern bridges, along with historic viaducts and aqueducts too.

Start // Bordeaux
End // Lyon
Distance // 338 miles (544km)

NORTH–SOUTH ROUTE, SWITZERLAND

Notable as the longest historic monument in Switzerland, the North–South Route takes you through many of the most scenic parts of this incredibly scenic country. You'll cross through the Jura, Mittelland, central Switzerland, the Alps and southern Switzerland. You'll follow historically and culturally significant trade routes, and hear the language change from German to Italian as you progress south. And you'll gain and lose significant elevation along the way, heading up to the Gotthard Pass, which peaks at 6890ft (2100m), and down to sea level at the end. Along with the exciting hairpin bends (37 of them), you'll also drive by points of interest such as the cities of Basel and Lucerne (and the lake of the same name), the Sasso San Gottardo museum in its 1940s bunker at the Gotthard Pass, the three castles of Bellinzona and Lugano (with another eponymous lake), before ending in Chiasso, alongside the Italian border.

Start // Basel
End // Chiasso
Distance // 227 miles (365km)

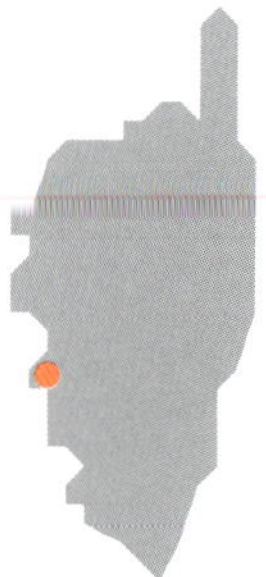

A CORSICAN GRAND TOUR

Rory Goulding goes in search of unspoiled Mediterranean scenery, finding rewards at every turn on a circuit of Corsica's vivid coast and remote hill villages.

On a beach south of Ajaccio, the cows and bulls are sunbathing. At least, it seems that way. Why else would a dozen-strong herd be standing placidly on the Plage de Mare e Sole – the Beach of Sea and Sun? Corsica faces the French Riviera across a hundred blue miles of the Mediterranean, but the island's coast has little in the way of high-rise hotels and beach condos. Most of it remains wild or at least – like the cattle – feral.

And as with the land (and its livestock), so too the road network. Corsica is the only region of metropolitan France without a single section of autoroute. There's a short stretch of high-speed bypass near Bastia airport on the east coast, but otherwise the island's rugged geography defeats all attempts to impose order on it.

Including mine. I had thought of driving a circular route around the coast, but it turns out there are inland sights I don't want to miss. I must also regretfully skip the northeastern promontory of Cap Corse, which points like an accusing finger towards Genoa, the island's former and unloved controlling power.

Having escaped the capital Ajaccio's very modest urban sprawl, and left the cows to their placid beach-time, I get my first real feel for the fragrant beauty of the coast along the D155. For much of Corsica's history, its inhabitants shunned the shoreline and kept inland, away from predatory foreign powers and raiders who would carry entire villages off into slavery. Even being up a hill didn't help the people of Sartène in 1583 though. I stop on the main square there for a pizza topped with slices of local *figatellu* sausage, and ponder the strange debt owed by modern Corsican tourism for its colourful postcard images of hilltop towns and Genoese watchtowers on dramatic headlands.

The road south towards Bonifacio goes through a landscape of Mediterranean shrub making what living it can on the pinkish rocks. The port on the far side of this near-deserted belt has the island's most impressive citadel. Bonifacio's Old Town occupies a splinter of land joined to the rest of Corsica by a neck less than 200 yards (183m) across, with houses confidently built right up to the edge of tall cliffs. Sardinia is a hazy prospect just 10 miles (16km) away on the southern horizon, but short of catching the car ferry, my journey must turn north again.

En route to Porto Vecchio I encounter the ultimate Corsican rarity – a long, straight road. The bayside town itself is Corsica's

closest answer to Saint-Tropez (though still dialled down several notches), with sand to suit all tastes. On the beach at Palombaggia and its neighbour Tamaricciu, umbrella pines and boulders make a natural sculpture garden, and when the sun hits the water, the sandy shallows are picked out, turquoise against sapphire. Along this charmed coast, the favourite eating spots and bars are beach shacks under roofs of cane or straw, known as *paillottes*.

Most Corsicans now live close to the sea, and driving through mountain villages it's common to see big houses firmly shuttered, empty except at Easter or Christmas when families return inland to their ancestral homes for a few weeks. The drive over the mountain spine to Zonza is my first taste of this hidden heart of the island. At the prehistoric site of Cucuruzzu, I walk a forest trail between mossy boulders to reach an isolated hill fort more than 3000 years old. And at the end of a rough road up to the Plateau de Coscione – closer in look to the Scottish Highlands than the classic Mediterranean – a herd of feral pigs take a shine to my rental car as a scratching post.

It would be possible to continue inland by road up the centre of the island to next stop Corte, but a brief return to the coast works out to be an hour faster. And that's including the hairpins below

"At the end of a rough road up to the Plateau de Coscione, a herd of feral pigs take a shine to my rental car as a scratching post"

the Col de Bavella. At this mountain pass, my route crosses that of walkers on the notoriously tough GR20 hike, descending from a path that runs along a jagged mountain ridge.

The next three staging posts illustrate a chapter of history that – outside Corsica – is fairly obscure these days, but which in its time captured the imagination of liberal-minded Europeans. The Corsican Republic was declared in 1755 in rebellion against Genoa, and managed to hold most of the island until the Genoese cut their losses and sold Corsica to France in 1769, just in time for a certain Napoleone di Buonaparte to be born a French subject. Corte, with its hilltop citadel, was the republic's inland capital while the Genoese hung onto their seaside strongholds such as Calvi; for that reason the Corsicans founded L'Île-Rousse, to have a port under their control.

GASTRUNUMIA CORSA

Corsica's cuisine has been shaped by its mountainous geography and complex history. Laws encouraging the planting of chestnut trees mean that this staple crop's influence is ever-present, from feeding the pigs that produce prized charcuterie, to the chestnut flour used in Pietra beer. Of the sheep and goat's milk cheeses, the most famous, *brocciu*, can be fresh or aged, and appears in desserts like lemony, cheesecake-like *fiadone*.

From left: Bonifacio's clifftop houses, and fishing boats; charcuterie for sale at L'Île-Rousse's covered market; Plage de Tamaricciu, Porto Vecchio. Previous page: driving northeast of Piana, past the Calanques

The drive from Corte to Calvi, via L'Île-Rousse, goes through the region of La Balagne. Corsica is often called a 'mountain in the sea' and the island frequently leaves no interval between the two extremes. But here, there's a gap for farmers to work with, making this stretch of my drive one of the most fertile parts of the island, known for olives, chestnuts, figs and other fruit trees. A signposted wine route loops lazily round a dozen estates.

The rural interlude doesn't last long. An hour south of Calvi, I pass over the Col de Palmarella to a primary-coloured panorama, where red rocks poke through beneath forested mountains that jut out into the azure sea. The road follows the kind of course an angry toddler's crayon might take, and as it passes above the coves known as the Calanques de Piana, I slow down not just for safety's sake, but to catch the shapes that appear in the rocks. Here is a blink-and-you-miss-it hole in an outcrop that reveals a sky-blue heart. There is a dog's head, ever alert.

Pulling into the umpteenth layby to get out for a better view, I notice a herd of goats on the boulders just above. They lock horns a few times for a tussle, before bounding off to mountain vistas even this most daring of Corsican roads can't reach.

DIRECTIONS

Start // Ajaccio
End // Ajaccio
Distance // 350 miles (563km)
Getting there // Ajaccio is the main airport for Corsica, though you can also fly into Bastia, Calvi or Figari. All have car rental availability.
When to go // Corsica is a year-round beauty, but many tourist businesses close between November and March. You'll find the island less crowded outside the main French and Italian summer holidays in July and especially August.
Tip // Locals may feel readier than you to take winding mountain roads at high speed – briefly pull into laybys if you find traffic building up behind you. It's a good chance to enjoy the views too.
Further information // www.visit-corsica.com

A Corsican Grand Tour

Opposite: tracing the wild slopes of
Mount Pantokrator, Corfu

MORE LIKE THIS
DRIVES AROUND MEDITERRANEAN ISLANDS

NORTH COAST GOZO, MALTA

Gozo is the second-billed island in the Maltese archipelago, but for scenic appeal it easily rivals Malta proper. A drive along Gozo's north coast reveals one of the country's least built-up corners. Begin with a dip at Ramla Bay, a wide and largely wild beach not to be confused with the resort of the same name on the main island. Once you've brushed off its characteristic orange sand, take a coastal drive through the small harbour of Marsalforn, beyond which the route passes a surreal landscape of seaside salt pans. The road gets gravelly after it ducks round the inlet of Wied il-Għasri, but stick with it if you can along the clifftops to reach Wied il-Mielaħ, a natural sea arch to replace the famous Azure Window that collapsed in 2017. The location of the latter still makes a fitting trip finale, with sunset views beside the Dwejra Inland Sea.

Start // Ramla Bay
End // Dwejra
Distance // 10 miles (16km)

MOUNT PANTOKRATOR CIRCUIT, CORFU, GREECE

Mount Pantokrator is the highest point in Corfu (2972 ft/906m), and a lap of its flanks brings generous mountain and coastal views as you round the northeast corner of the island. Start in Pyrgi village and proceed north and clockwise if you want to get the climbing done early. From Pyrgi the road zigzags up past olive groves through the villages of Spartylas and Strinylas. Here you can drive east on a road up to the summit of Pantokrator itself (a car with a nimble turning circle is an advantage) where there's a small but richly decorated monastery under a rather unfortunate communications mast. Return to the coast at the resort town of Acharavi, and head east as the road snakes round lushly wooded bays and charming villages such as Kassiopi and Kalami, with views towards Albania just two miles across the water.

Start // Pyrgi
End // Pyrgi
Distance // 41 miles (66km)

LIPARI LOOP, ITALY

Lipari is the middlemost of the Aeolian Islands, and as you drive the encircling main road, each of the other volcanic islands puts in an appearance on the horizon. Lipari Town is reached by car ferries and faster hydrofoils from Sicily, and heading out north the route is a palm-lined corniche running along a yacht-filled bay. From the road skirting the shingle beach at Canneto, you'll have views towards the islands of Panarea and – half-concealed behind it – the ever-smoking cone of Stromboli. Past the pumice quarries at Lipari's northeast corner, twin-peaked Salina lumbers into view, and after that, more distant Filicudi and Alicudi, if summer haze doesn't obscure them. Last to appear as you turn the southwest corner is Vulcano. It's visible from the main road, but for a close-up, end your drive at the viewpoint beside the Geophysical Observatory in San Salvatore, at Lipari's southern tip.

Start // Lipari Town
End // San Salvatore
Distance // 17 miles (28km)

OXFORD TO BATH VIA THE COTSWOLDS

Etain O'Carroll discovered a glut of medieval villages, grand country houses, gardens, museums and galleries in the rolling hills of the Cotswolds, between Oxford and Bath.

I ruminate on where to drive through the quintessentially English countryside of the Cotswolds for days but still can't decide. If I go north I can revisit some old favourites; if I go south I'll avoid the worst of the crowds. Whatever I decide, I'll miss places that hold fond memories of glorious summer walks through waist-high grass, wild swims under the shadow of manor-house ruins, pints with friends in pubs straight off the set of a period drama.

I'm torn. There are just too many beautiful options. If I were advising anyone else, I'd simply say to set off and follow your nose. The Cotswolds are so full of thatched cottages, rickety almshouses, elaborate houses and graceful churches that it doesn't really matter where you go.

The band of Jurassic limestone that defines the Cotswolds not only produces the warm, honey-coloured stone that makes these villages seem to glow at sunset, but also fertile grasslands that fed the thriving wool industry in medieval times. Cotswold sheep produced some of the finest wool in Europe and the region prospered on the back of it. The newly wealthy merchants ploughed their money into imposing homes and churches. But, as the wool trade declined and the Industrial Revolution began, the Cotswolds got left behind, and the bucolic scenes were left largely undisturbed. Lucky for us.

All that beauty doesn't go unnoticed though, and the region understandably attracts a lot of visitors. Fortunately, most tend to gravitate to a few well-known spots, and while towns such as Stow-on-the-Wold, Bourton-on-the-Water and Broadway are undeniably pretty, in the height of summer their lanes, tea rooms and antique shops are thronged. Lucky for us, again, it's easy enough to find alternatives.

Starting out in Oxford where august college buildings line the streets, you'll get a sense of what's to come. This genteel, conservative city is renowned as the home of one of the world's most famous universities. The first colleges were established in the 11th century and since then a host of Nobel prize winners, prime ministers and literary giants have studied here. Today, university buildings wrap around narrow cobbled lanes, tiny pubs play host to academic debate and rowing eights fight it out on the river.

Heading west, it's not long before I arrive in Woodstock, home to Blenheim Palace, an extravagant Baroque pile that was the

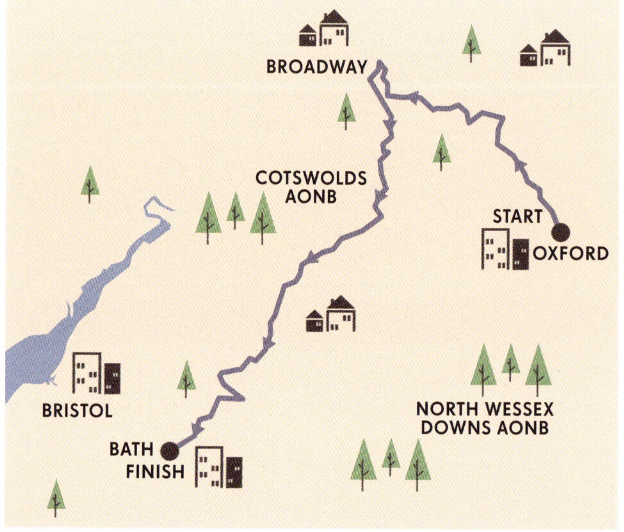

birthplace of Winston Churchill. Rather than touring its stately gardens and gilded halls, I wander the village streets where handsome townhouses and creeper-clad cottages with buckled roofs sit between art galleries and shops.

I can't help but make the detour to Great Tew, one of my all-time favourite places. The tiny village was built to house workers from the adjoining Great Tew Estate (now home to the Soho Farmhouse, the rural outpost of an exclusive London club) and looks out over extensive parkland. Slender streets wind past wonky cottages, thatched roofs pop out from behind banks of hollyhocks and horses graze in the meadows. The main attraction, however, is the 16th-century Falkland Arms, a pub so special I hope it never changes. Inside, uneven flagstone floors, open fireplaces and low beams hung with a dusty collection of mugs and jugs match a bar serving real ales drawn from ancient hand pumps. It provides the perfect end to a leisurely wander, sipping a pint before heading on past the ancient Rollright Stones and through the pretty village of Blockley to Chipping Campden.

Here, the graceful, curving main street is flanked by a wonderful array of wayward terraced houses and ancient inns. There's an imposing 17th-century market hall and a set of dignified almshouses, as well as the fine 15th-century St James' Church, built in the late Gothic style known as Perpendicular. The town is so beautifully proportioned and the buildings so harmonious it's unsurprising that Charles Robert Ashbee, leader of the Arts and Crafts movement, moved here along with the Guild of Handicraft in 1902. You can explore their work in the Court Barn.

PLAYING GAMES

First held in 1612, the Cotswold Olimpicks are a local take on the international event – highlights include welly wanging (throwing rubber rain boots), climbing a slippery pole, tug-of-war and relay races with wheelbarrows and hay bales. Most hotly contested is the World Shinkicking Championships, happily diminished in ferocity since steel-toed boots were banned. The games take place in late May or early June on Dover's Hill, near Chipping Campden.

Clockwise from above: Chipping Campden; the Roman Baths, in the city of Bath; vast Blenheim Palace in Woodstock. Previous page: Castle Combe is a contender for the Cotswolds' prettiest village

Lovely as it is, I decide to skip past Broadway and head south on the back roads, allowing fate to take me through quieter villages such as the Swells and Slaughters which sit between justifiably popular Stow and heavily commercialised Bourton.

From here, it's south to Cirencester, a town which was second only to London in Roman times. Although little remains from this period apart from the ruins of a grassed-over amphitheatre, the Corinium Museum brings the era to life. The medieval wool trade was also good to the town, with moneyed merchants funding the building of a superb church and townhouses. The cathedral-like Church of St John the Baptist stands on the Market Square, its flying buttresses and three-storey south porch leading to soaring arches and magnificent fan vaulting inside.

It's late afternoon when I reach Bibury, a place described by Arts and Crafts founder William Morris as 'the most beautiful village in England'. The day trippers have left and I wander along the river to the drunken cottages of Arlington Row. Built to store wool in the 14th century and converted into weavers' cottages in the 17th, this street is one of the most photographed in the area. I sweep south, detouring off the main road just to take a wander through Castle Combe, another stunner of a village, before heading on to the Regency wonders of Bath.

As the location of the country's only hot springs, the Romans built a city here in 44CE. The original baths still stand but today are surrounded by Georgian terraces built in the 18th century, when the city became the destination of choice for the high society set. There's also an imposing medieval abbey church and a host of museums, but my final treat is to soak in the rooftop pool at Thermae Bath Spa as the sun sets and the stars come out. As I look over the city's streets my mind is whirring, busily plotting a route back through all my other favourite haunts.

"Slender streets wind past wonky cottages, thatched roofs pop out from banks of hollyhocks and horses graze in meadows"

DIRECTIONS

Start // Oxford
End // Bath
Distance // 129 miles (207 km)
Getting there // The nearest major airports are London Heathrow and Birmingham from where there are regular bus and rail connections to Oxford as well as car rental facilities.

When to go // It's a glorious region to explore at any time of year but May and September offer the best balance between weather and crowds. Accommodation and restaurants get busy so book in advance as much as possible.

Tip // The region is laced with walking trails – park the car and set off on foot and you'll come across little villages tucked away among the hills that feel like they haven't changed in centuries.

Oxford to Bath via the Cotswolds

Opposite: a summer's day winds to a close in the Provençal village of Gordes

MORE LIKE THIS
DRIVES THROUGH MEDIEVAL SPLENDOUR

HILLTOP VILLAGES OF PROVENCE, FRANCE

Once a stronghold of Roman Gaul, Provence is overrun with amphitheatres and arenas, aqueducts and ancient vineyards. Among them lie medieval villages that tumble down steep-sided hills in a maze of cobbled streets and battered fortresses. It's a recipe for leisurely driving, the scent of lavender in the air and the promise of a top-class meal and fine wine at the end of the day. Start off in Nîmes with its magnificently preserved, twin-tiered amphitheatre and 2000-year-old temple, then tick off the ecclesiastical wonders of Avignon before heading on to the cobbled streets and medieval castles of the hilltop villages of the Luberon. Whether you choose to visit Gordes, Roussillon or Ménerbes, you'll find pretty lanes, great views and hilltop citadels. Head back through Les Baux-de-Provence, another gem of a village, to finish among the honey-coloured streets of Arles, so beloved by Van Gogh.

Start // Nîmes
End // Arles
Distance // 111 miles (180km)

TUSCAN HILL TOWNS, ITALY

After falling for the Renaissance wonders of Florence, head for the hills and cypress-lined roads of rural Tuscany to be seduced all over again. It's not just the landscape that does it, it's the medieval villages, excellent food and wine, and a pace of life that seems to make languid lunches and leisurely walks obligatory. The star of the show is Siena, a long-time rival of Florence that flourished in the early 14th century but was hit badly by the plague in 1348. Its spell of good fortune broken, the city went into decline, leaving its architectural riches preserved. In San Gimignano, medieval merchants showed off by building towers, each higher than the next, while Volterra offers Roman, Etruscan and medieval interest. Toast your Tuscan love affair in Montalcino or Montepulciano where you can sample the region's most prized wines.

Start // Florence
End // Montepulciano
Distance // 127 miles (205km)

MEDIEVAL SPAIN

At the crossroads of the Basque country and Castilian Spain, Navarra has long been a tempestuous place, its plains and vineyards hewn by the sierras that sit at the foot of the mighty Pyrenees. Between the limestone outcrops and sun-drenched fields lie medieval towns and villages, and a network of paths that led pilgrims along the Way of St James. Today, the area sees few visitors despite its obvious allure, and touring unpretentious towns such as Tudela and Cascante offers ecclesiastical splendour alongside down-to-earth charm. Visit quiet Olite and its Palacio Real, once home to the royal families of Navarra, then explore the otherworldly badlands of Bardenas Reales which doubled as a *Game of Thrones* location. Relax in tiny Ujué with its wonderful views and fortified church, before finishing with the vestiges of medieval pilgrim wealth in the convents, chapels, shrines and palaces that line the streets of Sangüesa.

Start // Tudela
End // Sangüesa
Distance // 82 miles (132km)

A DAY ON THE BELFAST LOOP

Brandon Presser finds the lonely shores of Northern Ireland – often overlooked for the classic cliffs and loughs of the Irish Republic – to be the perfect day-tripping antidote to Belfast's urban core.

Here's our best of the day,' the waiter says, pushing a porcelain dish across the table. 'We usually send the megrim to Portugal or Spain, but every so often we keep some of the finest catches for our customers.' I gently tuck into the white fish and glide my forkful through some tapenade. Moments later, barefoot in the sand, I toe the clear, curling tide as it rolls towards me, in the same gingerly manner with which I approached my lunch.

I need to rub my eyes. The beach is broad and filled with bathers, and the sea Caribbean-clear – but I'm not on a tropical island, I'm staring down the public beach in Portstewart along the upper crest of Northern Ireland. The cloudless weather seems more unlikely than it does unseasonable, forever turning my prejudiced imagination of a realm of beiges and grey into a vibrant scene of lapis and green like the one that lays before me.

For many, I would think, the small seaside town of Tudor-style row homes feels like a daytripper's coda along the coastal road due north of Belfast. But as I furiously inhale my honeycomb ice cream before it succumbs to the summer's heat I find myself strangely enraptured by my mini road trip's 'in between' experiences.

From Belfast, the so-called Causeway Coastal Route is a world-in-one circuit easily completed in a day's journey. It is, by design, a path to its namesake attraction, Giant's Causeway – a Unesco World Heritage Site of mythic hexagonal stone located about two hours away when following the seaside roads.

But as I begin the drive, it becomes immediately apparent – despite my urgency fuelled by years of ogling moody snaps of Giant's Causeway on Instagram – that it will take me far longer than a couple of hours to reach the intended destination. Each swerve

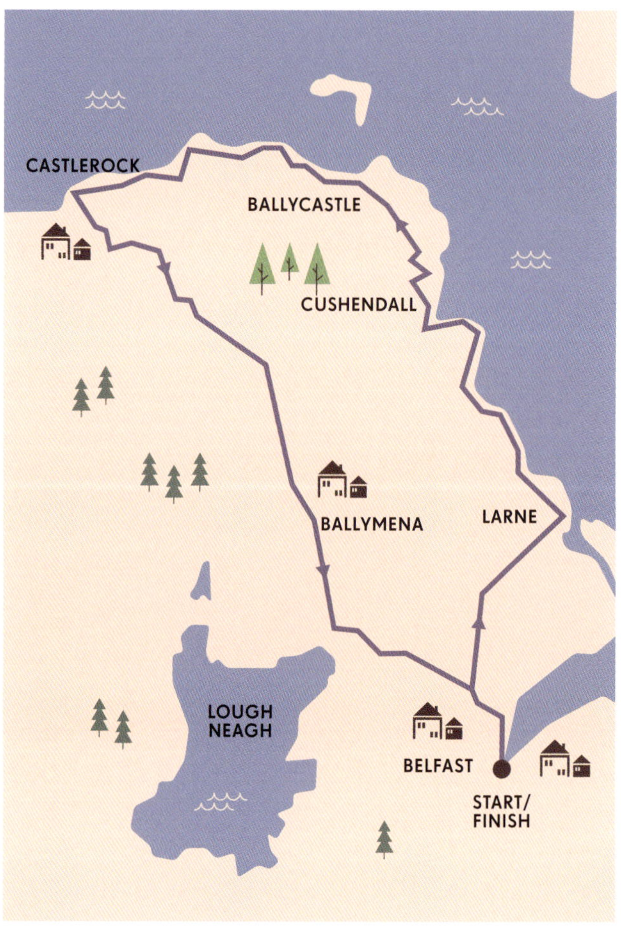

© Greg Sinclair | 500px

"Road signs advertise
the Dark Hedges ahead –
one of the many recesses
of Ulster made famous by
Game of Thrones"

on the coastal route begs me to turn off the road and explore its tangential attractions. And several times the road succeeds.

After Larne, stony cliffs – like fortress walls – flank seas for nearly 100 miles, breaking only nine times where deep glens burrow a verdant path to the countryside. Each valley, collectively known as the Glens of Antrim, promises a distinct and unique vibe, further exaggerated by the fickle North Atlantic weather casting a cloak of fog over one village while bathing the next in sun.

In Glenarm I pause to wander through the preserved village. In Carnlough, I have lunch along the scenic harbour, and in Glenariff I follow the boardwalk path through the lush, boggy forest to an inland constellation of secret waterfalls.

While the valleys are steeped in story (as locals will endearingly remind you in an unsolicited fashion) the ruins further north at Dunluce best bring the legends of sword-brandishing heroes to life. Built circa 1500 by the MacQuillian clan, the stronghold passed through several ruling parties until it became the County Antrim earls' seat in the 1600s. Perched on the cliff's edge, the gables of old stone are said to have inspired C.S. Lewis' *Chronicles of Narnia*.

Of the many other stops on the way to Giant's Causeway, Carrick-a-Rede is worth the longest detour, as it's only from here that one can fully appreciate the awesomeness of the Irish bluffs from below. A thin rope bridge connects the mainland to a rocky islet offshore that's home to soaring razorbills and kittiwakes. On a clear day, every crack and crevice of the cliffs are easily discerned, as are the Scottish islands skulking above the horizon in the distance.

I can feel the anticipation in my throat as I follow the final signs for Giant's Causeway, and seeing the rocky outcrop for the first time feels like one of those strange moments in travel when you can't help but weigh a big-ticket destination's worth against its hype. The counterculture of modern travel, too, further eschews classic attractions for local, un-touristy points of interest.

I clamber down Shepherd's Steps with the basalt stone rising like organ pipes around me – even more impressive than I'd imagined. From far away, the latticework of strange smooth stones resembles the scales of a beast sleeping along the water's edge. According to legend, the collection of rocks was created by giant hero Finn McCool to fight Benandonner, another giant from Scotland across the straight – a colourful reimagining of the scorching volcanic activity that carved up the area 50 million years ago.

After an hour of hopping from stone to stone like a frog leaping between obsidian lily pads, I find my way back to my car ready to turn inland back to Belfast. Road signs advertise the Dark Hedges up ahead – one of the many recesses of Ulster County now famous as a backdrop for the TV phenomenon *Game of Thrones*.

The infinite summer sky, however, encourages me to push on, just a little bit more down the shoreline to Portrush and perhaps all the way to Portstewart. Although no longer coasting through the 'in between' Belfast and Giant's Causeway, I continue on in search of more serendipity, rumours of fresh fish, soft sand, and perhaps even some honeycomb ice cream.

HIDDEN GEMS

It's not apparent when you zip through the coastal village of Glenarm that one of its local businesses, Steensons, is responsible for some of the jewellery featured on *Game of Thrones*, such as Daenerys' dragon brooches and Lannister's lion pendants. Fans of the show can grab their own pieces, made from the same moulds as the originals; the perfect souvenir after touring the sites where many pivotal scenes of the series were shot.

Opposite, clockwise from top left: local langoustines; the beech trees of the Dark Hedges road at Ballymoney; the Causeway coast road. Previous page: the Giant's basalt columns

DIRECTIONS

Start // Belfast

End // Belfast

Distance // 143 miles (230km)

Getting there // Fly into Belfast International Airport.

Where to stay // Splurge on Belfast's Merchant Hotel (www.themerchanthotel.com) set in a refurbished bank.

When to drive // Summer months offer the best chance for cloudless weather and Caribbean-clear waters offshore.

Where to eat // Try fresh fish at Harry's Shack in Portstewart, then top it off with some honeycomb ice cream at Morelli's down the street; or enjoy steaks and tunes at Berts Jazz Bar in Belfast.

What to take // Even in just one day the weather can be fickle – pack layers. And don't forget your zoom lens for cross-glen photo opps.

*Opposite: Lough Tay seen from Sally
Gap in the Wicklow Mountains
National Park, Ireland*

MORE LIKE THIS
ESCAPES FROM THE CITY

ROUND THE DANUBE BEND, HUNGARY

Before the Danube reaches Budapest, it makes one long turn to the right, cutting through a belt of mountains. In a country that's dominated by the Alföld (Great Hungarian Plain), these heights are a popular destination for hikers. Main road 11 follows the right bank of the Danube north from the capital, past Szentendre, with its quaint townscape and open-air museum, to Visegrád and its steeply perched medieval fortress watching the river's curve. Further upstream lies Esztergom, Hungary's ancient capital, with Slovakia on the far side of its Mária Váleria Bridge. This is the point to leave the river and curve back fishhook-style into the mountains of Danube-Ipoly National Park to get an overview. After a slow climb through thick forest, the road reaches the mountain resort of Dobogókő, 2293ft (699m) high, where roadside viewpoints and further trails reveal panoramas of Central Europe's greatest river.

Start // Budapest
End // Dobogókő
Distance // 52 miles (83km)

DUBLIN, IRELAND

The Emerald Isle is synonymous with its misty cliffs, but the rugged mountains of the interior are just as prone to those perfect #nofilter snaps on Instagram. Leave the gothic streetblocks of Dublin for Wicklow Mountains National Park, where stony peaks hide quiet loughs and windless forests of beech and pine. Thread the mountain pass at Sally Gap and wend your way through the Glenealo Valley – another realm of sacred stones, crumbling relics and flowing rivers. Follow the mirror-like lakes to find the way west towards workaday Portlaoise, or double back to the coast for a leisurely ride back to the capital. Coastal riders on the return leg shouldn't miss a stop in Bray at the very end of the day to visit the Harbour Bar for tea or tipples, and a some of the best local music around.

Start // Dublin
End // Portlaoise
Distance // 85 miles (137km)

FROM MAAS TO 'MOUNTAINS', NETHERLANDS

Technically the highest point in the Netherlands is on the Caribbean island of Saba, but most Dutch would think first of the 1056ft (322m) high Vaalserberg, which is also home to the Drielandenpunt – the border tripoint shared with Belgium and Germany. From Amsterdam (around 6.5ft/2m below sea level), a quest for giddy heights begins with a quick run past Utrecht and flat polder farmland as far as the old fortified town of Zaltbommel. Then it's time to switch to slower roads, following the N322 and N271 upstream along the right bank of the River Meuse (Maas in Dutch). Stops in the province of Limburg include the sandy heathland of De Maasduinen National Park, and the city of Maastricht, with the country's second-largest number of heritage buildings. After the villages of Sint Geertruid, Noorbeek and Epen, prepare for the final climb, including genuine hairpin bends.

Start // Amsterdam
End // Drielandenpunt
Distance // 183 miles (294km)

ACROSS ORKNEY IN AN EV CAMPERVAN

Phoebe Smith took her nine-month-old son on a road trip around Orkney, driving a futuristic electric campervan in search of these Scottish islands' Neolithic past.

The Standing Stones of Stenness rise like a giant hand from the ground, casting long shadows across the grass. I look up at them, feeling as tiny as my baby son who is secured in the carrier on my back. This ceremonial circle is just one of a collection of Stone Age remains that make up the 'Heart of Neolithic Orkney' Unesco World Heritage Site, a group of important monuments from around 3100 BC. Given Orkney's abundance of such places (200 at last count) and the density of their distribution (on average there are three sites of archaeological interest per square mile), it's little wonder the islands have become a byword for Ancient Britain.

As impressive as these old earthworks are, there are also modern structures that have drawn attention to this cluster of 70 far-northerly British islands – wind turbines. Ever since the first one to be connected to the UK's electricity grid was placed at Costa Head in 1951, wind turbines have become as ubiquitous to the Orkneys as historic monuments. Now Orcadians not only produce all the renewable energy they need, but are in the middle of a drive (pun intended) to encourage residents and visitors to use electric vehicles to get around.

When it comes to EVs, while most drivers are eager to be more environmentally friendly, 'range anxiety' – the worry that you'll run out of juice before reaching your next charging point – is still a factor. Here on Orkney things are different. In true green spirit I've come here all the way from London using public transport, stepping off the passenger ferry in Burwick, at the southern tip of the archipelago. I am met by Paul Hudd, whose Nissan Dalbury E campervan (aka Spoot) I've rented for the next three nights. Paul explains that the vehicle's range is 120 miles on a full charge.

For context, Mainland (confusingly the name of the largest Orkney island) is only 26 miles across, so that 120-mile limit seems more than adequate. Paul shows me where to plug the charging cable in, at the front of the campervan above its number plate, and I set to work getting the lay of the van. There are coat hooks that convert to hold devices so you can watch TV – although I plan for them to remain unused, as there will be so much scenery to admire instead. There's a swivelling passenger chair that, along with a hidden plank, helps set up a dining area. And there's a pull-flat double bed, and a roof that lifts just high enough to allow me to wedge the baby's travel cot

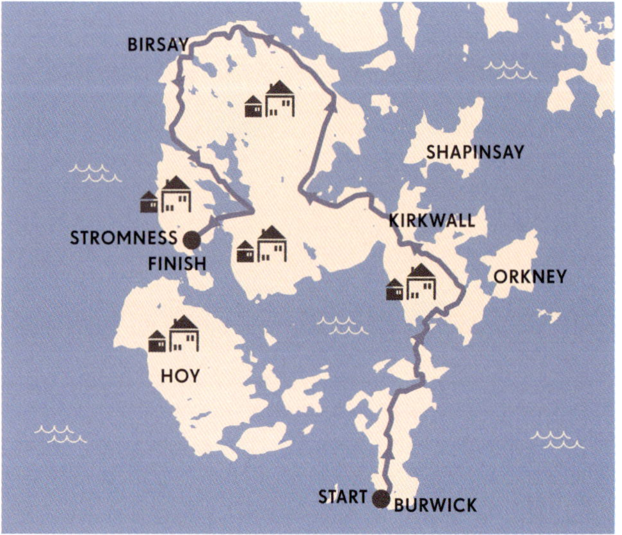

into it, where he will, I hope, be lulled asleep by the sound of the wind rocking the van each night.

I decide that the first night should be spent at a proper campsite where I can plug in, so head north across South Ronaldsay island to a campsite with credentials as green as my campervan's. Mike Roberts and his late wife Christina Sargent moved to Wheems Farm in the 1980s, establishing an organic farm and campsite here. It has run on wind turbines ever since. On my arrival there is a curry buffet in full swing, most of the food cooked from produce grown in the soil under our feet. 'The whole site is powered by just two turbines,' says Mike, as we take a tour of the gardens. 'We make more than enough electricity for ourselves, and the rest I give back to the grid.' The baby and I have full bellies and tired eyes as I put him in his cot, then sit with the back doors open to watch the light fade over the North Sea.

The following day we begin our exploration proper. South Ronaldsay is connected to Mainland via three smaller islands – Burray, Glimps Holm and Lamb Holm – along a series of causeways created in WWII to stop German U-Boats entering the body of water known as Scapa Flow. I drive over them in

"I drive in near silence, courtesy of the electric motor, as the water sparkles and rusted wrecks of battleships pop orange against the overcast sky"

near silence, courtesy of the electric motor, as the water sparkles a vivid turquoise and the rusted wrecks of WWI battleships pop orange against the overcast sky. We stop to wander along the beaches, watching kayakers paddle. Next we find the tiny yet ornate Italian Chapel, constructed by Italian prisoners of war during WWII.

In Kirkwall, Orkney's largest town, a juxtaposition between past, present and future greets us. I stroll with my son to see the magnificent, red sandstone Viking cathedral begun in 1137, while Spoot sits on rapid charge in a giant supermarket car park. Then we pass the Orkney Distillery, where use of hydrogen in place of fossil fuels is being experimented with to produce their spirit. We spend the night overlooking Kirkwall Bay, gazing out to the northern collection of islands that make up this chain, where

SUPERCHARGED

With 40-plus charge points across Orkney there should be no 'range anxiety' driving an EV around, especially as the islands are so compact and most EVs have a range of considerably more than 100 miles (160km). For the latest map of charge points on the archipelago see zap-map.com. Use Rapid Charge points where you can, as they take the battery of an EV like a campervan from empty to full in just 45 minutes.

From left: the Neolithic Ring of Brodgar, near Stromnness; grey seals bask on Copinsay; the beautiful interior of the tiny Italian Chapel on Lamb Holm; the Nissan Dalbury E campervan. Previous page: remains of a Norse settlement on Brough of Birsay

more hydrogen projects are being undertaken – including one that will see a ferry being powered by it alone.

Next day we continue north, oscillating between time periods. From the 5th century CE Pictish farm remains at the Broch of Gurness, we drive to the site of one of the first wind farms in the UK, constructed in 1983, at Burgar Hill near Evie. That night we camp at Birsay, where I strategically coincide sleep time for the baby with low tide so that, when he wakes, we can meander across a causeway to Brough of Birsay island. Here, Norse and medieval remains rest alongside Pictish history, while puffins and razorbills perch on the cliff faces before diving for fish.

The final morning sees us heading to Stromness, where we'll leave our EV campervan for Paul to collect while we take the ferry back to the Scottish mainland. En route, we visit more stunning ancient sites: the aforementioned Standing Stones of Stenness; Skara Brae Neolithic settlement; the Ring of Brodgar stone circle; and the Ness of Brodgar. The extent of the latter was only realised in recent times – its discoverer, archaeologist Nick Card, suggested that Orkney had been the centre of innovation in the British Isles 5000 years ago. Today, visionary ideas still emanate from this place.

DIRECTIONS

Start // Burwick
End // Stromness
Distance // 60 miles (100km)
Getting there // Take a train to Thurso, then a bus to John o' Groats for the passenger ferry to meet Paul and van in Burwick. To return to mainland Scotland, take the Stromness– Scrabster ferry, then a taxi back to Thurso.
When to go // June to September for long days, warmer weather and a reliable ferry service.
Further information // www.orkney.com
Campervan rental // The EV campervan (sleeps two adults) was provided through online sharing platform paulcamper. co.uk, and costs from £120 a night (3-night minimum).
What to pack // Campervan space is limited: pack layers and waterproofs. Bedding and crockery/utensils are provided.

Across Orkney in an EV Campervan

MORE LIKE THIS
DRIVING ELECTRIC

MOORS TO DALES, YORKSHIRE, ENGLAND

Moorland, coastline, waterfalls, gorges – exploring Yorkshire's moors and dales means constantly changing terrain. And you can enjoy it all in a classic 1973 VW campervan called Indie, lovingly converted to electric propulsion and available at edubtrips.co.uk. On pickup you're provided with a list of approved campsites that offer suitable charging points. Pretty Robin's Hood Bay has sandy beaches replete with fossils and makes an excellent start point, before meandering through the moors, taking in forests, valleys and Roseberry Topping, the hill from which a young James Cook found inspiration to explore the world. From the highlights of the moors, it's a scenic drive west into the Yorkshire Dales for limestone pavements at Malham Cove, the water-scoured Gordale Scar and the peaks that make up the backbone of England – the Pennines.

Start // Robin Hood's Bay
Finish // Malham
Distance // 134 miles (215km)

NORWAY'S NORTH

Norway is the nation with proportionately the world's highest level of EV-ownership. There are 16,000 charge points (3300 of which are rapid chargers), a scale of infrastructure that provides the freedom to tour fjords, wilderness and cities. In the country's winters, while EVs' battery range may reduce a little in the cold, use of special winter tyres helps still make them a workable option. Begin in coastal Tromsø, a place that hosts the annual Northern Lights Festival, then wind your way north towards Alta, which sits in the 'northern lights oval'. On the route you'll board ferries across fjords including Lyngen, where the Alps of the same name edge the scenery in a spectacular mountain fringe. Continue past lakes and bays, each crying out for a photo, with a stop in Kåfjord village for some aurora spotting. Then head on to Alta itself, where early studies of the northern lights were undertaken, and where the favourable inland climate still makes witnessing their displays more likely.

Start // Tromsø
Finish // Alta
Distance // 236 miles (381km)

LAKE CONSTANCE VIA FOUR NATIONS

Lake Constance is ringed by a road that takes in three (almost four) different countries. A lap of it covers 150 miles and is home to a sophisticated network of EV charging points. Beginning in Bregenz, Austria, take a cable car up Pfänder mountain for a panoramic view of the lake you'll be circling, before crossing into Switzerland and visiting the Saurer Museum's collection of vintage cars in historic Arbon. Continue clockwise and the town of Constance is reached next – and with it Germany – with a pretty waterfront lined with bars and restaurants. Border hop again through the Swiss town of Stein am Rhein, with its elaborately painted facades, before heading back into Germany for the long stretch of the northern lakeshore. Along the way are seaside-style towns with ample chances for lake bathing, as well as vineyards, churches and castles. While the fourth country isn't on the lakeside circuit, little Liechtenstein is impossible to resist, a detour just one hour south of Bregenz.

Start // Bregenz
Finish // Liechtenstein
Distance // 150 miles (242km)

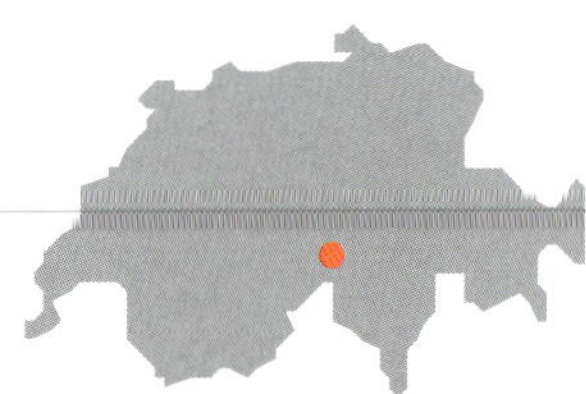

THE NAME'S PASS, FURKA PASS

Following in the tyre tracks of James Bond in the classic Goldfinger, Craig McLachlan headed, licence to drive in hand, across the pinnacle of Swiss Alpine passes.

Taking the road away from Fiesch, my wife Yuriko and I have no idea if we will even be able to drive over the Furka Pass. The less satisfying, less James Bond-ish alternative will be to board a car-train for the journey through the Furka Base Tunnel instead.

The only information we've found had said that the pass was closed through winter and would open in early June, depending on winter snowfall levels. It is the first day of June. We are cutting it fine, but the weather for the day looks good.

The owner of the pension we've just stayed in rolled his eyes – never a good sign – when I asked about conditions on the pass. 'We had a lot of snow this last winter,' he said, 'and no updated info on the internet. Good luck!'

Yuriko isn't as keen as I am about following where Sean Connery, in 007 mode, and his Aston Martin DB5 had hurtled across this truly epic pass. Apparently, the idea of coursing around switchbacks with precipitous drop-offs doesn't spark her sense of adventure as much as it does mine. She humours me though, saying that she also hopes the pass will be open.

Driving northeast through Upper Valais, and having done my homework, I try to build enthusiasm and interest in my passenger as we pass the small village of Niederwald. Yuriko had worked in hotels before we met so I exclaim: 'Caesar Ritz was born here. The youngest of 13 children. In 1850.' I delve deeper into what I'd read up on. 'He went from here to establishing the Ritz hotel empire across the world.' Yuriko gives me a sympathetic smile.

'And that's the Rhône River,' I say, pointing right at a waterway that is pleasantly lined with green meadows at low levels but which right now has alarmingly snow-smothered peaks rising on both sides.

'We're going to pass the Rhône Glacier,' I say. 'It's the source. The Rhône flows down this valley to Lake Geneva, then all the way to the Mediterranean. Over 800km in length.' I feel I am on solid ground here. Yuriko had studied French and is an enthusiastic Francophile. She smiles again.

'Don't worry, 007,' she says 'you can drive over the Furka Pass if they let us. Just don't drive like Sean Connery.' It is my turn to smile. We are in a tiny rental Toyota, a far cry from Bond's DB5.

We pass Oberwald, the western portal for the car train through

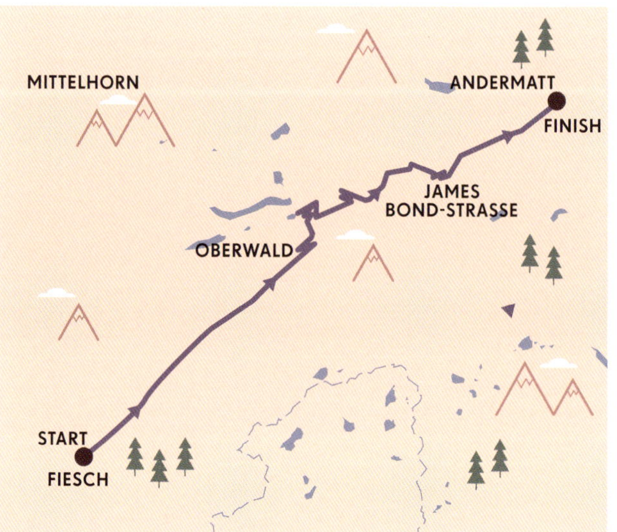

the 9.5 mile (15.4km) Furka Base Tunnel. There is a train waiting, but no vehicles in its carriages. An occasional car drives towards us, however, from the direction of the Furka Pass – a source of hope.

The road starts to climb up Furkastrasse, steeply gaining altitude through thick forest. The valley narrows as the twisting route crosses the Rhône a couple of times, the trees peter out and we arrive in the hamlet of Gletsch at a lofty 5771ft (1759m).

We park at a viewpoint next to the lovely Hotel Glacier du Rhône, built in the 1860s. Four hundred years ago the Rhône Glacier extended down to Gletsch, but over the centuries it has retreated over 1.5 miles (2.5km) up the valley and little of the ice can be seen from the viewpoint today. I decide to push my luck. I point out a mountain road that is snaking back and forth to the west.

'That's the route up to the Grimsel Pass,' I say. 'Do you think we could drive there and have a coffee at the café by the lake at the top? Since we're here. And might never come back.' Yuriko smiles again, which I take as a yes.

Back in the car, we climb over 1300 vertical feet (400m) in under 4 miles (6km), thanks to six incredible switchbacks, before arriving at the lookout at the top. We stare straight down on Gletsch and up the Rhône Valley towards the sinuous Furka Pass itself.

Coffee and diversion enjoyed, I crawl back down the road in low gear, barely touching the brakes. At the bottom, we turn left and started the main climb on a zigzagging road. After nine hairpin curves and steep straights, we park next to the long-disused Hotel Bélvèdere. There we take in more views of the Rhône Glacier before walking into an ice grotto inside the glacier itself.

On the road once more, another couple of miles of gentler climbing finally bring us to the Furka Pass, topping out at an impressive 7969ft (2429m). There is indeed plenty of snow all around, but the road itself remains clear and in excellent condition. Dropping down the pass's eastern side, and now in the canton of Uri, we drive through the hamlet of Tiefenbach, with its Alpine hotel.

My anticipation grows again soon after as we hit the first of eight descending switchbacks. Testing my 007 driving skills, I accelerate out of the first couple of hairpins. Yuriko is no longer even feigning a smile as she points out the limited guardrails. Knowing what's good for me, I ease back as we hit the patch of road now known as James Bond-strasse. This was where Tilly Masterson took a pot-shot at Bond from above with a rifle, in *Goldfinger*. I'd watched the scene on YouTube the previous week and recognised the spot, helped by an information panel with a photo of Connery and his Aston Martin. Along with my hit of Bond-fan appreciation, I am also entranced by the superb mountain views from this stretch.

I dawdle on the way down James Bond-strasse, savouring these last moments of cinematic homage. A couple of switchbacks, a gradual flattening of the descent, and we are past Realp – the eastern portal of the Furka Base Tunnel.

From here it is only a brief drive to the town of Andermatt, via a picturesque valley of soft grass, cows and yellow wildflowers. Yuriko is once again smiling, and I know I owe her one.

COLD STROLL

The trail to the Rhône Glacier Ice Grotto starts at the souvenir shop and car park next to Hotel Belvédère, 2 miles (3km) west of the Furka Pass. It takes 10-15 minutes to walk through stupendous glacial scenery to the Grotto, drilled through the ice each year since 1870. Enjoy the vivid hues of green and blue as you walk a tunnel through the glacier, with boarding beneath your feet. Go prepared with closed shoes and warm clothing.

Opposite, clockwise from top: the Rhône Glacier, source of the mighty Rhône River; the Hotel Belvédère; the ice grotto inside the glacier. Previous pages: an Aston Martin isn't essential for driving thrills here

DIRECTIONS

Start // Fiesch
End // Andermatt
Distance // 38 miles (62km)
When to go // The pass is generally open June to October, though this could be earlier/later depending on snowfall. Traffic can be busy on weekends and in the main holiday season of July/August.
Road conditions // You can check the latest at www.alpen-paesse.ch
Tips // Drive from west to east for the best views. Yellow Alpine Post Buses go over the pass from late June, so keep your eyes and ears open. The buses honk their three-tone horn as they approach tight corners, as a warning to drivers coming the other way. Be wary of motorbikes – this is a popular route.

MORE LIKE THIS
SWISS ALPINE PASSES

BERNINA PASS

The wondrous stretch of Alpine road over the Bernina Pass (7638ft/2328m) is open year-round and links the plush Swiss resort of St Moritz with Tirano in Italy. Allow plenty of time for the drive, whether you're doing it as a day trip or part of a longer European tour. On the northern side of the pass, consider stopping at the handsome resort village of Pontresina, or taking the Diavolezza cable car for views of the Morteratsch Glacier and Piz Bernina, highest peak in the Eastern Alps at 13,284ft (4049m). From Lago Bianco, the lake at the pass, the road descends with countless switchbacks and steep curves into Val Poschiavo and gorgeous little Lago di Poschiavo. Keep your eyes open for the Bernina Express train's Brusio Spiral Viaduct, where the track spirals to lose altitude before crossing the border.

Start // St Moritz, Switzerland
End // Tirano, Italy
Distance // 39 miles (63km)

GREAT ST BERNARD PASS

The lowest pass on the ridge between the two highest mountains of the Alps, Mont Blanc and Monte Rosa, the Great St Bernard Pass (8100ft/2469m) lies along the road connecting Martigny, in the Swiss canton of Valais, with Aosta in Italy. These days, most traffic avoids the pass road by paying a toll to go through the Great St Bernard Tunnel. Their loss, because this is a magical drive. Up to 32ft (10m) of snow sits here in winter – so the road is only open from late May through mid-October – and the lake alongside the pass is frozen for 265 days each year. Chances are you've heard of this place – the Great St Bernard Hospice at the pass dates from 1049 and the monks (a community still lives here) bred the mighty St Bernard dogs for rescue operations in the mountains during the 17th century.

Start // Martigny, Switzerland
End // Aosta, Italy
Distance // 50 miles (80km)

JULIER PASS

The road over the Julier Pass (7493ft/2284m) is an old Roman one, reconstructed as a cart road in 1820 to connect the Engadine Valley with the rest of Graubünden canton. These days, open year-round, it effectively connects St Moritz in the valley with Graubünden's capital Chur. The stretch heading south then east from Tiefencastel to the Julier Pass and down into Silvaplana forms a particularly spectacular scenic drive. In summer, the section from Tiefencastel to the pass is a steady climb past green fields, cows, wildflowers, road-hugging buildings, hamlets with ski lifts and high peaks on both sides of the valley. Once over the pass, the drop into the small Engadine resort of Silvaplana is dramatic, as are the Alpine views. Prepare with winter tyres and snow chains if making this drive in winter.

Start // Tiefencastel
End // Silvaplana
Distance // 27 miles (43km)

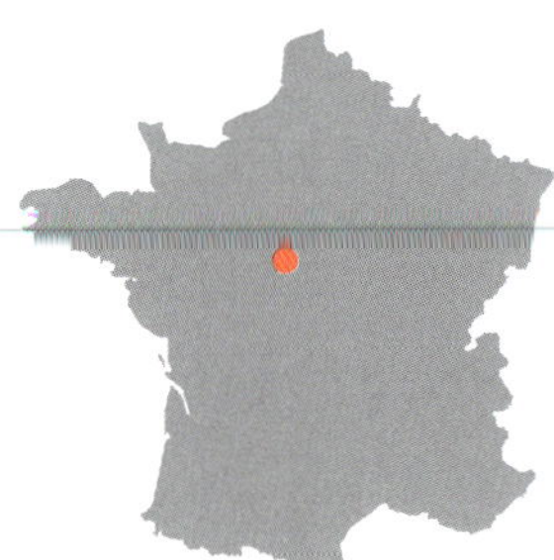

LOIRE VALLEY CHÂTEAUX

Nicola Williams took a Loire Valley drive in search of the French art de vivre, 'the art of living', visiting elaborate châteaux, sprawling vineyards and epicurean river towns.

Never is there such an incongruous din and commotion in regal Amboise as on market day. Chaotic honking sets the tempo as farmers, artisans, lorries and locals flock to the riverside town to trade creamy goats' cheese dusted in black ash, glass jars of rabbit pâté, stuffed pigs' trotters and other regional riches – as has been the case for the last 300 years. I indulge in a rainbow of *macarons*, brought to the Loire Valley by Catherine de Medici and her entourage of Florentine chefs in 1533, and congratulate myself on crafting a picnic fit for a queen.

I am driving along the Loire in slow gear, tracing the hypnotic course of France's longest and most royal river on part of its marathon expedition from the source at the foot of volcanic Mont Gerbier de Jonc in central France to the sandy beaches of the Atlantic Coast, 634 miles (1020km) west. The mighty Loire is acclaimed as the nation's last wild river and *le plus belle*, and as I pass wheat fields and asparagus crops, wildflower-tangled bridle paths and bird-speckled sand banks, its natural beauty cannot be denied. The river rarely dips out of sight, every bend in the road unveiling another Turner-esque vista. Transfixed by the Loire's extraordinary play of light and water, the English painter stayed in the valley on several occasions in the 1830s, famously capturing its magical light, oversized skies and burning sunsets in masterpieces of vermilion and chrome yellow that inspired Monet and the Impressionists a half-century later.

My own journey began on the Loire's rive gauche (left or south bank), in the graceful town of Sully-sur-Loire. A medieval fortress with thickset towers was built here in the 14th century to defend one of the river's few crossings, and today's resplendent 16th-century château – with its witch-hat towers, fairy-tale moat and manicured gardens – heralds the start of the Loire Valley proper. Over the course of five centuries, pleasure-seeking French kings, queens and aristocrats built the most extraordinary castles on the riverbanks here, rendering this entire stretch a Unesco World Heritage Site today.

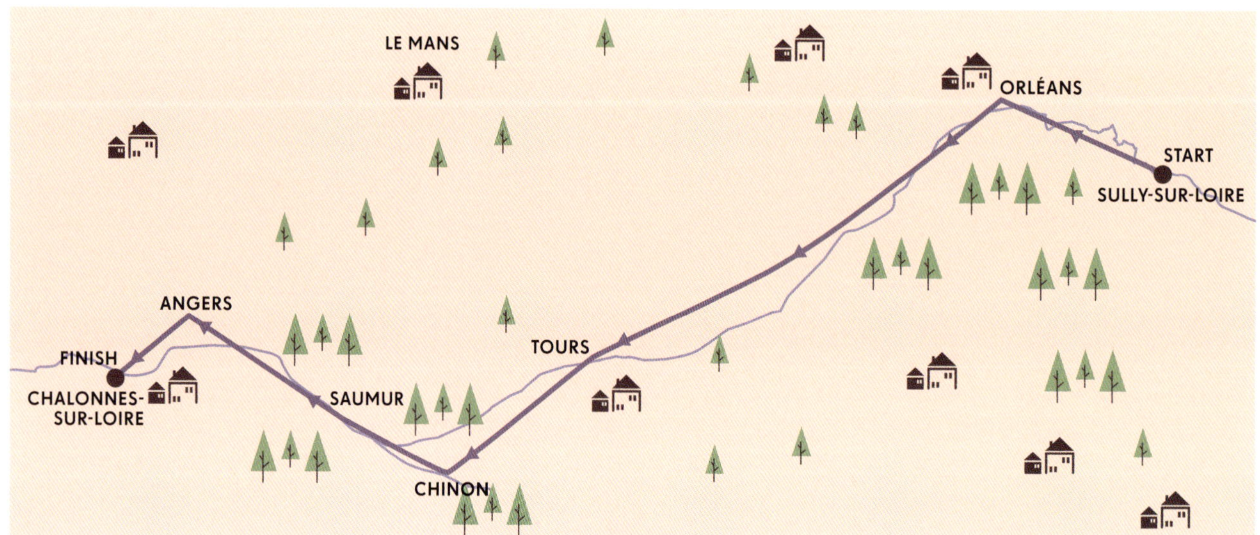

Over a late-breakfast coffee and croissant in Châteauneuf-sur-Loire I read up on the conceited adviser to Louis XIV who aspired to transform the town's medieval château into a mini-Versailles in the 17th century, only for French revolutionaries to sack, trash and destroy the bombastic creation in 1789.

Beyond the city of Orléans, cereal and potato fields frame the rural D951 with chessboard precision. Across the water on the right bank, the classical facade of 17th-century Château de Menars dazzles. The heady days of royal balls and lavish banquets are nothing but a memory for private châteaux such as this, which – with the upkeep of 34 bedrooms, 24 bathrooms, an orangery, nymphaeum and an alley of aged lime trees stretching 2.5 miles (4km) – face a Herculean preservation task. I later learn the château is on the market for €15.75 million – a snip of its original €31.5 million asking price.

Around the medieval town of Blois, the Loire Valley brings out its big guns. Of the hundreds of castles strewn along the river, Château de Chambord – built for François I from 1519 as a royal hunting lodge on the mosquito-plagued marshland of Sologne – is the biggest and most spectacular. The forest of chimney stacks, cupolas, lanterns and staircase turrets crowning the Renaissance pile is ethereal. As I cruise along its endless driveway, it's easy to picture the nomadic king and his retinue of several thousand courtiers clattering along here on horseback, carts overflowing with furniture, crockery, tapestries, linen, musical instruments and other provisions required for their short sojourn at the 426-room château. When François I was away, the château would be emptied. To think the king only stayed at Chambord 73 days in all beggars belief.

CALL OF THE STAG

Watching does grazing while they're stalked by bellowing stags at dawn and dusk during the rutting season on Chambord's huge estate offers a privileged insight into behind-the-scenes château life. Observation towers in the forest – which teems with boar, osprey and rare booted eagles too – ensure bold views of the deer in action on grassy prairies on the forest fringe. Rangers lead walks and other guided nature activities on the estate, www.chambord.org.

Clockwise from above: tarte aux pommes; a bedroom elaborately decorated for Louis XIV in the Château de Chambord; Château d'Amboise at sunrise over the Loire River; Château de Sully-sur-Loire. Previous page: the Château de Chenonceau

In every direction the road takes me, I am bombarded with more grandeur. Moored like a Neoclassical white ship in pea-green gardens, Château de Cheverny has sumptuous period interiors and kennels where I watch a pack of 90 hunting hounds devour 200lbs (90kg) of offal in seconds. The most magnificent stables of the 19th century and French gardens waltzing down to the water are the highlights of Château de Chaumont. At Chenonceau, I sample white Sauvignons from the castle's vineyards, relax on the moat in an old-fashioned rowing boat and snap the château's distinctive arcaded gallery mirrored in the serene Cher, a southern tributary of the Loire.

It was in château kitchens here that French cooking was refined, and quintessential dishes like *coq au vin* (chicken in red wine), *cuisses de grenouilles* (frogs' legs) and caramelised *tarte Tatin* (upside-down apple tart) were first cooked up. I drive west towards riverside Tours, depicted as 'the garden of France' by local writer Rabelais in the 16th century. I break at Château de Bourdaisière to discover hundreds of rare, ancient tomato varieties growing in its potager (kitchen garden). I admire more potagers at Château de Villandry, which overflow with cardoons, cabbages and beans cultivated in the 1500s. Crossing to the right bank, I explore wine-growing in Vouvray and uncover *champignons de Paris* (button mushrooms) farmed in troglodytic caves in Rochecorbon. And all the while, that Rabelaisian image of a green and fertile, utopian landscape laden with fruits, flowers, nuts and vegetables floats around seductively in my head.

Chinon, Saumur, Angers – so many grandiose châteaux mirrored in the glassy waters of the Loire, yet too little time. The succession of castles peters out in Anjou, where chalky tufa cliffs fringe the riverbanks instead. That evening for supper I dine on traditional river eels smoked in beechwood, and raise my glass to the valley's deck of preposterous kings and queens – and their brilliant contribution to French *art de vivre*.

"In every direction the road takes me, I am bombarded with more grandeur"

DIRECTIONS

Start // Sully-sur-Loire
End // Chalonnes-sur-Loire
Distance // 175 miles (280km)
Getting there // Paris Charles de Gaulle Airport is 125 miles (200km) away. Trains link Paris Bercy with Gien, 15 miles (25km) southeast of Sully, from where car rentals can be picked up.
When to go // May and June are mellow, with many wildflowers. September and October usher in autumn's grape harvest and rutting season, with unforgettable *dégustations* (wine-tasting) and wildlife encounters.
Where to stay // Blois, Tours, Saumur and Angers have a decent choice of budget and midrange hotels. For a unique Chambord experience book Le Relais de Chambord and stay in either the château's former kennels or afloat a boat on the moat.
More info // www.loirevalley-france.co.uk

Opposite from top: the Cathar
Château de Peyrepertuse, high
in the French Pyrénées; the
Château de Beynac looms over
the Dordogne River

MORE LIKE THIS
IN SEARCH OF
GRAND CHÂTEAUX

CATHAR CASTLES,
LANGUEDOC-ROUSSILLON

In France's sun-baked southwest, this drive
trails the medieval Cathars – religious
fundamentalists, persecuted and burnt as
heretics from 1208 by Pope Innocent III.
Forced to flee into arid mountains once
marking the frontier between France and
Aragon, the Cathars sought refuge in
fortresses atop rocky crags, built to defend
the French border. From Languedoc's
blockbuster fortified city of Carcassonne,
follow the valley of the River Aude between
steep cliffs and spectacular gorges to pick
up signs for ruined Château de Puilaurens.
Expect a hair-raising drive to Château de
Peyrepertuse, the largest, most impressive
Cathar castle, with a high, sheer drop on
all sides. From its battlements, spy the
next stop, pinnacle-teetering Château de
Quéribus. The final leg is a scenic drive
through Roussillon's tempting Corbières
vineyards to Château d'Aguilar, and
beyond to Perpignan.

Start // Carcassonne
End // Perpignan
Distance // 130 miles (205km)

VALLÉE DE LA DORDOGNE,
THE LOT & DORDOGNE

This countryside trip plunges into the
rural Lot and Dordogne region, taking
in limestone cliffs and canyons, forest-
covered hills and fantasy châteaux
overlooking the Dordogne River. Begin in
medieval Loubressac with its gorgeous
Dordogne Valley panorama. Wind south
along quiet lanes to Autoire and hike up
to the cliff-wedged ruins of Château des
Anglais for more views. Trace north to
the castle-crowned village of Prudhomat,
then meander west along the Dordogne,
passing through pretty Carennac, Gluges
and Creysse. Break for Michelin-starred
dining at hotel-restaurant Château de
la Treyne, teetering cinematically on a
cliff above the river. Or continue west to
a trio of dramatic châteaux: 12th-century
Beynac on a limestone bluff; quintessential
medieval fortress Castelnaud, with
its warfare museum; and 15th-century
Milandes, where risqué Paris showgirl
Josephine Baker lived in the 1940s and 50s.

Start // Loubressac
End // Château des Milandes
Distance // 75 miles (120km)

BORDEAUX WINE COUNTRY

In gourmet Bordeaux learn about Médoc
wines at La Cité du Vin, then motor north into
the vineyards along the Gironde Estuary's
western shore. Taste artisan chocolate at
the château in Margaux village, and sail
to island-vineyard Île Margaux to explore
its vineyards and overnight in its château.
Back in Margaux, drive north to Pauillac for
exceptional food at hotel-restaurant Château
Cordeillan-Bages. Cruise north along the D2
– past château-wineries Mouton Rothschild,
Lafite Rothschild and Cos d'Estournel – to
St-Estèphe for tastings and wine classes at
Château Ormes de Pez. Backtrack south to
Lamarque and take a car ferry across the
Gironde to Blaye, with architect Vauban's
citadel and vineyards. Cognac aficionados
can head 50 miles (85km) north to Cognac,
before dipping south to delightful St-
Émilion, a medieval village ringed with
wine-producing châteaux. For wine, dining,
vineyard biking and accommodation, Premier
Grand Cru Classé winery Château Troplong
Mondot is the oenophile jackpot.

Start // Bordeaux
End // St-Émilion
Distance // 180 miles (290km)

FINDING SOLITUDE IN THE VALE OF EWYAS

The remote road through Wales' Vale of Ewyas took Kerry Walker on a drive full of wild romance, unruly sheep and literary legends.

Wales has valleys too countless to name and number, but the Black Mountains' Vale of Ewyas is special. In the southeast of the country, on the fringes of the Brecon Beacons, this valley hides deep in the pleats and folds of craggy, dark-browed hills, where in winter gales howl across the moors and in summer breezes ripple through the heather.

It might be the 21st century elsewhere, but this valley didn't get the memo. Here, drystone walls sprawl over a tapestry of fields to tiny chapels and ramshackle farmhouses. Unruly sheep dawdle on single-track lanes, oblivious to tutting drivers. This is a landscape as bleak as it is beautiful; a landscape that speaks to the soul. The valley feels ancient – and it is. Strike up to windy plateau on the heights and you'll find Iron Age hillforts and perfectly aligned standing stones: the indelible etchings of mysterious ancestors.

Since moving to Wales several years ago, the Vale of Ewyas has pulled me back time and again for long, often wet walks and road trips with mood-lifting views. The hills to the east rise up like natural fortifications between Wales and England, with the valley acting as a drawbridge. England is but a crossbow shot away, but the Vale of Ewyas feels staunchly, defiantly Welsh.

And now here I am again, back on the joyous road to nowhere. My first stop at the start of the valley is the 900-year-old Skirrid Mountain Inn, just north of Abergavenny. This is billed as Wales' oldest and most haunted pub and I can well believe it – the woodsmoke-charred stone walls, dark beams and hangman's noose allude to a long and bloody past. Shakespeare apparently dreamed up the character of Puck for *A Midsummer Night's Dream* over a pint beside its great inglenook fireplace. Now the inn brims with locals with lilting, singsong voices and hikers ready to hit the hills – me included.

Close to the inn is the trail up to the summit of the Skirrid. Topping out at 1594ft (486m), it's a modestly sized peak, but that detracts nothing from its drama. I walk up through old-growth woods bursting into spring bud, and as I emerge on the wind-buffeted ridge, the

clouds part and the sun spotlights fields chequered with hedgerows. The Brecon Beacons sit like the prows of great ships to the west. To the east, the River Severn Estuary glimmers.

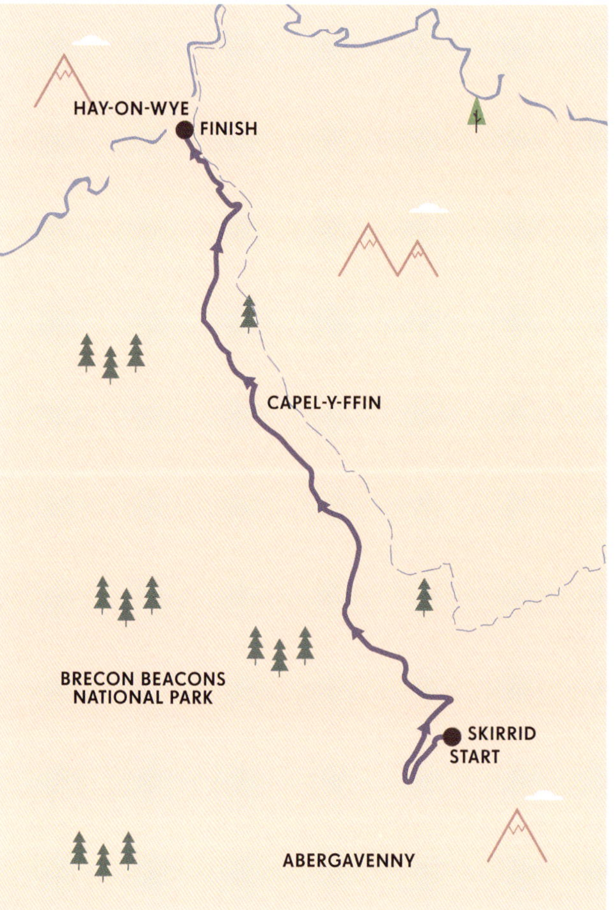

© Peter Adams | Getty Images

"The further north I drive,
the more isolated the valley
becomes, the hills closing
in, the moors brushed gold
and green"

The Skirrid stews in myths. Its Welsh name, Ysgyryd Fawr ('great shattered mountain'), refers to the massive landslide that shook it during the last Ice Age. But some prefer the legend that it was formed when a bolt of lightning hit it during the crucifixion of Jesus, giving it the nickname 'Holy Mountain'. The idea stuck, with pilgrims flocking to its now-ruined chapel over the centuries. Superstitious farmers once carted off its red soil to guarantee a good harvest.

From the Skirrid, a road cuts north through the Vale of Ewyas, a 35 mile (56km) drive to Hay-on-Wye. There's something magical about the way the scenery unfolds. The River Honddu slips secretively through the valley, emerging from behind a stand of trees then disappearing again. A shaft of sunlight illuminates a slope at random. The road narrows until it becomes a single-track lane that whips its way deeper into the moors and higher into the mountains. Getting stuck behind a tractor or being forced to reverse is par for course, but who cares? This is one drive you won't want to rush.

Pilgrims certainly didn't when they made their way to the 12th-century Augustinian abbey of Llanthony Priory, which has now fallen into romantic ruin, its nave and cloisters exposed to the sky. According to the medieval archdeacon of Brecknock, historian and chronicler Gerald of Wales, the priory was 'truly suited to the monastic life' in a 'wilderness far removed from the bustle of mankind'. And so it is still today, I think, as I survey the same views that Turner captured in his dramatic 1794 painting.

The further north I drive, the more isolated the valley becomes, the hills closing in, the moors brushed gold and green. It was this lonely beauty that fired the imagination of Bruce Chatwin, who found inspiration for his novel *On the Black Hill* here. He was particularly drawn to the Vision Farm, which sits on a gentle rise above the hamlet of Capel-y-ffin – where, local lore has it, the Virgin Mary appeared to local farmers back in 1880. Adding fuel to this religious fire was Father Ignatius of Jesus who, haunted by a lifelong fear of hellfire, subsequently came here to found the New Llanthony Abbey.

Down by the river is the far humbler St Mary's Chapel, one of Britain's smallest churches, which the diarist Reverend Francis Kilvert so eloquently described as being like a 'grey owl among its seven great yews' in his 1870s reflections on rural life.

Pushing north from Capel-y-ffin, the road gets steeper and narrower. This is the Gospel Pass, Wales' highest mountain road, clambering up to 1801ft (549m), with an average gradient of 5%. I marvel at a cyclist negotiating the incline. As there is precious little traffic, I make use of the passing places to survey the view: Hay Bluff to the right; Twmpa or – as it is more amusingly known – Lord Hereford's Knob to the left.

The Wye Valley spreads out before me, with Hay-on-Wye – of literary festival fame – but a couple of miles distant. It's a view that William Wordsworth and his sister, Dorothy, loved. I roll down the window. There's silence but for the muffled bleat of sheep and the whistle of a red kite. I fancy that if the poet had his chance to wander lonely as a cloud again, there would be no better place than here to do just that.

HIKES IN THE BLACK MOUNTAINS

Stretch the legs on this drive with some great Black Mountains walks. The 4.5 mile (7km) circular hike up to Hatterall Ridge combines views of the valley and Llanthony Priory with the chance to spot wild ponies. The 6 mile (9.5km) circular route to Hay Bluff tempts with a greater uphill challenge, beginning with a short, steep climb to the summit of Hay Bluff and along the ridge to Twmpa for spirit-lifting views of the Black Mountains.

Opposite, clockwise from top left: the Skirrid; the 900-year-old Skirrid Mountain Inn; Llanthony Priory is similarly ancient. Previous page: sheep find shelter on the valley floor

DIRECTIONS

Start // Skirrid Mountain Inn/the Skirrid
End // Hay-on-Wye
Distance // 35 miles (56km)
Getting there // Abergavenny has excellent rail connections to London, with regular services to Paddington. Hereford is the nearest train station to Hay-on-Wye.
When to go // The drive is best tackled from April to October to avoid the wettest, iciest conditions.
What to pack // Though short, this is a remote drive, so bring snacks, drinks and a map in case the GPS goes haywire. A topographic map, warm layers, waterproofs and sturdy boots are advisable for hikes en route.
Where to stay // Finish the trip in glamping style in Hay-on-Wye in one of By the Wye's off-grid safari tents perched in treetops above the river.

MORE LIKE THIS
BRITISH HILL PASSES & SINGLE TRACKS

TORRIDON TO DIABAIG, SCOTLAND

Everyone raves about the single-track Bealach na Bà on the Applecross Peninsula in the Northwest Highlands. Just as beautiful though is the lesser-known drive from Torridon to end-of-the-road Diabaig, where a small handful of whitewashed cottages nestle in the crook of a shingle bay. The slip of a road unravels along the shores of fjord-like Loch Torridon, passing spectacularly rumpled munros and flint-blue lochans. It's remote and bumpy, wending up and down over crags deeply scarred by the elements, with a moody loveliness that gets under your skin even if the Scottish weather misbehaves. The finale is the pretty fishing and crofting village of Diabaig, where you can fill up on local langoustines and scallops at charmingly converted schoolhouse Gille Brighde ('The Oystercatcher').

Start // Torridon
End // Diabaig
Distance // 8.5 miles (14km)

SNAKE PASS, ENGLAND

The clue is in the name: the Snake Pass flicks and wriggles its way through the crumpled, heather-cloaked hills, bog and bleakly beautiful moors of the Peak District National Park. Such wilderness is exhilarating, particularly given how close this steep stretch of the A57 is to the big cities of Manchester (to the west) and Sheffield (to the east). One of civil engineer Thomas Telford's masterpieces, the high road through the Pennines opened in 1821. Capping out at 1673ft (510m) above sea level, the drive goes deep into the Dark Peak area of the park, with its desolate uplands, lonely moors and windy ridges. Factor in time for hikes up to the plateau of Kinder Scout, where views reach all the way to Snowdonia in Wales on cloudless days, and Derwent Edge, with its remarkable gritstone tors and uplifting views of the Ladybower Reservoir and its Ashopton Viaduct.

Start // Glossop
End // Ashopton Viaduct
Distance // 11 miles (18km)

HARDKNOTT & WRYNOSE PASS, ENGLAND

When you see the signs warning of 'narrow routes' and 'severe bends', you know you are in for one heck of a drive. Twisting and turning precariously through the Lake District National Park, Hardknott Pass is a heart-pumping, hairpin-riddled single-track that is one of England's steepest roads. The views are magnificent, stretching across gold-green moors and fells to the ragged outline of Scafell Pike, the country's highest mountain. But don't get distracted: there are roving Herdwick Sheep, sharp bends and oncoming cars to look out for. At its steepest, the road has a gradient of 33%, rendering it treacherous in dark, wet or icy conditions. At the top of the pass, keep an eye out for a ruined Roman fort, with views to the coast. From the Duddon Valley, the Wrynose Pass takes over, zigzagging to Langdale Valley and Ambleside at the northern tip of Lake Windermere.

Start // Eskdale
End // Ambleside
Distance // 17 miles (28km)

ROLLING THROUGH THE DOLOMITES

Driving through some of Italy's most dramatic scenery, Glenn van der Knijff somehow managed to keep his eyes on the road, just with breaks to soak in the memorable views.

The towering heights of France's Mont Blanc massif and the glacier-carved grandeur of Switzerland's Matterhorn might be better known, but thanks to a blend of limestone peaks, local culture, bucolic valleys and timeworn villages, Italy's Dolomites make an undersung and worthy rival.

This immense mountain range falls within the Alto Adige (Südtirol in German), Trentino and Veneto provinces and is a wild, beautiful and accessible region offering many attractions for adventurers, including challenging opportunities for road cycling, hiking and climbing. In winter, the numerous ski resorts unite to form the Dolomiti Superski, one of the largest linked winter sports areas in the world, famous for its near 25 mile (40km) Sella Ronda circuit. German and Italian are widely spoken, but many residents also speak the local Ladin language. Given all these attributes, it's not surprising that much of the Dolomites has been given Unesco World Heritage status. Or that my family and I would be drawn to it.

We start our drive in Val Gardena, setting up base in Santa Cristina, a small village near Ortisei, the valley's principal service town. It's soon clear that, like many villages in the region, Santa Cristina maintains its tradition of woodcarving, particularly of religious figures, which dates back to the 17th century. Shops selling finished products abound.

© Glenn van der Knijff

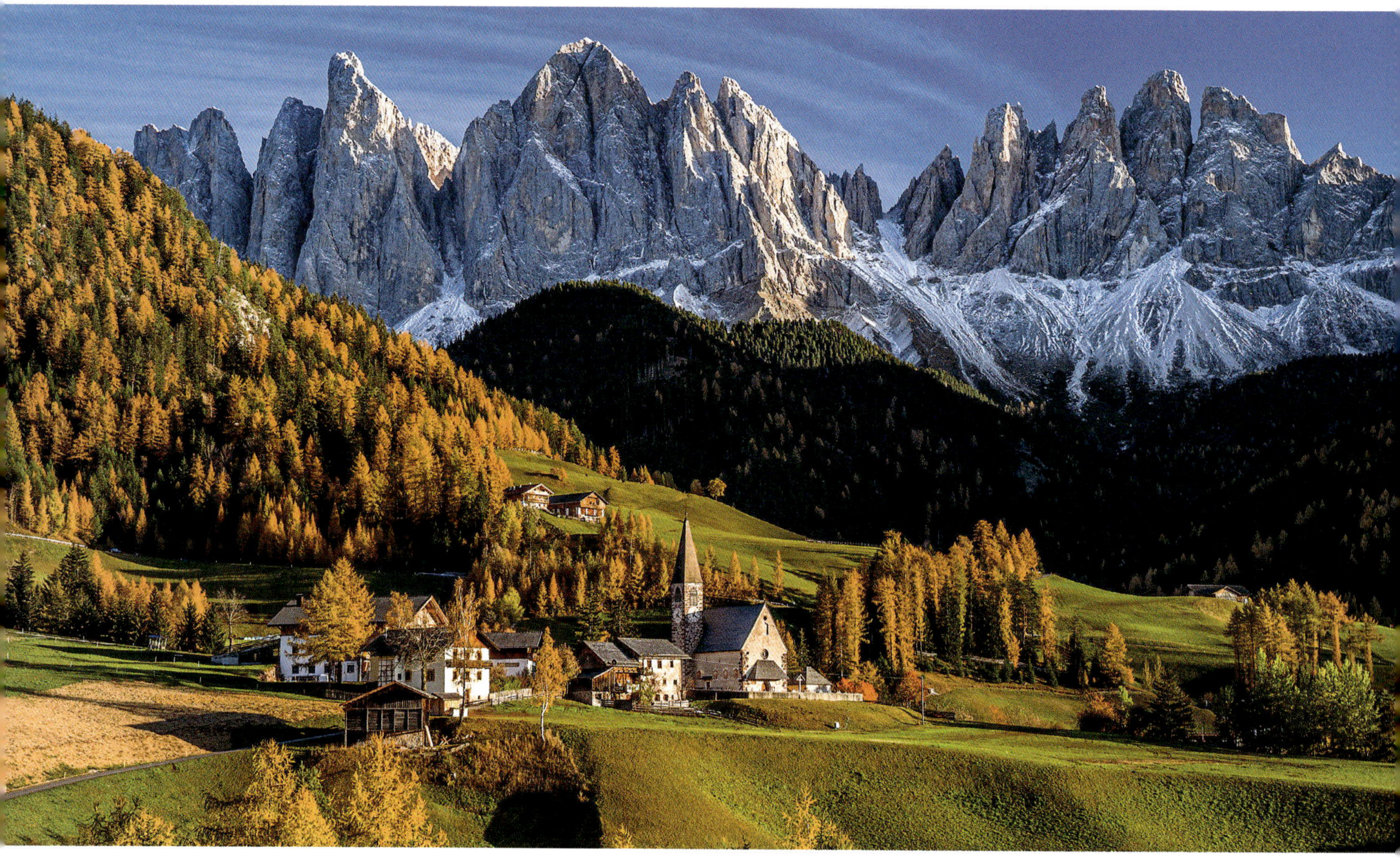

Though we are definitely in Italy, my senses tell me otherwise. Town and street signs are multilingual; architecture has a distinct Tyrolean style; and local cuisine has a definite Austrian influence. Digging deeper, I learn that this region was once part of the Austro-Hungarian Empire until formally annexed by Italy in 1919 after the end of WWI.

Back in the present, with time permitting, little beats immersing yourself in the Dolomites by hiking the network of trails and making use of the region's *rifugi* (mountain huts). On our briefer schedule, driving is an excellent alternative. Despite the number of apparently impassable peaks and valleys, there are many good roads that wiggle across the range, typically delivering outstanding vistas. As we depart on our self-devised tour, our map suggests we are in for a sinuous drive, with all the twists and turns normally found on a theme park ride. I start slowly – winding roads, travel-sick kids and rental cars don't mix – and under sunny skies we drive east through Selva and head toward Passo Gardena. Increasingly impressive views of the region's landscapes have me pausing frequently at roadside lay-bys. One peak in particular, Sassolungo (10,436ft/3,181m), looks outrageously impressive with its grey, orange and yellow-coloured

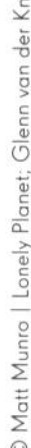

cliffs. This and the other mountains here become yet more beautiful at dawn and dusk, when the soft, warm hues of alpenglow, or *enrosadira* (Ladin for 'to turn pink'), take hold.

On reaching Passo Gardena we stop again to let the children play in a few tiny patches of snow, the remnants of a recent cold snap. The crags of the Gruppo di Sella range are close by, giving this seasoned hiker itchy feet.

The curve-strewn road from the pass to Corvara demands attention, and at every turn another array of precipitous summits comes into view, begging for more photo stops. Despite the drama of the scenery there are surprisingly few formal viewpoints, although thankfully there's no shortage of places to safely pull over.

Past Corvara we head through Val Badia before climbing to Passo di Valparola. Amid still-more expansive views, hunger sees us pushing onwards to Cortina d'Ampezzo. One of Italy's most famous and luxurious ski resorts – home to the 1956 Winter Olympics – Cortina is for jetsetters, ski-bums, climbers and hikers, along with the likes of us. We fuel-up at a café, where I make a mental note to one day return for a winter visit.

Beyond Cortina, a secondary road guides us to Lago di Misurina, a lake high on a pass that was used for skating events during the Winter Olympics. Wanting to explore deeper into the mountains, we detour east onto a side-road and stumble upon idyllic Lago d'Antorno, where the southern face of Tre Cime di Lavaredo is photogenically reflected in tranquil waters. As one of the Dolomites' – and all of Italy's – most adored peaks, the triple-summited Tre Cime di Lavaredo is a popular climbing and hiking destination. My deeper exploration of this mountain will have to wait, as we backtrack to the main road and descend north.

October days are short and we find ourselves pressing on against the dwindling afternoon sun to reach Val di Funes before nightfall, briefly halting again when Tre Cime's northern cliffs loom into view from a bend in the road.

As we dip into the Val Pusteria and become caught in a slow-moving line of vehicles progressing towards Bolzano and Innsbruck, our focus is on the day's final stop. We drive through Brunico, then bypass Bressanone on a motorway, before taking the next exit onto a narrow road which leads into the heart of remote Funes Valley.

The superlative view of the day is our last. The sun is about to set as I bring the car to a stop on a lane above the hamlet of Santa Maddalena. As I look across the valley, the final few rays highlight the autumn foliage of larch-forested hillsides. Behind a cluster of traditional buildings, the skyline is pierced by the grey crags of the Odle range. I grab a few photographs as the shadows of dusk extend over a church, and then I pause. I take time to absorb the memory before the chill of evening descends.

Our road trip's end lies just over the far side of the Odle range. With darkness overtaking us, we begrudgingly return to the motorway rather than take the circuitous route there. Exiting the rush of traffic, we wind back down to Val Gardena. The dark buttresses of the Dolomites once again lean over us, like protective friends.

SPEAKING LADIN

An ancient language with origins dating to Roman times, Ladin was once widely spoken in a region that stretched from the River Danube, north of the Alps, to Lake Garda, near Trento. These days though it's mostly confined to the secluded valleys that surround the Gruppo di Sella range. As a traditional dialect that is proudly protected and maintained, Ladin is recognised as one of the region's three official languages, along with German and Italian.

Opposite from top: walking trails wind out from the Passo Gardena; the Santa Maddalena church in the Val di Funes. Previous page: the peak of Sassolungo, seen from near Plan de Gralba

DIRECTIONS

Start // Santa Cristina
End // Santa Cristina
Distance // 133 miles (214km)
Getting there // Bolzano is accessible by train and has car rental. Venice is the closest international airport.
When to go // The mountain passes are closed by snow in winter, so May to October is the best time to go.
Where to stay // Villages in the Val Gardena and Val Badia have hotels, pensions and apartments but, for a full range of services, Ortisei makes an ideal base.
Further information // www.dolomites.org and www.valgardena.it/en
What to pack // A camera and warm clothes (especially for the high passes) are a must; a map and good boots for short walks; snacks and drink for roadside picnics.

Opposite from top: Lake Garda with the gloriously situated town of Riva del Garda in the foreground; reaching the high altitude plateau of Campo Imperatore, in Italy's Abruzzo region

MORE LIKE THIS
HIGH ALTITUDE ITALY

PASSO DI GAVIA

The highlight of this relatively short route through the Ortles-Cevedale range of the Central Alps is the crossing of 8599ft (2621m) Passo di Gavia. The scenery along the way is pretty wondrous too, taking in valleys and peaks. Though it might not have the white-knuckle infamy or exhausting switchbacks of nearby Passo dello Stelvio, Passo di Gavia is still one to be reckoned with. The road is tight in places, and shut by the likelihood of wintry weather right the way from November to June. This drive departs deep within the Camonica Valley at Edolo and passes Ponte di Legno, where the SS300 road climbs to the pass. Overshadowed by towering Corno dei Tre Signori (11,023ft/3360m), the views from up here are as memorable as on the Stelvio but, usually, the road sees far less traffic.

Start // Edolo
End // Bormio
Distance // 41 miles (66km)

BRENTA DOLOMITES

Northwest of Trento, the picturesque crags of the Brenta Dolomites are a high point of the region in both senses, while, further south, the lakeside town of Riva del Garda has an enviable position at the northern end of Lago di Garda, a place for relaxation and water sports. Combining both in this drive, your route follows the SS240 southwest out of Riva, chasing valley views at Lago di Ledro and the Cascata d'Ampola waterfall. Bearing north into the Valli Giudicarie, the roads climb to the village of Madonna di Campiglio, a ski resort known for its summer hiking and vie ferrate – exposed climbing trails protected by cables and ladders. Be sure to spend a night or two in Madonna di Campiglio, your base for walks above into the dramatic Brenta Dolomites.

Start // Riva del Garda
End // Madonna di Campiglio
Distance // 56 miles (90km)

THE APENNINES OF ABRUZZO

Taking the form of a dividing spine through central Italy, the Apennine mountain range encompasses characterful hilltop villages, much wildlife and untamed landscapes. East of Rome, the Apennines pass through the Abruzzo region and are easily accessible, providing a perfect destination for scenic drives. Beginning at the medieval valley town of Sulmona, one beautiful option climbs through the range to L'Aquila. Highlights along the route include the pretty village of Santo Stefano di Sessanio and mountain vistas from the high plateau of Campo Imperatore, both within Parco Nazionale del Gran Sasso e Monti della Laga. At Campo Imperatore, experienced hikers can don boots for the ascent of the Apennines' highest summit, Corno Grande (9554ft/2912m), a 5.6 mile (9km) roundtrip.

Start // Sulmona
End // L'Aquila
Distance // 94 miles (151km)

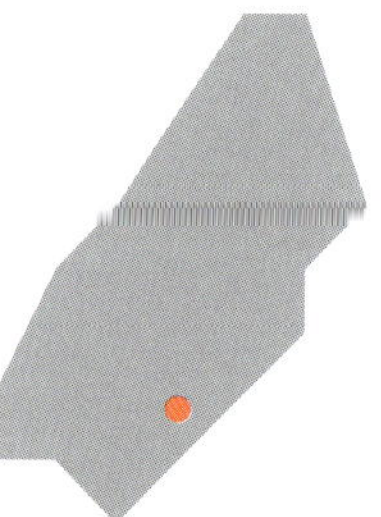

AROUND THE ISLE OF MAN TT COURSE

Matt Master circled the course of the world's most challenging and treacherous road race, on an island equidistant between England and Northern Ireland.

Beyond the memories of most, the Isle of Man was once a busy holiday destination, until its Victorian seafronts were abandoned for package trips to sunnier climes in the second half of the 20th century. For some its draw today is as a tax haven – its curious status as an autonomous dependency of the British Crown attracting both big businesses and high net worth individuals. Yet for me and many others, the principal image conjured up by this dot of land in the Irish Sea is one of leather-clad bikers, charging full throttle around its perilous mountain roads, battling extremes of speed, physical endurance and weather on the Isle of Man TT, or Tourist Trophy.

This route is the stuff of international sporting legend, a race so demanding and dangerous that many professional motorbike riders refuse to take part. But, for a select few of their more determined contemporaries, it's the only race they care to run. Held annually between May and June for over 100 years, the TT sees a variety of racing bikes – ranging from spindly classics to the latest technological pioneers – take on a course that weaves through the centres of towns and villages, along narrow country roads and high into the remote mountains that define much of the island's windswept topography.

My arrival on the Isle of Man was preceded by a three-hour ferry ride from Liverpool docks, time enough to fully appreciate the isolation of this island sat squarely between the east coast of Northern Ireland and the western fringes of the Lake District in England. Such isolation has shaped the history of the island and its Manx population, and continues to add a certain mystique to the enthralling, terrifying TT.

Throughout the summer months, the Isle of Man, and the TT course in particular, is a driving destination for motorsport fans from across Europe. All come to marvel at the immensity of the meandering clockwise circuit from and to the capital of Douglas, and many intend to exploit the fact that there is no speed limit on most of the island's unrestricted country roads. It's worth reading up on exactly how this plays out in reality, however. The local police still take the subject of dangerous driving very seriously and the Isle of Man's own Highway Code is peppered with aphorisms such as 'Better to arrive late than never' and 'Normal speed meets every need'.

All ferries arrive in Douglas, allowing you to head with minimal preamble onto the TT route itself, pointing northwest on the A1 through the hamlets of Glen Vine, Crosby and Greeba towards the Tynwald National Park. This first stretch of the course is narrow, two-

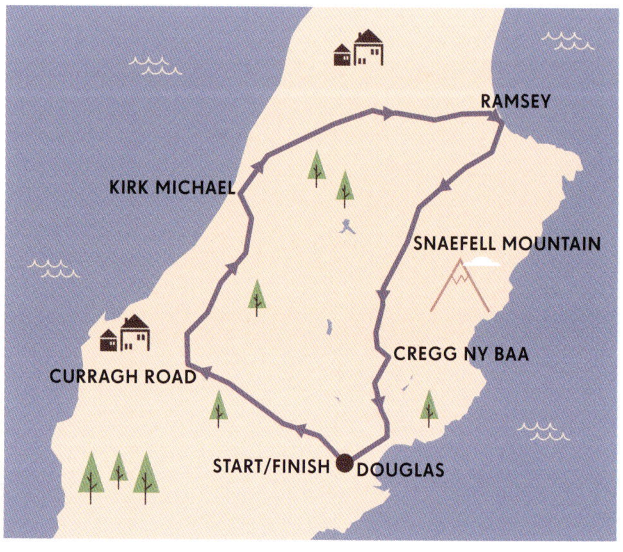

© JazzyGeoff | Shutterstock

"The TT is the stuff of sporting legend, a race so demanding and dangerous that many professional riders refuse to take part"

lane country road, lined with trees and apparently unremarkable in a car at sensible speed – although a pre-emptive visit to YouTube had refreshed my memory as to what it looks like at full power on a sports bike, tyres coming within inches of the raised kerbs that appear suddenly from among the shadows, the rider's shoulders comparably close to the rough stone walls of outlying farms and cottages.

Where the A1 dissects the A3 Curragh Rd, the course takes a hard right and climbs steeply uphill towards Ballig Bridge. It's at this point that the views begin to open up to the west, out towards the sea, and the first of the high hills loom from the north. Jinking left and right, the road continues to ascend, the sky expanding exponentially above as the trees fall away around Cronk Y Voddy, a straight and flat out section of the course that allows riders in full race mode to regain their senses before plunging into the next series of hugely physical bumps and bends.

Beyond the town of Kirk Michael, the A3 spears on through long and winding tunnels of densely planted trees, bumpy and incredibly technical for the TT competitors, with even small sections of the course taking years to learn well enough to be attacked at meaningful speed. The route then drops towards the town of Ramsey, the most northerly point on the circuit, before turning due south for the final and most famous stretch of all, the Snaefell Mountain Road.

Leaving Ramsey, it's a near-continuous climb on the A18 through corners with names like Waterworks and Gooseneck, some three quarters of the way around the circuit now but with much of the drama still to come. Here, the course becomes truly remote, with far reaching views to left and right and Snaefell peak in the distance, closing fast. Just after the Bungalow Bridge is the highest point of the circuit, 1400ft (427m) above sea level, and on a clear day a glorious vantage point from which to appreciate the setting for such an unlikely race. It's well worth stopping to catch your breath, drink some coffee and smell the crisp air, usually blowing in hard and relentlessly off the Irish Sea.

From here, the A18 continues to sweep between the high and barren peaks around Snaefell before a sudden downhill section leads off the mountain for good at Creg Ny Baa. A tight right hander precedes an immediate return to typical country roads, lined with low hedges, then more kerbs and the outlying sprawl of suburban Douglas as the lap comes to an end.

It's a process well worth repeating, as I found myself doing several times in a single day, with differing agendas. Sometimes to take in the scenery. Sometimes to drive the road a little more concertedly, to wonder at the superhuman levels of concentration required to do it at race speed, on two wheels, and to sample the occasional, visceral thrill of a derestricted rural road.

Even if you've no interest in motorbike racing, the Isle of Man is a remarkable place to visit. For those drawn precisely by the mythology of motorsport, it sits alongside Le Mans and the Nürburgring as one of Europe's most potent and evocative driving destinations – beautiful, haunting, and touched by madness.

CHANGEABLE WEATHER

Thanks to its unique position and exacerbated by its mountainous terrain, the Isle of Man enjoys famously unpredictable weather. The reality of four seasons in one day has played its part over the decades in making the TT such a dangerous race. It's not uncommon to leave Ramsey in full sun, only to find it sleeting hard on the other side of Snaefell Mountain. Take nothing for granted except your need for waterproofs.

Opposite, clockwise from top left: a memorial statue to 26-time TT race winner Joey Dunlop; motorcycle-with-sidecar riders skim feet from houses; the Port of Douglas. Previous page: practice laps in the TT

DIRECTIONS

Start // Douglas
Finish // Douglas
Distance // 38 miles (61km)
Duration // The course record might be just under 17 minutes but you should allow at least a couple of hours, with stops to take in the scenery.
Getting there // Steam Packet runs twice-daily ferries from Heysham and Liverpool to Douglas between late March and October; prices start at £56 for foot passengers. Or you can fly to Isle of Man Airport (7 miles south of Douglas) from UK and Irish cities including London, Dublin, Belfast and Edinburgh.
Where to stay // Hotel Halvard, a short walk from the ferry terminal, has suites with sea views.
Where to eat // 14 North Restaurant on the Douglas Quayside specialises in seasonal local produce.

Opposite from top: the Military Road wiggles past Compton Bay on the Isle of Wight; a 'tombolo', or natural sand causeway, links St Ninian's Isle with Shetland's Mainland

MORE LIKE THIS
BRITISH ISLAND DRIVES

ISLE OF ARRAN, SCOTLAND

The Isle of Arran's sole A road performs a near perfect loop along this island's wild and varied coastline, offering unhindered views over the Firth of Clyde and the distant Scottish mainland on two sides. Leaving the ferry terminal at Brodick, Arran's capital, head south on the A841. From the pretty seaside town of Lamlash, with its views of Holy Isle to the east, the road runs through Whiting Bay west towards Kilmory and Blackwaterfoot. This southern stretch is along cliff tops with far reaching outlooks, while the next, northwest section towards Lochranza runs at shore level, allowing easy access to beautiful beaches. The scenery changes again for the final third of the journey, the road edging up Goatfell Mountain before rejoining the sea at Sannox and hugging the coast back to Brodick.

Start // Brodick
Finish // Brodick
Distance // 56 miles (90km)

ISLE OF WIGHT, ENGLAND

Sat in the English Channel due south of the hectic ports of Southampton and Portsmouth, the Isle of Wight offers a unique sense of island life the minute you drive off the ferry in Cowes. Much of the southern part of the island is a dedicated Area of Outstanding Natural Beauty, with the A3055 Military Road running most of the way along its verdant coast between Chale, near the Victorian resort of Ventnor, and Afton. The rest of the island is made up of a haphazard network of local roads that can be joined up to make a clockwise circuit, taking in Osborne House (Queen Victoria's seaside bolthole in Cowes), the Culver Battery near Bembridge, Ventnor's Botanic Gardens and the remote outlook of St Catherine's Oratory, in an approximate semi-circle, before enjoying the dramatic cliffs that lead towards the chalky outcrop of The Needles.

Start // Cowes
Finish // The Needles
Distance // 45 miles (72km)

SHETLAND, SCOTLAND

Shetland is sufficiently far from what is already the most northerly point of the British mainland that most visitors choose to fly in and rent a car. The island's own Mainland is dissected by the A970, a spine road which begins conveniently at Sumburgh Airport in the south and terminates at the northern tip in North Roe. Striking north, the ferry from Leebitten will whisk you across to Mousa for a visit to its famous broch, one of the best-preserved Iron Age round towers in Europe. Continuing north, largest town Kirkwall has the Shetland Museum for background on the archipelago and then it's more ferry crossings as you aim for your ultimate goal, the view from Hermaness of wonderfully named Muckle Flugga Lighthouse, built just off the isle of Unst in 1854. It's Britain's northernmost lighthouse, closer to the Norwegian town of Bergen than it is to Aberdeen.

Start // Sumburgh
Finish // Hermaness
Distance // 83 miles (134km)

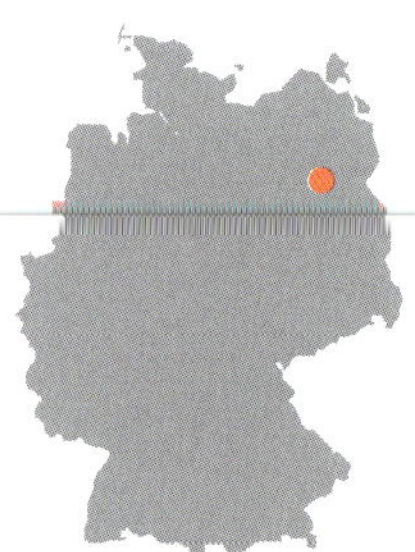

SOUTHBOUND IN GERMANY'S EAST

On a drive from Berlin to Dresden and beyond, Rory Goulding discovered that the lands of the former DDR are rich in sights whose fame outside Germany remains muted.

I had been to Berlin only once before, on a German exchange trip when half the city seemed to be under scaffolding in its post-unification rebuilding spree. Now, I'm curious to return and delve more into the history of the surrounding region, beyond the depictions of the DDR (the former East Germany) that I saw in films such as *Good Bye Lenin!*, *The Lives of Others* and *Deutschland 83*. Street-level distinctions are steadily blurring: mostly it's the eastern legacy that's fading, although the DDR's Ampelmännchen – a jaunty, hat-wearing variant of the traffic-light man – has started to pop up at pedestrian crossings west of where the wall once ran.

The rental car office is close to the Kaiser Wilhelm Memorial Church, with the stump of its stone tower preserved as a memorial to what was lost in a 1943 bombing raid. From here, I head out of the city past the old Tempelhof Airport, a representative piece of Nazi architecture that later became a symbol of freedom during the Berlin Airlift. Shortly after this, I pass into what was once DDR territory, where I'll stay for the rest of the trip.

The reputation abroad of the German autobahn network rests heavily on the 'no speed limit' policy – and also its history. Contrary to popular lore, these highways were first planned before the Nazi rise to power, and yet that regime's association inevitably colours aspects of the design, such as the way curves were often placed for maximum scenic drama. As it happens, Autobahn 13 down which I'm headed runs through largely flat lands. In the former East, you mostly have to head south to find mountainous scenery, with the major range running along the Czech border – my ultimate destination.

That's not to say the countryside between Berlin and Dresden has no beauty, but the best of the landscape is of the get-out-and-look kind. Less than an hour after leaving the capital, I exit the autobahn

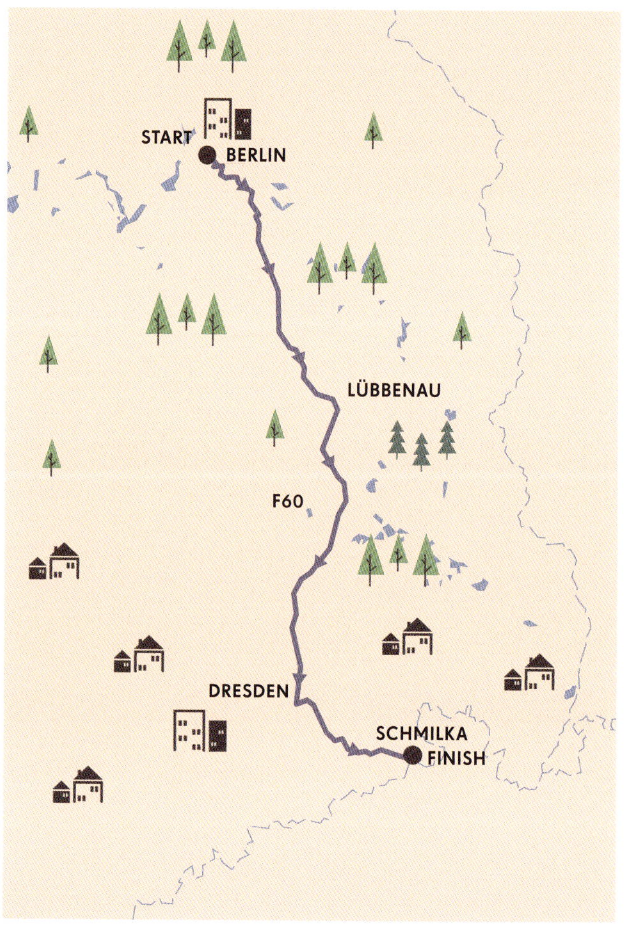

at the town of Lübbenau, on the edge of the Spreewald. Here, the Spree River, on its way to Berlin, unravels into dozens of channels that thread through water meadows and forests of alder, ash and willow. It's a biosphere reserve, ideally explored by canoe, but also a place where pockets of traditional culture hold out. The bilingual signs at the entrance to Lübbenau/Lubnjow and the neighbouring village of Lehde/Lĕdy show that I'm now in the historical region of Lusatia, where some 25,000 people still speak Sorbian languages related to Czech and Polish. Easter eggs painted in intricate Sorbia patterns are on show in the Lehde Open-Air Museum, but really the whole village is museum-worthy, with its waterside houses topped – in a rather Viking way – by crossed wooden gable ends in the shape of crowned snakes, a traditional good-luck sign.

Further surprises lie off the A13. Earlier, I'd skipped the opportunity for some beach time at the Tropical Islands Resort, a former airship hangar of record vastness, now done up to look like a wayward piece of Bali. But in this region where the landscape has been deeply altered by the strip-mining of lignite, I make a diversion to gawp at Overburden Conveyor Bridge F60, a steel mining monster proudly touted as an Eiffel Tower on its side, only taller/longer. It's the world's largest moveable piece of machinery, though one which has been at rest since 1992. The panorama from its top platform gives a hint of the future, with many old strip mines being flooded to create the Lusatian Lake District –a huge contrast with the area's industrial past.

As a symbol of rebirth, however, there is little to match the city of Dresden. Crossing a bridge over the curve of the Elbe River, I see a skyline both older and newer than it was when the Wall fell.

LAND OF PICKLES

If you've watched the 2003 movie *Good Bye Lenin!*, set in the last months of East Germany, you might have seen the lead character's mother hanker after Spreewald gherkins, which now have EU-protected status. In the SpreewaldRabe factory tasting room near Lübbenau, you can compare flavours, including dill and mustard. And at Lübbenau's Restaurant Hanschick, you can stay in a cabin shaped like the big wooden barrels once used for pickling.

Clockwise from above: painted Easter eggs at the Lehde Open-Air Museum; the Augustus Bridge and Frauenkirche in Dresden; the city's Striezelmarkt Christmas market. Previous page: exploring Spreewald around Lübbenau

The capital of Saxony was the Baroque jewel of German art and architecture until the devastating bombing raids of 1945. Although much restoration was done even under the DDR, the city's beloved Frauenkirche, with its bell-shaped dome, had been deliberately left as a pile of rubble, in memoriam. City guide Anett Orzyszek explained to me: 'Every year in February we went to remember the families who died. In the last years of the DDR, it was a place where you discussed politics. You could say a revolution started right here.' Even after the end of communism, Anett, like many others, thought the church would never be rebuilt. Since 2005, however, the Frauenkirche has stood once again, its pale golden form speckled with stones from the original.

Before the turmoil of the 20th century, Dresden was one of Europe's travel magnets, a Florence of the North. I have a soft spot for places that got through their picture-postcard phase early, and my final stop is another classic. The rugged landscape of Saxon Switzerland inspired Romantic artists including Caspar David Friedrich 200 years ago. Despite the fanciful name, the mix of vertiginous rocks and grasping pines that now constitutes a national park looks more like a Chinese landscape than a scene from a Heidi story. On the drive from Dresden to Bad Schandau, gateway to the park, the road bends to the rhythm of the Elbe and I watch vintage paddle steamers ply its waters as I drive its banks. The river carves between tablelands that are often wrapped in cloud, like a South American lost world.

The furthest stop south on my road trip is the village of Schmilka, where I'm due to meet a rock-climbing guide for an introductory course in one of the specialities of Saxon Switzerland. I can see – just seconds down the road – the customs post before the Czech border. I must resist the temptation to drive on and explore further. But in a region defined for decades by razor wire and watchtowers at its limits, there's a humbling joy to know that the choice is mine.

DIRECTIONS

Start // Berlin
End // Schmilka
Distance // 146 miles (235km)
Getting there // Berlin Brandenburg Airport is now the sole hub serving the city. Dresden Airport at the southern end of the route is much smaller, though it does have a handful of international flights. Berlin to Dresden takes around two hours by train. Car rental companies can be found at Berlin Brandenburg and throughout the capital itself.
When to go // The region looks at its best in spring or summer. Winter is the only season that imposes restrictions, as some visitor facilities in Spreewald and Saxon Switzerland shut down, though frost and snow bring their own beauty to those landscapes, and Dresden's Christmas market is famous.
Further information // www.germany.travel

MORE LIKE THIS
OTHER SIDES TO GERMANY'S EAST

THURINGIAN FOREST NATURE PARK

Thuringia is called the 'green heart of Germany', thanks to the range of thickly forested hills that runs through the state and because the region has cropped up at key moments in the country's history. A touring route follows mostly minor roads through the park from Hörschel, its northern tip, near the sprawling hilltop castle of Wartburg where Martin Luther took refuge, to the ethereal Saalfeld Fairy Grottoes. The track weaves like a shy forest creature, emerging at the lowland edge before ducking back into the folds of the hills, where the woods might suddenly reveal old mine workings, a ski jump or a rustic tavern in a clearing. And if all the half-timbered towns such as Schmalkalden put you in mind of a Christmas story, wait until you get to Lauscha, which has built a small industry upon decorative glass baubles since the 1840s.

Start // Hörschel
End // Saalfeld
Distance // 280 miles (450km)

UPPER LUSATIAN HOUSE ROAD

Around the town of Zittau, tucked in where the borders of Poland and the Czech Republic meet, lies Germany's perhaps most overlooked corner. Apart from quirkily eroded sandstone mountains to the south, the area is one of rolling farm country, famous for a version of half-timbered house, Umgebindehaus, distinct from the typical Fachwerkhäuser style found elsewhere. As such, the region has been honoured with a detached section of the German Timber-Frame Road, a momentous route which otherwise runs far to the west. This more manageable loop begins in Ebersbach-Neugersdorf, which has fine examples of the style (log-cabin-like ground floor, half-timbered upper floor), including one that's now home to a coffee museum and roasters. There are more than 6000 of these handsome houses dotted across this part of Upper Lusatia, many of them in six more towns and villages visited on this circular route.

Start // Ebersbach-Neugersdorf
End // Ebersbach-Neugersdorf
Distance // 70 miles (112km)

GERMAN AVENUES ROUTE

If only you could swap your car for a carriage, a trip along the Deutsche Alleenstrasse (German Avenues Route) would feel like a series of opening scenes to a lavish costume drama. The route's guiding theme is the kind of stately, tree-lined avenue you might expect leading up to an aristocratic country mansion. The whole route is actually a mightier endeavour than laid out here, running in branching segments for some 1864 miles (3000km) diagonally across Germany, from the Baltic Sea to Lake Constance. For a straight run down the centre of the former DDR, however, opt for the stretch between the beloved holiday island of Rügen and the cultural heavyweight of Dresden, via Wittenberg, where Martin Luther helped launch the Reformation. Skirting chestnut woods and golden fields of rapeseed, the route sticks determinedly to slower roads, at one point taking a chain ferry across the Elbe in preference to nearby highway bridges.

Start // Rügen
End // Dresden
Distance // 416 miles (670km)

Garten

ACROSS THE TOP OF SCOTLAND

Tracing the wild reaches of Scotland's north coast, Adam Weymouth discovered that one of Europe's most sparsely populated regions makes for one of its most beguiling drives.

The top of Scotland is remote and unforgiving and has the lowest population density in the country. Despite having lived in Scotland for several years, I had never made it this far north. I was not quite sure why I would want to, or what would tempt me there.

On my road trip ahead there will be many times when I will crest a mountain pass and see a single farmhouse backed by a towering landscape, no one else in view, and think, 'Who on Earth lives here?' But by the end of this drive, having met the people who do make their home in this isolated corner of the UK, I will come to be envious of their deep connection to their community and land, and see that perhaps it is my own life in the city that has become somehow remote. There will be no shortage of opportunities along this journey to pull over at some dramatic spot and ponder such thoughts.

The land changes as soon as I leave the start of this drive, the town of Ullapool. To reach this point, I have driven all

morning through the sort of Highland landscapes with which I am familiar. But heading beyond Ullapool I encounter something entirely different.

Within a mile, I have parked and am standing beside the car, looking out over the sea. The air is fresh. A single row of cottages follows the curve of a small bay, and looming beyond is the immensity of Ben Mór Coigach. This place feels far more northern, as though I have driven out onto tundra, and as I cruise along again I cannot shake the sense that I have crossed into a different, Arctic country. Barren, rolling land stretches away, scattered with fallen blocks of granite. Thin rivers run through the moorland, shining in the sun. Over it all, like whales breaching, are the mountains, great stark mounds of rock with their evocative Gaelic names: Glas Bheinn; Canisp; Breabag; Cùl Mòr. Belted Galloway cattle stand around, indifferent to these glorious surroundings.

And this is a lived landscape, too. Each of the little village harbours I go on to encounter – Kylesku, the curiously named Badcall, Scourie – is full of fishing boats. Late in the evening I pull up outside the hotel in the first of them, Kylesku, balanced on a little piece of land between Loch Gleann Dubh and Loch a' Chàirn Bhàin. The hotel's restaurant menu describes itself as 'ultra-local'. As if to prove the point, my waiter points out the beds, visible from where I'm sitting, where they source their mussels. The fish are landed locally, the scallops hand-dived round the corner from the hotel. A local diet doesn't feel much of

"As I cruise along I cannot shake the sense that I have crossed into a different, Arctic country"

a sacrifice here, and many of the restaurants in the region hold to the ethos: why travel far for food when it's available in such good quality nearby? As I tuck into some delicious venison, I recall that earlier that afternoon I had seen a herd of red deer, pouring across the hills as I drove, and consider that what I'm enjoying must be some of the most sustainable meat on the planet.

The next day I follow a huge estuary, the Kyle of Durness, northwards. The dramatic and powerfully named Cape Wrath lies off to my left. Angry it might sound – and look, in bad weather – but its name is actually derived from the Norse for 'turning point', this cape being the northwest tip of mainland Scotland. And here I turn too, the road now heading east of Durness and striking out for the coast, running high up on the cliffs above immense and windswept beaches. The morning light picks out the pinks of the heather and the rock. Rising above me off to the right is Ben Hope – I'm told that from the summit on the summer solstice, you can see the sun all night. All along this stretch there are exquisite spots to camp, and as long as you take everything home with you and don't damage the landscape, you are generally free to pitch up where you like. I spend a night at Armadale Bay, where I have

a swathe of sand and sea and sky entirely to myself. My swim here, in the tossing swell of the Atlantic, is wild and bracing, even in August.

In the morning I drive on. Occasionally I pass an isolated house or church, a few graves beside the road, but mostly there is only rolling moor and sheep and views out across the ocean. A two-and-a-half-mile causeway and bridge form a spectacular entrance to the village of Tongue, where the cosy Brass Tap bar at the Tongue Hotel beckons me in. From there, the drive takes me to places whose names I have known my whole life but never thought I'd get to. Thurso, a busy little town with a high street full of local shops and cafés, and, via a short detour, John o' Groats, because its name is the stuff of legend, the end of so many trans-British journeys, the farthest point from Land's End in southwest England. It's named after a 15th-century Dutchman, Jan de Groot (John the Large) who ran the ferry from here to Orkney.

Just to the west lies Dunnet Head, the most northerly point of mainland Britain. This is it, I can go no farther. I park and follow the path out to the lighthouse. The sea is far below me. Fulmars blow around like spume. Gannets dive from great heights into the water. It's a clear evening when I arrive and the islands of Orkney, offshore to the north, are caught in a beautiful light. This is not remote, I think. This is a place where people and place, the food they eat, the work they do, all feel intimately connected, part of one community. With the wind at my back I look out across the Atlantic, not ready to turn around just yet.

COASTAL CAVERN

Smoo Cave can be found on the beach just outside Durness. This huge cave has been eroded by both sea and river, and artefacts uncovered here suggest that it was occupied as far back as Neolithic times. The Vikings built and repaired their boats within its series of chambers, and it continued to be used by local fishermen up to the 20th century. Summer boat tours explore the parts that cannot be reached on foot.

From left: local mussels; the shoreline in Ullapool village; Smoo Cave; Sango Bay at Durness. Previous page: the Kylesku Bridge spans Loch a' Chàirn Bhàin

DIRECTIONS

Start // Ullapool
End // Dunnet Head
Distance // 158 miles (254km)
Getting there // Ullapool is an hour's drive from Inverness, which is served by trains (including the sleeper train) from London and other cities in Scotland.
When to go // The road is beautiful year-round. Summer means long evenings and stopping on every beach; winter, snowy landscapes and maybe even the northern lights.
Where to stay // If you're into wild camping, read up on how to do it responsibly before you go. Otherwise, there are all manner of campsites, hotels and self-catering options.
Further information // If you fancy extending the trip, this road is part of the much longer North Coast 500, which begins and ends in Inverness

Opposite: 'The Jacobite' steam train service crosses the Glenfinnan Viaduct

MORE LIKE THIS
REMOTE SCOTTISH DRIVES

ARGYLL'S SECRET COAST

Dunoon is only a short train ride and ferry out of Glasgow, but the road from here that hugs the coast of the Cowal Peninsula feels a world away from city life. The scenery is wonderful, and the roadside viewpoint between Glendaruel and Tighnabruaich, gazing out over the Kyles of Bute, reveals one of the most memorable panoramas in Scotland. The huge sandy beach at Ostel Bay, a short walk down the track from the little cafe at Kilbride Farm, is a must. If the sea looks too chilly, stop in at Portavadie Marina for a soak in their heated outdoor infinity pool instead. Hikes round here wind through hunched and dramatic Atlantic oak woods, some of Britain's last remaining temperate rainforest. Finish with a dinner of locally sourced seafood at Inver, just south of Strachur.

Start // Dunoon
End // Strachur
Distance // 52 miles (84 km)

THE OUTER HEBRIDES, FROM BARRA TO LEWIS

Most of the roads that thread together the islands of the Outer Hebrides are single track and the going is slow – the perfect pace for exploring everything that this archipelago has to offer. The white-sand beaches and turquoise waters can trick you into thinking you have landed somewhere much more tropical (the water temperature and the wind speed soon bring you back to reality) and even in the height of summer you can bag a whole beach to yourself. Begin on Barra, the Outer Hebrides' most southerly inhabited island, and set your sights north. Each island along the way has a distinct character, from the pretty lochs scattered across North Uist to the austere moonscapes of Harris. And don't miss the Callanish standing stones on Lewis, a grouping of close to 50 megaliths that date back to around 3000 BC.

Start // Castlebay
End // Port of Ness
Distance // 168 miles (270 km)

FORT WILLIAM TO MALLAIG

The so-called 'road to the Isles' begins in Fort William, within sight – mist allowing – of Ben Nevis, Scotland's highest peak. It then unwinds through some truly lovely countryside, hemmed in by mountain summits and giving views out over Loch Shiel and Loch Eil. For Harry Potter fans, the railway viaduct at Glenfinnan forms an iconic part of the route taken by the Hogwarts Express, and it isn't uncommon to see young wizards lining the road here in the hope of catching a glimpse of a steam train chugging by. Take the turning at Arisaig to follow a narrow road past exquisite beaches, keeping an eye out for seals and gannets. At Arisaig you can hire kayaks, should you want an unobtrusive way to approach such wildlife for a closer look. Continue your Scottish driving adventure by taking the ferry from Mallaig onwards to Rum, Eigg or Skye.

Start // Fort William
End // Mallaig
Distance // 46 miles (74 km)

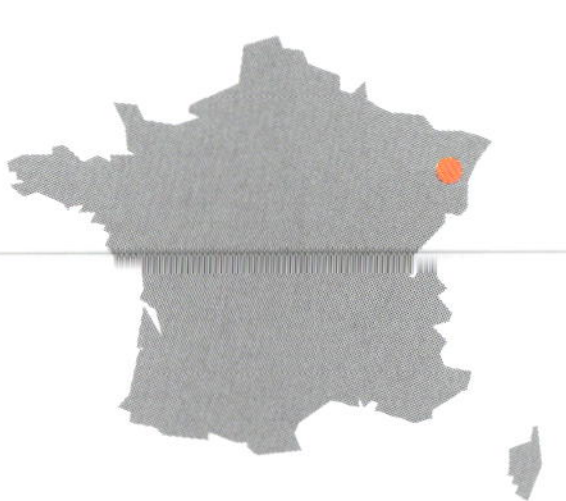

THROUGH THE GRAPEVINE: ROUTE DES VINS D'ALSACE

On one of France's finest drives, Kerry Walker found that every turn reveals hamlets with storybook appeal, vine-swathed views and cellars with glasses for tastings at the ready.

I have the peculiar sensation that I've somehow been drafted as an extra on a Disney film set. The village I'm exploring is too ludicrously cute to be true – there are half-timbered, wonky-gabled houses in colours as bright as liquorice allsorts, their window boxes overflowing with geraniums. Storks are balancing protectively on the huge nests they've built atop chimney pots. Cobbled lanes polished smooth with centuries of boot leather weave past patisseries scented with gingerbread and displaying *macarons* in every shade. Beyond the medieval town walls, row after neatly tended row of vines march up hillsides watched over by the hazy Vosges Mountains in the distance.

This is northeastern France, but not as many people know it. Alsace does things a little differently. Sidling up to Germany, it has ping-ponged between the two countries over hundreds of years, finally being returned to the French post WWII. Listen carefully and you'll hear the Germanic cadence of Alsatian, the local dialect. Look carefully and you'll notice the mix of French and German cuisine on menus – *choucroute garnie* (a gutsy dish of sauerkraut garnished with sausage and smoked meats), *wädele* (pork knuckle in pinot noir) and *lewerknepfle* (liver, shallot and parsley dumplings).

Even the oft-blasé French go misty-eyed at the mention of Alsace, considered something of a national treasure for its cross-cultural idiosyncrasies. And the 105-mile (170km) Route des Vins wine route, which corkscrews largely along scenic backroads between Marlenheim – 13 miles (21km) west of Strasbourg – and Thann, is the region's pièce de résistance. It's easy driving; the landscapes are soothingly green and you are never more than a few miles from a village with fairy-tale looks, an excellent restaurant, or a *cave* (cellar) where you are welcome to stop and sample the local wines. Unlike

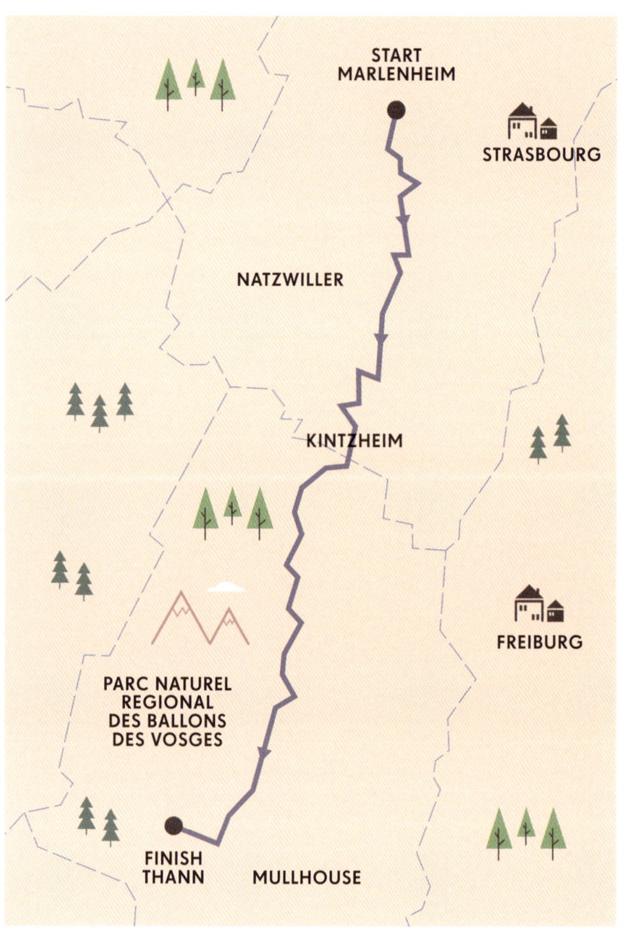

in more prestigious regions like Champagne, say, or Bordeaux, no appointments are usually necessary for a *petite dégustation* (tasting), and the wines on offer are often surprisingly good. At the white end of the spectrum are light, citrusy sylvaners, tangy rieslings, spicy gewürztraminers and aromatic, honeyed muscats. Light-bodied pinot noirs, full of ripe fruit notes, dominate the reds.

Like a fine meal, the Route des Vins is best broken down into several courses and savoured slowly. Stopping overnight not only allows you to see the towns and villages at their lantern-lit best, it also means you can sensibly factor in the wine tastings post-drive.

After a spin of Strasbourg's historic centre and Gothic giant of a cathedral, I'm ready to drive south. It's early autumn and already the vine-draped hills are beginning to turn gold and the scent of new wine is drifting from roadside *caves*. The road wends past sleepy villages that recline at the foot of rolling, low-browed hills. This is gentle countryside that grows on you with its quiet beauty. There are no grand chateaux. The delightfully old-world villages I pass have an air of model railway perfection and they smell like Christmas.

In Obernai, I wander aimlessly in the backstreets of a town where life still revolves around the market square – this one sports a Renaissance-style six-bucket well and a bell-topped corn exchange. I follow a trail that takes me beyond the town walls and up into the vines, and am later rewarded for my efforts with a slab of *zwiebelkuchen* (onion tart) and glass of effervescent new wine at a cosy *winstub* (wine tavern).

Grand cru wines can be found in the nearby village of Mittelbergheim, none of which are finer than those sold at Domaine

COLMAR CHARM

Strasbourg is better known, but Colmar is a delightful base to explore the Route des Vins. Its old town is crammed with half-timbered houses in chalk-box colours, but its canal-woven Petite Venise (Little Venice) quarter steals the show – rent a rowboat in summer. Colmar's other claim to fame is as the birthplace of Frédéric Auguste Bartholdi, the Statue of Liberty sculptor. The Musée Bartholdi (www. musee-bartholdi.fr) is where the legend was born in 1834.

Clockwise from above: grapes ripen on the vine; the canal in nearby Strasbourg; Riquewihr, one of the route's prettiest villages. Previous page: the vast vineyards of Alsace

Gilg, hailing from the slopes of Zotzenberg and Moenchberg. The 16th-century stone cellars are their pride and joy, as are their rieslings and sylvaners, which have won many accolades.

Heading on further south brings me to Dambach-la-Ville, another chocolate-box village, this one lined with late-medieval houses painted in shades of pistachio, caramel and raspberry – they look almost edible. Lifted high on a wooded crag above a sea of vines is Dambach-la-Ville's most evocative sight: the nearby 12th-century Château du Haut-Koenigsbourg. A riot of red towers and turrets, it was elaborately rebuilt by Kaiser Wilhelm II in 1908. On cloudless days, the views reach west as far as the bluish-green Vosges and east to the rolling mountains of Germany's Black Forest. Occasionally, if visibility is really good, the faint outline of the Alps is distinguishable to the south.

Competition is stiff for the prettiest town title on the Route des Vins, but the twin settlements of Ribeauvillé and Riquewihr are both as lovely as they come. They brim with history, too – the former with its Pfifferhüs which once housed the town's fife-playing minstrels, and the Tour des Bouchers (Butchers' Bell Tower); the latter with its ramparts enclosing a maze of twisting lanes and half-timbered houses that twist up to the Tour des Voleurs (Thieves' Tower). For an insight into Alsatian wines, I opt to visit the museum and cellars of the Cave de Ribeauvillé, leaving an hour later more the wiser and several glasses of wine merrier.

But it is in the tiny hamlet of Kaysersberg that time really stands still and I get a sense of what makes this region tick. After trying organic wines at Vignoble Klur, I strike out on foot on trails that taper off into the hills, now burnished by the last light of day. Up here I find myself alone, surrounded by row after row of ripening grapes. There is much harvesting still to be done. And though the open road and Colmar await, I'm in no hurry to leave.

© Cultura Exclusive / Walter Zerla | Getty Images

DIRECTIONS

Start // Marlenheim

End // Thann

Distance // 106 miles (170km)

Getting there // Strasbourg (www.strasbourg.aeroport.fr) is the closest airport, served by a raft of airlines. All major car hire companies are represented at the airport.

When to drive // The road is accessible year-round and each season has a different appeal – from summer wine festivals to golden autumn days to the festive sparkle of some of France's best Christmas markets.

Where to stay // The villages on the route all have plenty of hotels and restaurants. Tourist offices can provide details of local *chambres d'hôtes* (B&Bs).

More info // For the lowdown on sights, attractions, hotels and restaurants on the drive, visit www.alsace-wine-route. com. Local tourist offices can supply you with the excellent English-language map/brochure *The Alsace Wine Route*.

Route des Vins d'Alsace

*Opposite from top: terraces of vines
along the Douro River; wine barrels
at Quinta do Pacheca*

MORE LIKE THIS
GRAPE TRAILS

DOURO VALLEY, PORTUGAL

Portugal kept this one up its sleeve
for a long time, but oenophiles have
finally clocked on to the romance – and
increasingly outstanding wines – of
the Douro Valley. The world's oldest
demarcated wine region (in 1756, for the
record) is a real beauty, with mile after mile
of twisting, terraced vineyards that rise
sharply from the Douro River. Its true heart
is the Alto Douro (Upper Douro), a Unesco
World Heritage Site. The drive kicks off in
the grand port lodges of Porto, gradually
inching east to the Spanish border. En
route expect to find an abundance of
historic wine estates – Quinta Nova and
Quinta do Crasto are names to remember.
And you'll want to linger at the Casal de
Loivos lookout, where the gasp-eliciting
view over the vines is the Douro reduced
to postcard format. Allow five days to a
week to do the drive justice.
Start // Porto
End // Miranda do Douro
Distance // 222 miles (358km)

CHIANTI ROAD, ITALY

Toscana simply doesn't get more *bella* than
this classic drive on the SR222 through
Chianti country. Linking two great medieval
cities, the road meanders languorously
through gently rolling countryside striped
with cypress trees, olive groves and vines.
After an art and architectural feast in
Florence, it's time to head south to Siena,
crowned by its magnificent cathedral
and 12th-century Piazza del Campo. In
between are honey-coloured hill towns,
where life revolves around the town square,
and is punctuated by the chiming of the
campanile. Stop by *enotecas* (wine shops),
open for tastings of the region's revered
red wines, including Chianti Classico, a
sangiovese-dominated drop. The road
is technically drivable year-round, but is
perhaps at its most photogenic during the
late springtime eruption of poppies and
other wildflowers.
Start // Florence
End // Siena
Distance // 44 miles (71km)

LAVAUX VINEYARDS, SWITZERLAND

Easily doable in a day trip from Geneva, this
short but sublime drive takes in the Unesco
World Heritage-protected Lavaux vineyards,
which stagger up from the northern shores of
Lake Geneva in a series of sheer, stone-
walled terraces that beggar belief. The road
trip along Rte 9 begins in the higgledy-
piggledy French-speaking city of Lausanne
and takes in pretty lakeside towns like Vevey
before swinging southeast to Montreux (of
summer jazz festival fame) and Château
de Chillon, an extraordinary 13th-century
fortress, brought to world attention in 1816 in
Lord Byron's poem 'The Prisoner of Chillon'.
Painters William Turner and Gustave
Courbet subsequently immortalised the
castle on canvas. In the vineyards, pause
at a cave to taste beautiful chasselas white
wines that are crisp, minerally and usually
only produced on a small, artisanal scale.
Lavaux Vinorama in lakeside Rivaz whisks
you through the region's 300 wines and
offers insightful tastings.
Start // Lausanne
End // Château de Chillon
Distance // 25 miles (40km)

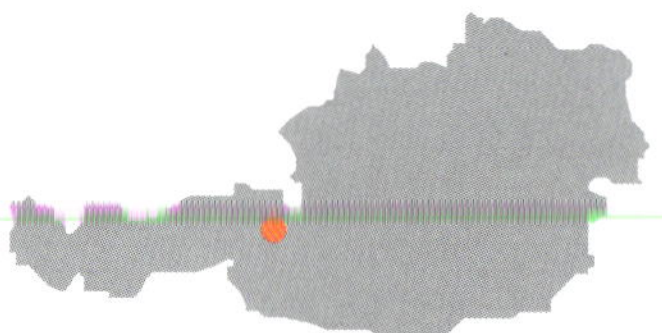

RIDING HIGH ON THE GROSSGLOCKNER HOCHALPENSTRASSE

*Being the passenger on the highest surfaced road in Austria suited Ann Abel just fine –
she could admire the scenery while her husband handled the many hairpin bends.*

Truth be told, I was grateful that I was in the passenger seat on my trip along the Grossglockner Hochalpenstrasse ('high alpine road', if you don't speak German). It was an exciting, sometimes scary drive on whichever side of the car, and I was more than happy to sit back and enjoy the views without having to concentrate on the driving.

I was in western Austria at the time, as a journalist on assignment for an American magazine. My husband, who speaks German, as the son of a German immigrant, had decided to join me for this stretch of my trip. He had become intent on seeking out a driving challenge. The Grossglockner Hochalpenstrasse was that challenge and, up for the adventure too, I would ride along with him. Trusting that he'd find his way around the hairpin turns – all 36 of them, not that I was counting – I would take the opportunity to appreciate the Alpine scenery as the twisting road led through lower slopes covered in emerald-green meadows, then climbed towards snow-capped peaks. It would reach stately heights, all the way to the highest point in Austria, the Grossglockner. Here is a recap of our drive...

We buy our access pass for the road at the entry point in Fusch an der Glocknerstrasse, a tiny town whose main appeal is that it's the gateway to the road. My husband begins driving uphill and I roll down my window to drink in the views and refreshing air. Pretty quickly, the curves become tight and the drop-offs steep. It's a popular road, with some sections where uphill and downhill traffic need to share the tarmac. Also, we are there at a busy time of year, meaning there sometimes are pauses to wait for the car ahead to move on – which sounds easy enough, but we are on a steep incline in a car that isn't especially performance oriented and which is fitted with a manual transmission.

My husband, though, is having fun, learning to juggle the gas pedal and the clutch as it is our turn to move ahead in those few spots where we are sharing the road. Actually, he is having more than fun. As we drive higher, I can see that he is having

the time of his life, accelerating and braking as the turns demand, flicking his eyes away from the road's surface to glimpse those high Alpine views I am so admiring.

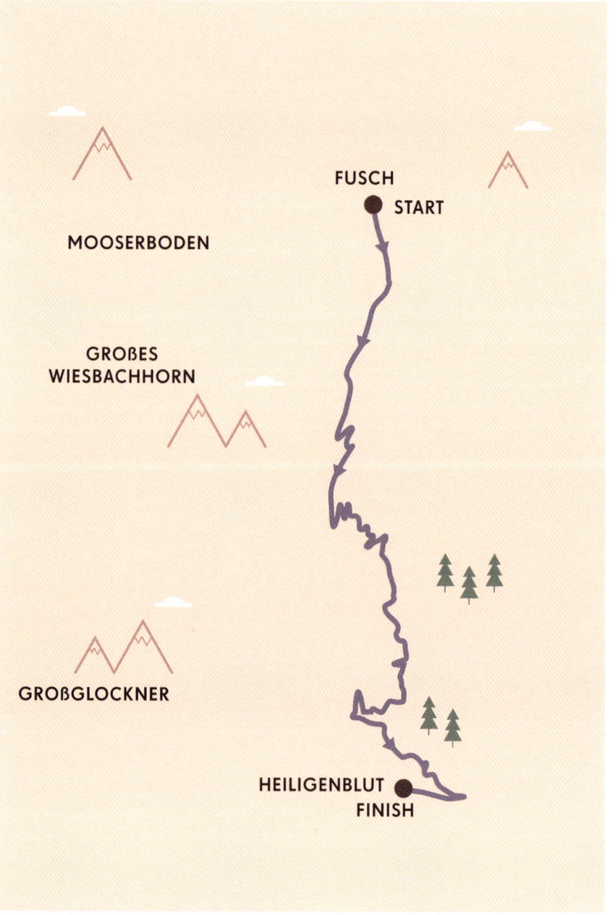

*"My husband was having the
time of his life, accelerating and
braking as the turns demanded,
flicking his eyes away from
the road's surface to glimpse
those high Alpine views"*

I admit this surprises me because I'd barely ever seen him drive.
We'd lived in New York City for well over a decade, and driving had
formed no part of our day-to-day lives. Watching him at the wheel
now, I see a different side of him, one that might have been at home
as an adventurer in the Alps rather than an art director in Manhattan.
It wasn't his usual challenge, but he was clearly embracing it.

I like observing this in him as much as I enjoy the road, and as
we make our way along the 30 miles (48km) the route stretches, I
fall more and more in love with its beauty and this shared experience.
Such immense nature surrounds us: the meadows are a vivid green,
the sky is so blue, and the mountains are so jagged, heavily snow-
capped and steep.

As we hug the road around another tight bend, the nothingness
that falls beneath the passenger side of the car seemingly begins
just a foot from the tyres. And then the gigantic nerd – and failed
engineering university student – in me comes to life. Peering out the
car window at a section we are on, a thought crosses my mind that
had crossed it before on other winding high-altitude drives – how did
this road even come to exist?

I looked it up right after we finished the trip, of course. The
Grossglockner's high pass was once reserved for ambitious and
experienced mountaineers. There was no road at all, so the only way
to get up to the pass was to hike all the way, and the treacherous
paths never lent themselves to easy hikes. They still don't.

The first version of the road opened in 1935. It had its roots in a
moment of Austrian history – the crowning glory, the ultimate point

AN IMPERIAL LOOKOUT

One of the high points (in every sense) of the Grossglockner Road, the 7772ft (2369m) Kaiser-Franz-Josefs-Höhe viewpoint is named for the Austrian emperor who stopped by in 1856. It commands astonishing ringside views of the mighty Grossglockner and the snaking Pasterze Glacier. Get the inside scoop on Hohe Tauern NP at the interactive visitor centre, then follow the 30-minute trail across the Pasterze Glacier to get a close-up of this icy wonder.

Clockwise from left: a statue of Kaiser Franz Josef I; St Vincent Church in the village of Heiligenblut am Großglockner; climbing into the clouds; the highest point, at the Edelweißspitze. Previous page: one of the 36 hairpin bends ahead

for many of those making this drive, is the Kaiser-Franz-Josefs-Höhe viewpoint near the summit, so called by the mapmakers who wanted to pay homage to the Habsburg regent who had famously visited the region nearly a century before.

This 1935 route remained for experienced adventurers only through those early years, but, over time, the road became wider, less hazardous and more comfortable to travel along, despite the turbulent decade that followed the initial opening, a period that saw the Nazi takeover of Austria and WWII.

Thanks to the commitment of the local people here, there are now plenty of options for drivers – and passengers – who might want to stop along the way: exhibitions, museums, mountain huts (the area is still a great base for hiking), inns, visitor centres and information points, all of which blend with surprising harmony into the landscape.

Even without knowing all that history, I still swoon as we head on over the passes. The Hochalpenstrasse gives arguably the best views of Austria's greatest peaks, the 5.2-mile (8.4km) long Pasterze Glacier (the longest in the Eastern Alps) and the 12,460ft (3798m) summit of the Grossglockner itself, the highest mountain in Austria.

Having peaked, literally, at the viewpoint, driving down is lovely but less memorable. We pass by the snow-shrouded Johannisberg, continue through the special conservation areas of the Hohe Tauern National Park, and eventually arrive at the finish line of the road in Heiligenblut. I feel proud of my husband for meeting the challenge, for showing me a side of him that I'd not seen before, and for treating us both to something truly epic.

DIRECTIONS

Start // Fusch an der Glocknerstrasse
End // Heiligenblut
Distance // 25 miles (41km)

Getting there // Austria has excellent air connections with much of the rest of the world, and some airports in Germany and Italy are close enough to also give easy access to the country's delights. The nearest airports to Fusch an der Glocknerstrasse are Innsbruck (Austria) and Munich (Germany). It's easiest to rent a car at the airport.

When to go // This corner of Austria is best driven and explored in April, May, September and October, when the days are long, the weather is generally pleasant and the crowds are smaller.

Tip // Tickets for the road can be bought in advance from www.grossglockner.at

*Opposite: tackling the 48 switchbacks
and ever-changing weather of the
Stelvio Pass, Italy*

MORE LIKE THIS
HIGH ALTITUDE ADVENTURES

STELVIO PASS, ITALY

Brushing right up against the Swiss border
in northern Italy, the Stelvio Pass peaks
at some 9045ft (2757m) above sea level,
making it the highest-altitude paved
mountain pass in the Eastern Alps, and
the second highest in all of the range.
Zigzagging up and around and over some
26 miles (42km) of Italy's Ortler Alps, it's
considered one of the most dramatic and
challenging passes through the mountains.
Those challenges include avoiding
sightseer congestion in the summer (tip:
go as close to sunrise as possible) and
ferocious, wintry weather – possible in any
season at the road's highest points – which
can at times cause blockages through
landslips or snow drifts. And for anyone
who is keeping score, the route has 48
notoriously tight hairpin bends.
Start // Stilfs
End // Bormio
Distance // 26 miles (42km)

MONT VENTOUX, FRANCE

Mont Ventoux, the highest point not just in
the Provence region but across all of the
South of France, looms above the plains
near Carpentras to a height sufficient –
6263ft (1909m) – to have earned it the
nickname 'the Beast of Provence' (it's
also known as 'the Bald Mountain' thanks
to its barren terrain). Nicknames aside,
the smoothly surfaced route up and over
the mountain came to prominence after
being spotlighted as a stage in the Tour
de France. The top of the mountain is bare
limestone, with no vegetation or trees,
which can make it look snowcapped from
a distance and a bit bright up close. It can
become extremely windy up there – gusts
of up to 200mph (320kph) have been
measured. No surprise then that the Col
des Tempêtes – the Storm Pass – often has
to be closed.
Start // Bédoin
End // Mont Ventoux summit
Distance // 14 miles (22km)

OBERJOCH PASS, GERMANY

This 3865ft-high (1178m) mountain road
– once a crucial trading route across the
Bavarian Alps – is known for its panoramic
views over the cross-border German/
Austrian Nagelfluhkette Nature Park, the
mountainous Austrian state of Vorarlberg
and the Swiss Alps. Access to the Oberjoch
Pass is via the shores of beautiful Grosser
Alpsee lake and the traditional mountain
towns of Immenstadt, Sonthofen and
Bad Hindelang. The high mountain pass
itself wends its way towards Wertach,
forming the centrepiece of Germany's
oldest touristic route, the 280 mile (450km)
Deutsche Alpenstrasse (German Alpine
Road), which starts in the town of Lindau
by Bodensee (aka Lake Constance) in the
west and ends in Königssee in the east.
After taking in this most memorable stretch
of that route, consider extending your
journey to the Deutsche Alpenstrasse's
more distant extremities.
Start // Immenstadt
End // Wertach
Distance // 38 miles (61km)

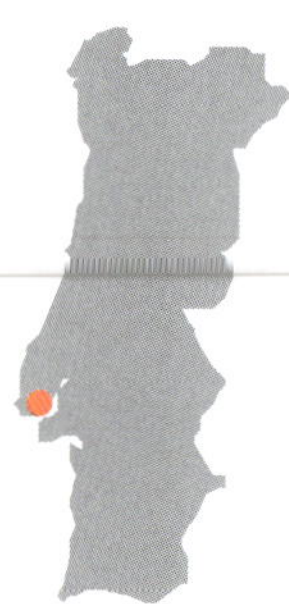

PORTUGAL'S ATLANTIC COAST

Searching for the seaside-loving soul of Portugal, Regis St Louis plotted a route that would take him to clifftop promontories, white-washed villages and historic city neighbourhoods.

Mid-morning, and the sun is at my back as I walk carefully up to the edge of a cliff, peering over the low stone wall at the watery horizon of the Atlantic Ocean. Far below me, swells smash against the rocky coastline, while off to my right stands the red-topped lighthouse that has been guiding ships since the 1700s. This is Cabo da Roca, continental Europe's westernmost point, and a fine vantage point for contemplating the way geography can so deeply shape a nation's identity.

The previous evening, I had wandered the streets of Lisbon, taking in equally dramatic views over the Tejo River from hilltop perches and riverside promenades. I lost myself (literally and often) in the maze-like lanes of the Alfama, where the strains of *fado* music spilled out of terrace cafés while swallows darted overhead. There seemed no better place to start my journey than the seafaring city of Lisbon, said to have been settled by the equally seafaring Ulysses. From here, I would wind my way north to Porto, clinging as much as possible to the coastline.

In the morning, I set off as fog clings to the hillsides, and the far side of the Ponte 25 de Abril (a near perfect copy of San Francisco's Golden Gate Bridge) seems to disappear into a misty abyss. In Belém, I pull over to pick up flaky custard tarts fired up at Pastéis de Belém, a bakery that's been going strong since 1837. Breakfast in hand, I drive past two of the district's grand attractions, the soaring Jerónimos Monastery and the Belém Tower, both built in the 16th century during Portugal's glory days in the Age of Discovery.

The fog is beginning to lift as I head west along the ocean-hugging N6, palm trees and snatches of sandy beaches coming

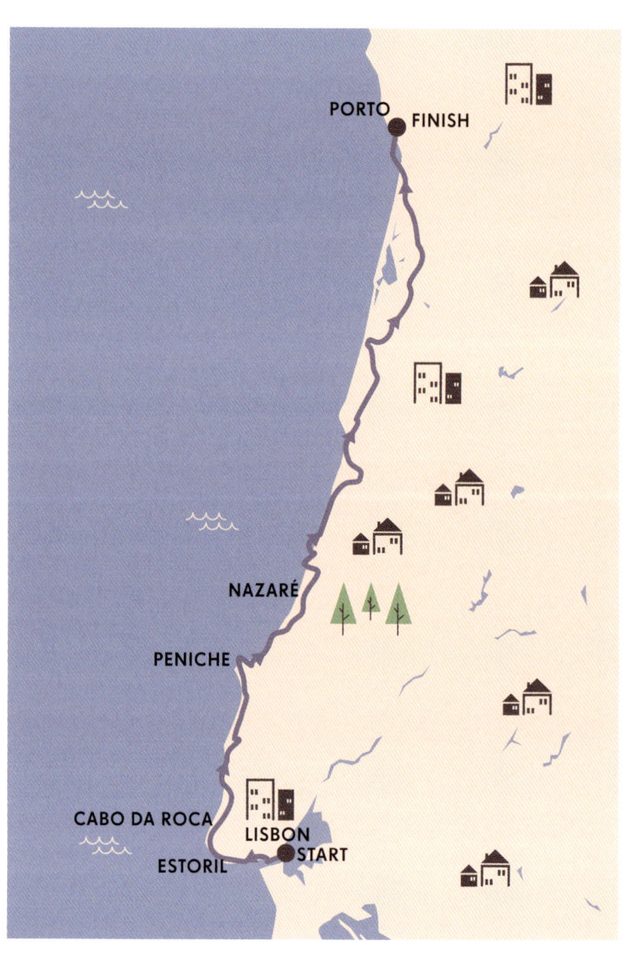

into view against the suburbs that hug the hills. When I drive past the faded Estoril Casino, I squint to imagine it as the luxurious playground of high-rollers, a magnet for the wealthy which earned this coastal stretch the moniker of Portuguese Riviera. King Luís I made the area fashionable when he built a royal summer residence here in the 19th century, and the area was awash with aristocrats and espionage during WWII (and inspiration for a martini-loving spy named James Bond, after Ian Fleming's stay here in 1941).

I leave the four-lane highway behind as I pass the former fishing village of Cascais and pick up a smaller two-lane coastal road. I roll past umbrella pines and scrub, and soon escape the trappings of civilisation altogether, with the foamy ocean lapping the shore just beyond the roadway. The waves grow fiercer as I curve north, following the edge of Iberia along beautiful but wind-blasted beaches like Praia do Guincho, where shadow-filled dunes stretch inland.

The N247 leads me onto a ridge lined with eucalyptus trees that soon fill the car with their fragrance. I've driven this stretch in the past, and turn-offs along the way – many unmarked – sometimes led precipitously down narrow roads toward hidden coves fringed by wave-battered rock formations. The turn-off to Cabo da Roca, however, is well indicated, and I soon reach the cross-topped stone monument announcing the continent's end. Looking out at the Atlantic, I wonder who was the first to spy Vasco da Gama's ships returning from his epic voyage to India,

or witness the grand send-off for Cabral who – though he didn't know it at the time – was bound for Brazil.

Wedged into a narrow corner of Europe, with the vast ocean before them, the Portuguese naturally cultivated a fascination with the sea. Visionary explorers helped shape the nation's psyche, along with the great epic poets like Camões (the Shakespeare of Portugal) who celebrated their discoveries. Geography also shaped the nation's appetite. *Bacalhau* (salted cod), ideal for long ocean voyages, is the beloved national staple that's served up in hundreds of different ways. Even the mournful music of *fado* was first popularised by sailors singing of anguished longing for loved ones while far from home.

I stop for lunch a few miles north at Adraga, a famous but unfussy seafood restaurant overlooking a picture-perfect beach. Nearly everything on the menu is caught nearby, and the *percebes* (goose barnacles), with their salty tang, taste like a mermaid's kiss.

The sun is high overhead as I drive north, passing through Azenhas do Mar, its collection of lily-white houses coiled around

a clifftop. I pause to stretch my legs at Ericeira, a town so famous for its *ouriços* (sea urchins), it was named after them.

The coast-hugging road continues past slumbering villages and the green fields of Estremadura. Enticing beaches lie just beyond the bitumen, with paths leading down to the wave-pounded shore. I pause in Peniche for a look at the 450-year-old fortress transformed into one of dictator Salazar's infamous jails for political prisoners in the 20th century. From there, I skirt around the placid Lagoa de Óbidos to the white sands fringing Foz do Arelho, a town overlooking the largest saltwater lagoon in Portugal. A short hop along is Nazaré, famed for its promontory shrine that houses one (miraculous by some accounts) 8th-century carving of the Virgin Mary. Nearby, the ramparts of the São Miguel Arcanjo fort provide a perfect platform for watching the tremendous swells that periodically crash ashore. It was here in 2011 that Hawaiian surfer Garrett McNamara rode a 78ft (24m) wave, at the time the largest ever ridden. Since then, thrill-seekers have come to fire down eight- and nine-storey behemoths – the biggest surfable waves on the planet.

It's nearly sunset when I roll across the lower deck of the Ponte Dom Luís I and into Porto's riverfront district of Cais da Ribeira. In the setting sun, the tile-clad buildings blaze with colour and the Douro River sparkles. I'm already looking forward to evenings spent wandering the lamplit lanes of this enchanting riverside city, so full of secret histories.

THE LEGEND OF DOM FUAS

According to local legend, on a foggy day in 1182 near present-day Nazaré, nobleman Dom Fuas was in pursuit of a deer when the animal disappeared over the Sítio precipice. Dom Fuas almost followed, crying out to the Virgin Mary, but his horse miraculously stopped at the cliff's edge; the mark of one of its horseshoes is still visible. Afterwards, Dom Fuas built the small Ermida da Memória chapel in gratitude, later visited by Vasco da Gama.

From left: pasteis de nata (custard tarts) fresh from the oven; rock stacks at Ursa Beach, Cabo da Roca; cloisters of the Jeronimos Monastery in Lisbon; outdoor dining in the city's Alfama district. Previous page: the seaside town of Azenhas do Mar, near Lisbon

DIRECTIONS

Start // Lisbon
End // Porto
Distance // 220 miles (354km)
Getting there // Lisbon Airport has lots of international connections, and all major car rental companies.
When to go // This drive is possible year-round. The best beach months are June to August; less crowded are spring (March to May) or autumn (late September to November).
Where to stay // Towns along the route provide ample sleeping and dining. You can also pitch a tent at one of a dozen or so campsites – check www.orbitur.pt for locations.
Further information // Tourism offices in Lisbon, Ericeira, Peniche, Nazaré and Porto provide helpful intel.
Tip // Bring good shoes/boots to walk the rugged paths along the coastline, and swimwear for a dip in the ocean.

Opposite: cheerfully painted houses and boats in the harbour of Portovenere, Liguria, Italy

MORE LIKE THIS
SEASIDE SPINS

THE LIGURIAN COAST, ITALY

Stretching from the French Riviera to Tuscany, Liguria is home to a coastline of cliffs, forested peninsulas and sparkling coves that have long entranced visitors. A road trip from La Spezia to Ventimiglia takes you on a curvy drive along the Mediterranean, with ample opportunities for taking in the region's natural and cultural draws while overnighting in pastel-hued villages set along the water's edge. A favourite of the English Romantics, Portovenere makes a fine gateway for boat trips to the island-dotted Bay of Poets, while the Cinque Terre nearby has fabulous views above the rugged shoreline. At Camogli, you can walk a cliffside trail to the Romanesque monastery of San Fruttuoso. Afterwards, get your fix of old palaces in the medieval lanes of Genoa, then linger on the beaches fronting historic Noli in the less visited western reaches of Liguria before reaching Ventimiglia.

Start // La Spezia
End // Ventimiglia
Distance // 193 miles (310km)

THE ALGARVE, PORTUGAL

Anchoring southern Portugal, the Algarve offers sunny beaches, white-washed villages and biologically rich wetlands. Most people come to bask on the sand, though the Algarve has allure beyond the beach, including historic sites like the mosaic-filled Roman ruins of Milreu. The journey begins at Sagres, where you can explore a 16th-century fortress perched dramatically on a cliff overlooking the Atlantic. The scenic N125 runs east to Lagos, a lively base for dining and water adventures. Near Faro, you can ferry out to a pristine island or go birdwatching in Ria Formosa Natural Park. Tavira, one of the Algarve's prettiest towns, has an inviting riverside, excellent seafood restaurants and intriguing architecture from centuries past. It's also a short hop to the dunes and white-sand beaches of Ilha de Tavira. Finish (or extend your drive) at the border with Spain in Vila Real de Santo António.

Start // Sagres
End // Vila Real de Santo António
Distance // 122 miles (196km)

THE HIGH COAST OF SWEDEN

Though it runs for barely 60 miles (100km) along the Gulf of Bothnia, the Höga Kusten (High Coast) sets the stage for one of Sweden's most memorable road trips. Sheer cliffs plunge down to the sea, and narrow roads take you past lakes, fjords and wooded islands. From the small town of Härnösand – once a pre-Viking trading post – follow the forest-lined E4 to the Höga Kustenbron, a grand suspension bridge over the Ångerman River. From there, you can leave the E4 behind and explore back coves and country lanes as you wind your way toward Nordingrå, a small village surrounded by lakes and mountains. More cinematic beauty awaits in Skuleskogen National Park, where you can walk amid towering old-growth forests, green valleys and the red-rock canyon of Slåttdalsskrevan. At journey's end in Örnsköldsvik treat yourself to a Swedish feast – those with daring palates might even try fragrant *surströmming* (fermented herring).

Start // Härnösand
End // Örnsköldsvik
Distance // 68 miles (110km)

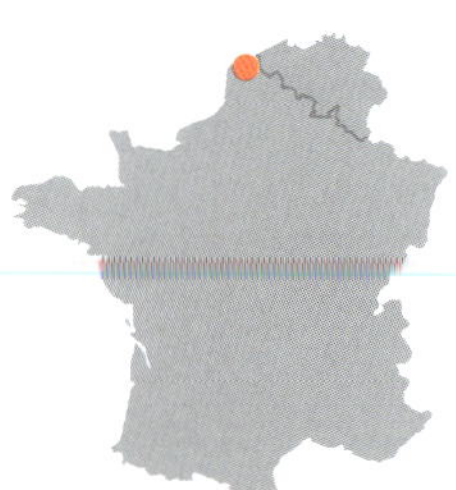

ON THE FRONT LINES
IN BELGIUM AND FRANCE

On a drive through the countryside of Belgium and northern France,
Stephen Lioy visited the battlefields and monuments of the two World Wars.

I begin where British and French soldiers exited mainland Europe in early summer 1940: Dunkirk. Here, on the northern edge of France, a combined military and civilian armada carried out the evacuation of over 338,000 soldiers in what Prime Minister Winston Churchill called a 'miracle of deliverance' – one that would ultimately prove a pivotal moment in WWII. While the World Wars may now seem remote to our daily lives, on these coasts of France and Belgium the poignant memorials live on, reminding us of the horrors that engulfed Europe and the rest of the world twice in the twentieth century.

If Dunkirk's modern harbour and sandy shores mask the town's dark history, a reminder of the drama of those few days over 80 years ago can be found in the Dunkirk War Museum. Housed in a fortress from the 1870s that became the headquarters of the Allied forces, the museum offers context on the city, the fighting that raged in and around it and on the evacuation, codenamed Operation Dynamo, itself.

From the flat coastal plains near Dunkirk, I follow the road east into Belgium and then south as it avoids the last small ridges that separate the town of Ypres from the sea. This is territory connected to an earlier, equally brutal conflict, WWI. For the Allied Powers of Britain and France during that war, control of this landscape would come at significant cost, most terribly in the 1917 Battle of Passchendaele, with hundreds of thousands of soldiers sacrificed. Retracing their steps, I follow the contours of many of the same slopes the armies themselves once marched along. Down, to the forested cemetery at Polygon Wood. Up, to hilltop Tyne Cot, previously a fortified German outpost with strategic views across the countryside and now a sombre Commonwealth

Cemetery, with a small museum of artefacts recovered on site. Then underground, to the replica trenches of the Memorial Museum Passchendaele, into a recreation of the landscape that defined the Ypres Ridge.

Trading the darkness of the museums for the sunny skies and bucolic Belgian countryside, I find it hard to imagine these villages and fields as the centre of a continent-spanning war. Driving to Ypres, memorial plaques and small roadside cemeteries are scattered reminders of history. I pass the Menin Gate, where each night at 8pm the war is remembered in a bugle call, and visit the In Flanders Fields Museum which

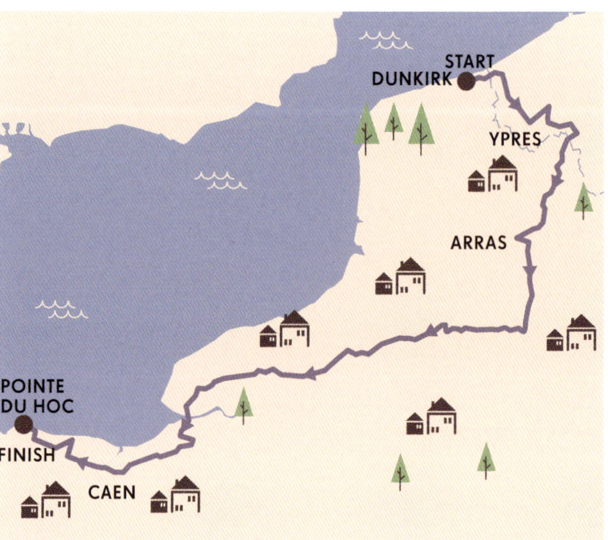

© Sergey Novikov | Shutterstock

PONT DE NORMANDIE
ADAPTEZ
VOTRE
VITESSE
90
RAPPEL

attempts to forge more intimate connections with those battles long ago. Recorded for a modern audience are stories of the soldiers, locals and medical staff who lived through the Battles of Ypres, their words adding faces and voices to the recollections of mundane daily routine punctuated by terrifying bursts of warfare.

Back across the border, atop Vimy Ridge in France, I drive through an area that itself tells the story of battle. Among woods so dense the growth of them speaks of the decades that have passed, the forest floor is still pockmarked with scars from the vicious shelling which reached a rate as high as 3000 explosions per minute in the final desperate hours before the assault on Vimy in 1917. Moving carefully along manicured paths, safe from the unexploded ordnance that more than a century later still poses a risk to visitors, I head up to the imposing limestone pillars of the Canadian Memorial that dominates the ridge, visible from miles round. The limestone is slowly dissolving with the passage of time, just as memories of the wars fade and the forest grows over impact craters.

Leaving the ridges where some of the worst fighting of WWI took place, I continue west past other towns – Arras, Amiens – whose names are intricately connected with the war, towards France's flat coastal plains again, now in search of memories of later momentous events. I pause in the city of Caen, in Normandy, and visit its excellent Memorial Museum, displaying an absorbing collection on WWII and the region's role in the D-Day Landings. It's to these landing sites I then head, through more countryside whose contemporary peacefulness,

LA TELLE DU CONQUEST

Just inland from the beaches of Normandy, 230ft (70m) of embroidery tell the tale of a much earlier epic struggle. *The Bayeux Tapestry* (La telle du conquest in French) depicts the Norman invasion of England in 1066 through richly-coloured scenes showing William the Conqueror's armies as they march to war and the Battle of Hastings. Unusual for both its size and content, the tapestry is priceless both as a work of art and a piece of military history.

Clockwise from above: the Normandy American Cemetery in Colleville-sur-Mer; the Les Braves memorial on Omaha Beach; Tyne Cot Commonwealth Cemetery. Previous page: the Pont de Normandie spans the Seine, from Le Havre to Honfleur

whose quiet country lanes and quaint villages, belie the horrific struggles seen here in summer 1944 when Allied troops came ashore and opened a second, western front against the occupying Nazis.

The seafront town of Arromanches-les-Bains was at the centre of the British attack on D-Day, 6 June 1944. Known as Gold Beach, it's also remembered for its role in the war effort beyond the initial landings. On the town's beach and trailing off into the waves, the ruins of Mulberry harbours stand as slowly decaying monuments to the complex logistics demanded by such a colossal battlefront, hastily constructed to allow troops and vehicles to pour into northern France. I walk towards the bulk of one section of the artificial harbour, trying to picture the scale of the fighting here in Normandy.

Further west, on a bluff overlooking Omaha Beach, the Normandy American Cemetery helps me understand. Nearly 10,000 graves of US soldiers lost in the fighting are marked by white marble headstones. The ordered lines stretch towards the horizon – a deeply sorrowful sight, representing only a fraction of the casualties of both World Wars. As the American flag flying over the cemetery is retired to the sound of a lone bugler, I leave for the final stop of this reflective road trip.

Pointe du Hoc has a rugged beauty, yet must have been a place of dread for the elite US Army Rangers tasked with scaling the 100ft (30m) high cliffs that rise straight from the sea. Fortified gun positions defended the German lines and strafed the American troops climbing the cliffs with deadly fire. They now stand empty, silent witnesses to the former horrors of war. Here, on the edge of the continent with the English Channel as a backdrop, the Allies' final bloody push began, and I end my drive, thinking of those whose lives were so affected by the World Wars.

"The contemporary peacefulness, country lanes and quaint villages belie the horrific struggles seen here in summer 1944"

DIRECTIONS

Start // Dunkirk
End // Pointe du Hoc
Distance // 357 miles (575km)
Getting there // The closest major airports/train stations to Dunkirk are Brussels (Belgium) and Lille (France), though it may make sense to start and finish in Paris to add the city to an itinerary. Visitors from the United Kingdom can arrive by sea in a historical nod to the sites themselves – with regular sailings from Dover to Dunkirk and Caen to Portsmouth, both of which accept vehicles.
When to go // Travel in late May/early June to mark the anniversaries of the evacuation from Dunkirk and the D-Day Landings in Normandy, or July to November to coincide with important dates from the WWI battlefield sites.

On the Front Lines in Belgium and France

Opposite: an obelisk on Moscow's Poklonnaya Hill marks Russian victory in WWII

MORE LIKE THIS
THE ROADS TO WAR

THE GALLIPOLI CAMPAIGN, TURKEY

Join the Antipodean crowds for 25 April ANZAC Day commemorations on the edge of Europe, in Turkey's Dardanelles. Circle around the peninsula, from Anzac Cove to Cape Helles and back, in the footsteps of the Australian and New Zealand Army Corps' storming of (then crawl to stalemate in) Gallipoli (Gelibolu in Turkish) in 1915. Though ANZAC forces were eventually evacuated after the campaign proved unsuccessful, the fighting in Gallipoli is popularly viewed as a foundational element of both countries' modern identities. Dotted along the rugged coastline are memorial sites, museums and historic battlefields – locations of fierce fighting between the ANZAC and Ottoman forces. Many are accessible directly by car, though the New Zealand government's Ngā Tapuwae walking trails offer a deeper insight into the history and personal stories of the conflict through a series of audio guides.

Start // Gallipoli
End // Gallipoli
Distance // 108 miles (174km)

MEMORIES OF TERROR, POLAND

Begin an exploration of the devastating impact of WWII on Poland with the harrowing history of the concentration and extermination camps at Auschwitz-Birkenau and Treblinka, before driving on to the glimmer of hope and humanity that was Oskar Schindler's factory in Krakow. Continue to Warsaw, former site of one of the largest segregated ghettos established by the Nazis during the war. The city is home to the excellent Warsaw Uprising Museum, which documents the resistance of its Jewish residents to German occupation. Finish the journey north in Gierloz, at the ruins of the infamous Wolf's Lair – site of the failed 1944 attempt by Nazi officer Claus von Stauffenberg to assassinate Adolf Hitler and so change the course of the war.

Start // Auschwitz
End // Gierloz
Distance // 412 miles (663km)

WAR AND PEACE IN RUSSIA

Take a tour of military and literary history on a drive through the Russian countryside, visiting the major battlefields of Napoleon's invasion in 1812, many of which are dramatised in Leo Tolsoy's War and Peace. Start at the steps of the Victory Museum on Moscow's Poklonnaya Hill, where Napoleon once waited in vain for the surrender of the city. Just outside the capital, trace the course of the frustrated French emperor and triumphant Russian tsar on roughly the same route the Russians used to retreat from Borodino to Tarutino, followed by shows of Russian strength at Maloyaroslavets, Vyazma and Krasny. Though the tsar's forces would continue to pursue Napoleon's to the Berezina River and one final engagement, the modern-day border of Belarus complicates this final leg for would-be road-tripping historians – a satisfying closure to the story just eludes most visitors, as it did the French forces.

Start // Moscow
End // Krasny
Distance // 422 miles (679km)

SHORE TO SUMMIT FROM GENEVA TO ZERMATT

Vardhan Kondvikar let noble dogs, hospitable monks, chocolate-shaped mountains and a diagonal railway guide his trip around this lake-to-mountains stretch of Switzerland.

There's a cow flying above. Switzerland throws up such strange distractions. This suspended sculpture of a winged bovine looks ecstatic as she welcomes me to the restaurant La Vache Qui Vole, in Martigny. I end a long but satisfying day of driving with a hearty meal and an aerial cow looking on.

Turning the (Swiss) clock back to my road trip's start in Geneva, the scene is equally surreal. Wealthy and stylish, Geneva gleams. The sunlight turns the namesake lake into a sparkling display to rival Tiffany's, then softens in parks full of beautifully-dressed people, then lights up the only Bugatti Veyron – a million-euros-plus hypercar – I've ever spotted in the wild, outside the sort of hotel that charges you just for looking at it. Beyond such displays of wealth, the city has a more humanitarian side – it's home to the Red Cross and the emotive *Broken Chair* sculpture, a reminder of the harm land mines can cause.

Heading east along the lake, I approach the Lavaux area's Unesco-listed terraced vineyards and quiet villages, to pick up a bottle and some local cheeses, Gruyère and Vacherin Fribourgeois

among them. Onwards, then, to the handsome town of Montreux, known for its music history – Queen spent a lot of time here, and Deep Purple composed *Smoke on the Water* after the local casino burnt down while they were in town to record an album.

Late afternoon, I drive into Martigny, built around a delightful little square, all cobblestones and pretty buildings. The nearby Abbey of St Maurice has Roman origins; its cloisters, excavations and museum are open to visitors. There is a waterfall to hike to, and a St Bernard museum full of both actual dogs and the cuddly toy variety.

As I love both driving and dogs, my goal is loftier – the Great St Bernard Hospice, south of Martigny along a storied mountain pass, the Col du Grand St Bernard (Great St Bernard Pass). If that name inspires cute canine images, remember that St Bernards became famous for rescuing pilgrims caught in blizzards while trying to brave this section of the Alps. The Col reminds me of this fearsome history in no uncertain terms when, the next morning, I set off at dawn. It's a grey, chilly day. Alpine weather is notoriously fickle and it starts

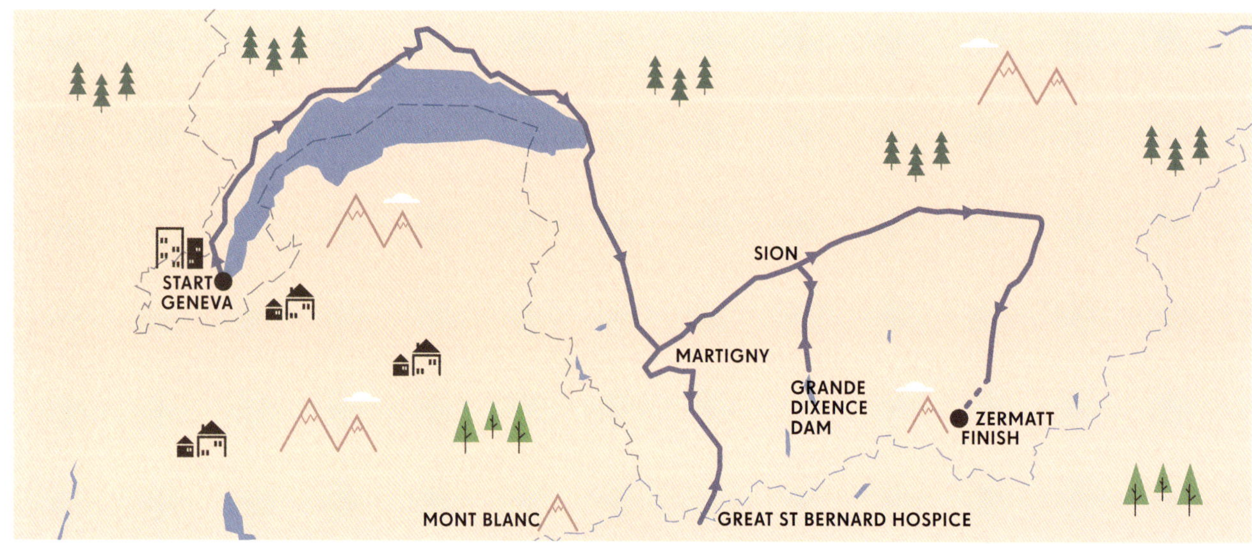

© Matt Munro | Lonely Planet

ADLER HITTA

"Alpine weather is notoriously fickle and it starts snowing, little puffs of powder"

snowing, little puffs of powder. As I drive past fortress-like concrete structures built by the Swiss Army, the flakes really start coming down. The scene is utterly gorgeous – the sinuous road almost empty, the snow-dusted views making my jaw drop a bit more with every minute.

The monastery of Great St Bernard is almost invisible in the snowfall. The wind whips across a nearby lake the colour of blueberry frappe. A helpful temperature readout at the hospice's museum says it's −2.4°C, and, outside, the wind takes control of my feet on the icy path. The famous dogs, sensibly, are inside the museum. Monks with hooded faces bowed against the wind hurry across the road. Being famed for their hospitality (along with the care of stranded pilgrims) they direct me to a café where I can get a hot chocolate.

Back down in Martigny, I drive east to Sion, the capital of Valais and, like Martigny, dating back to Roman times. There are hidden ruins here, accessible with a guide. These include a site near the main square that used to be a Roman bath, a sort of spa-cum-social club, ingeniously designed and heated, and built with the typical flat Roman bricks I spot under so much else here. In later centuries, Sion became an important walled city, controlling the St Bernard Pass into Italy. I take a walk around, admiring the ornate town hall and maze of cute streets, all especially so at this moment in the autumn, with drifts of golden leaves and steeples picked out in rosy sunlight.

A side trip south from Sion takes me up to the Grande Dixence Dam: apart from it being a fabulous drive, the dam itself is spectacular. I park near the Hotel du Barrage and take a cable car to the top of the dam, seeking views of snow-capped peaks beyond the reservoir. A group of elderly women stumble shakily off the cable car – then take off at top speed up a near-vertical hiking path, while I hobble and wheeze about in wonder.

My journey ends, Swiss-style, with chocolate and the Matterhorn, the distinctive mountain whose shape inspired Toblerone bars. Zermatt, the base for exploring the Matterhorn and surrounds, is actually not accessible by car so I park in the town of Tasch and take the shuttle train. Zermatt itself is gorgeous and busy, but literally and figuratively overshadowed by the Matterhorn's mesmerising presence.

I've been advised to wake early and take the first train up to Gornergrat. It's steep, so the electrified cog railway runs on a sharp diagonal and I have the novel experience of trying to decide what angle the cows are standing at. And then the sunrise turns the tip of the Matterhorn red, which is just nature showing off.

I'm faced with a choice: get off at Rotenboden station and walk to beautiful Riffelsee lake, looking for its reflections of the Matterhorn, or continue up to Gornergrat, which promises a 360-degree view of dozens of peaks over 13,100ft (4000m). I'd best choose right now, because the next train, an hour later, will bring a great many tourists.

I use my precious time to let the views sink in atop Gornergrat. There's an observatory and cafés, and a lovely spot where stones have been piled up, Buddhist-style. It's quite something – the 29 mighty peaks encircling the summit, the vanilla-foam smoothness of the glaciers, the light twinkling off everything. All that's missing, I think, is a flying cow.

AN UNDERGROUND LAKE

Valais is a region of lakes, and some of them, like the one at Saint-Leonard, are underground, to be explored on an eerie 30-minute boat ride. If you've read the *Harry Potter* books, this is Voldemort's Horcrux lake – there's even a sunken boat in the clear waters, with a weird greenish glow to complete the fantastical impression. Saint-Leonard is just outside the town of Sion, an easy addition to your trip.

Opposite, clockwise from left: St Bernard dogs at home in the snow; the Matterhorn rises above Zermatt; the Glacier Express sets out from Zermatt. Previous page: diners look across to the Matterhorn from a restaurant in Findeln

DIRECTIONS

Start // Geneva
End // Zermatt
Distance // 242 miles (387km),
then train from Tasch to Zermatt.
Getting there // Geneva airport has flights to dozens of international destinations, and is the place to rent a car.
When to go // From June to October you should have no problems with snow – though mountain passes may open earlier or later, depending on winter weather. Traffic builds on weekends and in the holiday season of July/August.
Road conditions // For the latest see www.alpen-paesse.ch
Tip // Make sure your car's tank is full/your EV is fully charged and that you have food and blankets with you when you venture into the mountains, where the weather can suddenly change.

Opposite, clockwise from top:
the Stegastein Viewpoint above
Aurlandsfjord, Norway; hills of the
Black Forest, Germany; Alexander
Nevsky Cathedral in Sofia, Bulgaria

MORE LIKE THIS
DRIVING ROUTES
TO SCENIC TRAINS

ROAD AND RAIL TO MYRDAL, NORWAY

The drive west from Oslo to Flåm is filled with mind-blowing landscapes. Taking the E16, you'll pass gorgeous Lake Krøderen and go through the Lærdalstunnelen, at 15 miles (24.5km) the world's longest road tunnel. Stop at the Stegastein Viewpoint, and then drive along the Aurlandsfjord to Flåm. There, swap your car for one of the most beautiful train journeys on Earth, to Myrdal, enjoying the comfort of a vintage train compartment. You'll watch the scenery change from the Flåm Valley's farmland to impassable mountains. The vivid blue Flåmselvi River follows the railway for large parts of the trip, passing small farms in locations you'd think no one could live. Myrdal is a remote outpost popular with hikers – you can hike (or cycle) back downhill to Flåm, with views of cascading waterfalls and sharp peaks along the way.

Start // Oslo
End // Myrdal
Distance // 217 miles (349km) driving, then 1hr on the train.

A FAIRY-TALE DRIVE IN THE BLACK FOREST, GERMANY

Beyond cake, ham, the Brothers Grimm and any number of storybook cottages in the woods, the Black Forest also has a fabulous driving route to offer – the B500 highway, part of which has the much more romantic name of Schwarzwaldhochstrasse (Black Forest Way). The road's many sweeping curves make it a biker's and driver's dream – set off early to avoid the crowds. The best itinerary is between Baden-Baden and the village of Kniebis, taking it easy through the forest, past lovely little towns and villages that inspired the Grimms. At Titisee-Neustadt, park and hop on the train through the craggy Hell Valley to the town of Freiburg im Breisgau, passing Lake Titisee, the Hirschsprung (deer's leap) rock formation and Ravenna Gorge. Spend the night exploring Freiburg before taking the train back to pick up the car.

Start // Baden-Baden
End // Freiburg im Breisgau
Distance // 89 miles (143km) driving, then 50min on the train.

A NARROW-GAUGE RAILWAY TO BANSKO, BULGARIA

This multi-day route covers some of Bulgaria's historical highlights, along with great driving in the Rhodope Mountains. Start in Sofia, with its grand Alexander Nevsky Cathedral, Yellow Brick Road (really) and beautiful murals in Boyana Church. Head east to the medieval capital Veliko Tarnovo, chock-full of lovely cobbled streets and lorded over by the Tsarevets fortress. Then take the Shipka Pass to Plovdiv to see its Roman amphitheatre and huge Dzhumaya mosque. Next are the crumbling fortress at Asenovgrad and the serene Bachkovo Monastery. You can explore for days in the Rhodope Mountains, southwest of Plovdiv, but make three lake towns a priority – Trigrad, Dospat, Golyam Beglik – and finally the village of Septemvri. Here, catch Bulgaria's last narrow-gauge railway to the ski resort of Bansko, a scenic journey that lets you wave to fishermen by the rivers and have a beer while you do so. Stay overnight in Bansko, and take the train back to Septemvri the next morning to pick up the car.

Start // Sofia
End // Bansko
Distance // 416 miles (669km) driving, then 4hr30 on the train.

TOP MARKS FOR BRITAIN'S LONGEST ROAD

Richard Porter travelled between the Big Smoke and Auld Reekie, on an under-appreciated, country-spanning, capital-connecting drive from south to north in Great Britain.

If you want to escape north from London the quickest way is up the M1, the motorway that starts on the capital's northern fringes and doesn't stop until 193 miles (310km) later in Leeds. But the quickest way is not the most interesting. That would be the M1's strange and varied sibling to the east, the A1. Where the M1 is smooth and consistent, the A1 is quixotic, one minute vast and multi-laned, the next narrow and wiggly. If you want to see bits of Britain you'd never spot from a proper motorway, take the A1. Its route even once had a better and more epic name: The Great North Road.

My journey starts not on the edge of London but deep in the heart of the city, in the shadow of St Paul's Cathedral among streets with grubbily Dickensian names like Cheapside and Poultry. I get moving and find myself trundling past the kitchenware shops and sourdough outlets of Islington before quickly dropping onto less gentrified Holloway Rd, skirting Arsenal's football ground and bizarrely boastful kebab shops – how can they all be London's number one? – before doglegging around Highgate Hill and passing under the glorious Victorian span of Archway Bridge.

A few miles on, the A1 crosses a vast and bewildering junction with its inner London cousin, the North Circular, then slinks down the side of the M1 and makes its break for the north. At this point I'm rewarded with quirky treats that make the A1 so much more interesting – the multiple domes of the UCL Observatory and the little town of Borehamwood, home to multiple film studios. The original *Indiana Jones* and *Star Wars* movies were shot here, as was *The Muppet Show*. There's not much to see from the road, however, so I keep moving, past South Mimms services where

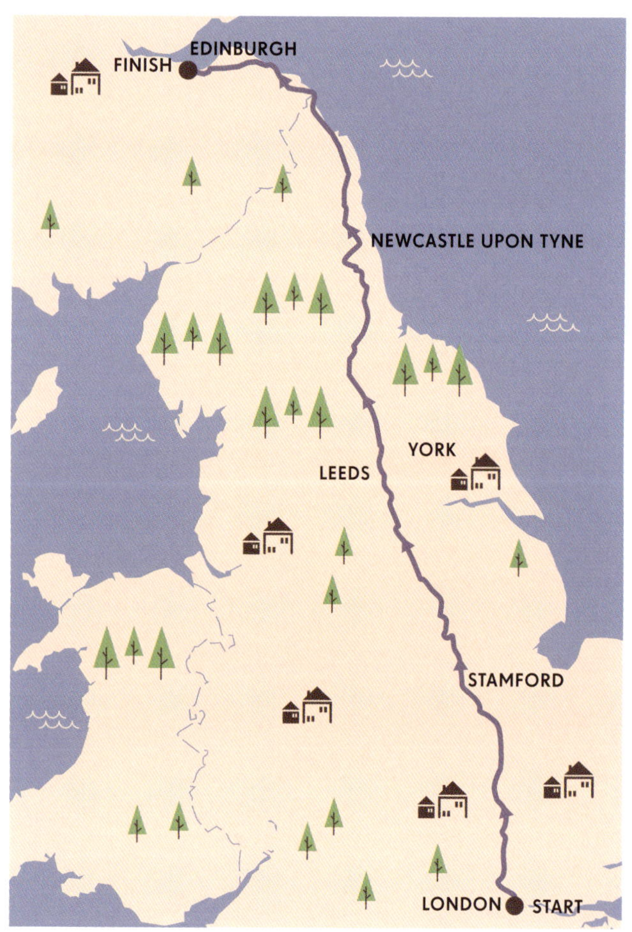

"If you want to see bits of Britain you'd never spot from a proper motorway, take the A1"

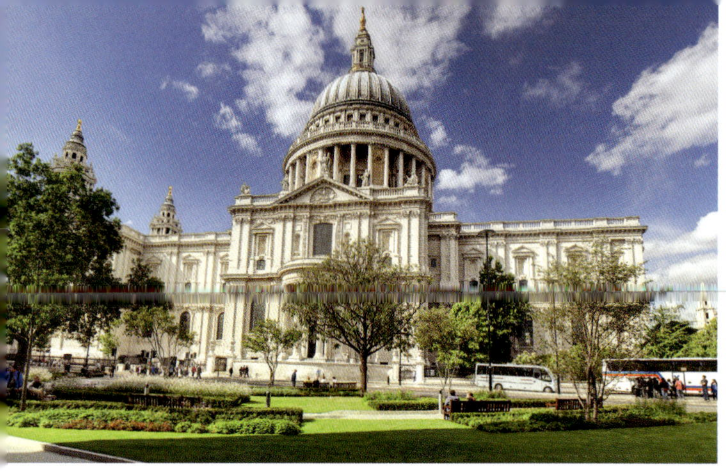

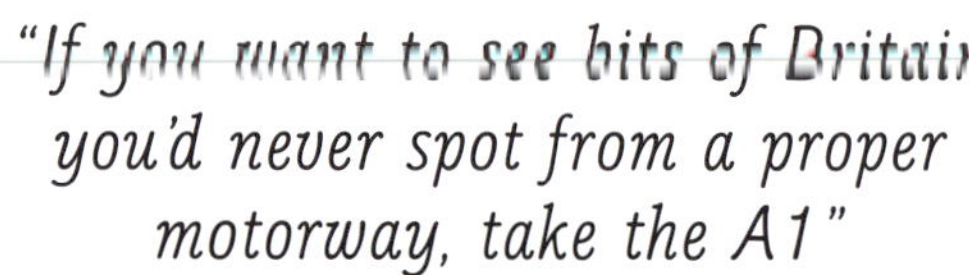

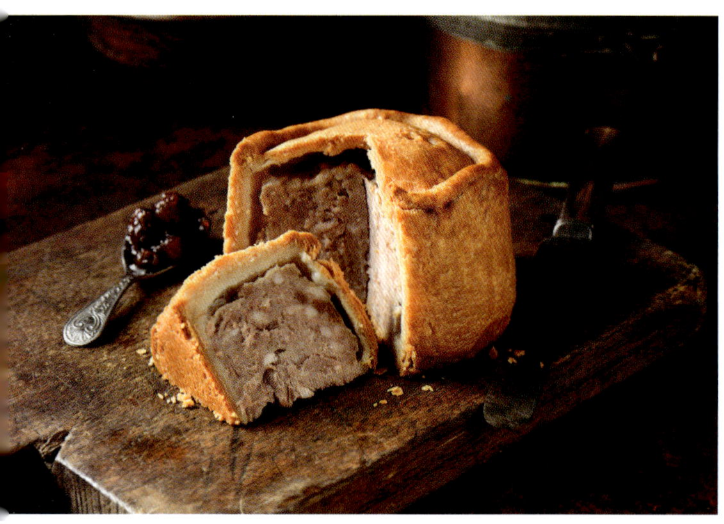

hirsute truckers get haircuts inside an old bus, near Knebworth stately home, and around Stevenage, birthplace of Formula 1 champion Lewis Hamilton.

I'm on a fast-paced dual carriageway now until the Wodehousian-sounding town of Biggleswade, where a series of roundabouts slows my progress and by the time I reach Sandy in Bedfordshire, all pretence of driving a business-like express road evaporates. I'm passing so closely in front of cottages I could knock on their doors from the car window. Sandy is also home to an inexplicably high number of used car dealers and a giant sex shop called Happy Lovers A1, a local landmark for 20 years.

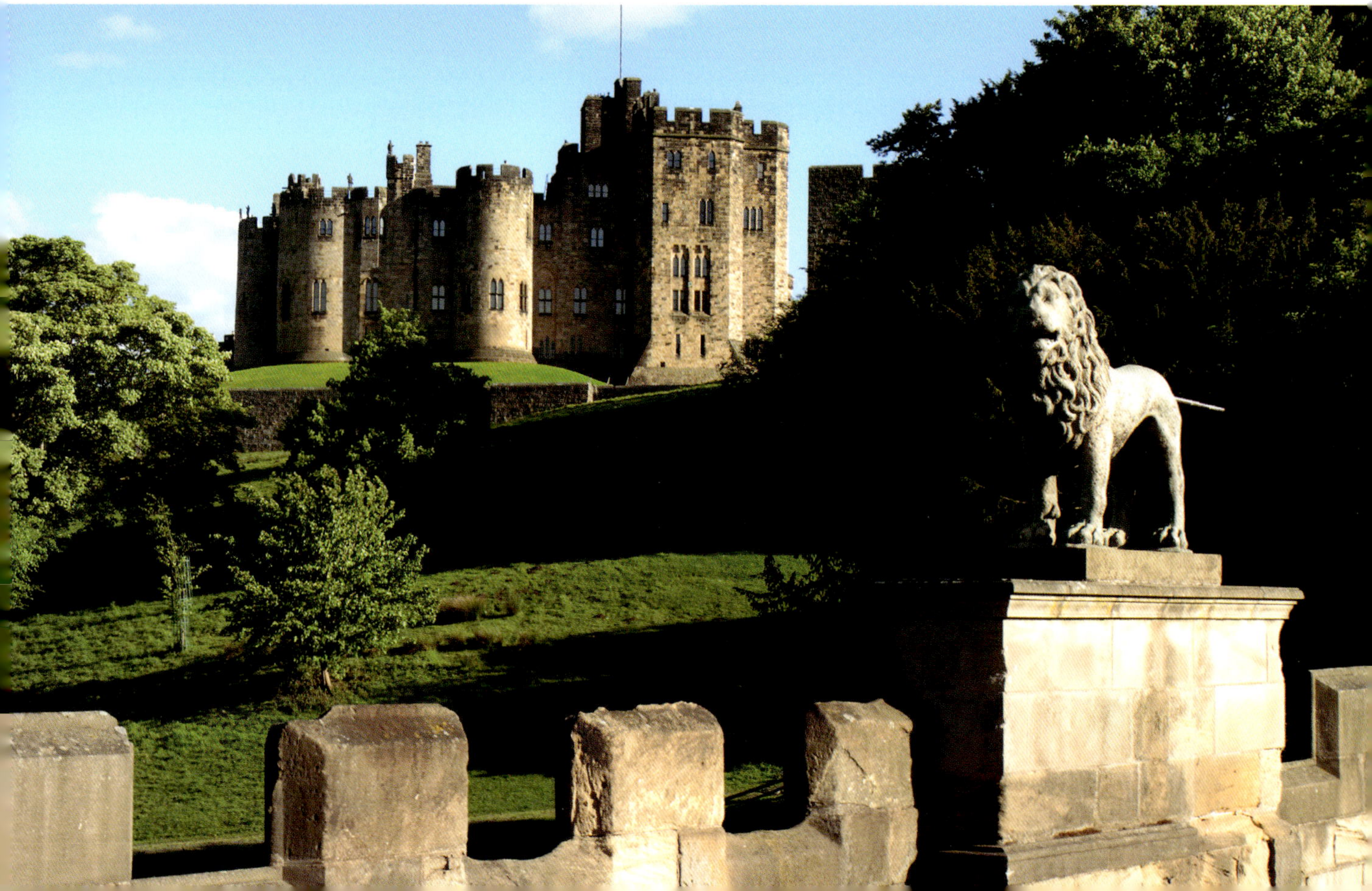

Perhaps out of embarrassment, or maybe just because it needs to negotiate the contortions of the Great Ouse River, the A1 becomes twisty and restless here before pulling itself together in order to headbutt into the A14 north of Buckden, at which point it morphs into an eight-lane mega-motorway to thunder across the flats of Cambridgeshire. One of the joys of the A1 is that there's plenty to see and do either side of it, beyond the usual stops for fuel and lube. During this section of the journey you could visit Cambridge, or stick with the A1 until Stamford, a handsome coaching town and England's first designated conservation area. Not far northwest there's Melton Mowbray, Britain's pork pie capital (and home to one of just six dairies allowed to make Stilton cheese), and impressive Belvoir Castle, its roots dating back to the aftermath of the Norman Conquest. Detour to Sherwood Forest, forever associated with Nottingham (and the Sheriff thereof) though actually closer to Mansfield and home to a Center Parcs family resort – so you can honour the legend of Robin Hood by swimming inside a geodesic dome.

Not tempted? Drive on to Yorkshire, swerving around Leeds where the M1 gives up and merges into the A1, and surge onwards into North Yorkshire where there are a couple of interesting options: the charming spa town of Harrogate and delightful history-packed York. If you fancy a longer diversion, tumble east across the moors to Scarborough or Whitby, solid coastal towns where fabulous portions of fish and chips await.

Great sections of the A1 spear north under the big skies of open countryside until the road draws closer to Newcastle and is fringed with buildings moments before yielding one of its treasures. There, looming over its lanes, is *The Angel of the North*, Antony Gormley's 66ft (20m) tall statue on the site of an old colliery, glorious in its scale and the soft colour of its patinated steel skin. After this landmark the A1 arcs around the Tyneside conurbation before bursting once more into rural bliss. I'm now 300 miles from London but there's still a chunk of England to go so I keep on trucking until I reach Alnwick, where you might enjoy a trip to the castle, used as a filming location for movies such as *Harry Potter* and *Robin Hood: Prince of Thieves*.

I keep on across Northumberland's emptiness, eventually catching sight of the sea and Lindisfarne, a tidal island settled by monks in the seventh century and later christened Holy Island. Not long now until Berwick-upon-Tweed, England's most northerly town, where you might stretch your legs on the old town walls before entering Scotland. When this happens you'll get some wondrous views of the North Sea before the A1 turns sharply inland and buries itself in the undulating beauty of the Scottish Borders ahead of the final run west to my ultimate destination, Edinburgh. Here the A1 becomes a disjointed urban road, casually offering views of Arthur's Seat and the Robert Burns monument until, in the shadow of the magnificent Balmoral Hotel and within sight of the Scott Monument, the road merges seamlessly into Princes Street, Edinburgh's main drag, and the A1 is officially at an end.

There are faster ways to get from London to Edinburgh but if I'd taken them I wouldn't have seen observatories and holy islands and public art and unexpected sex shops. I wouldn't have seen a vivid snapshot of the real Great Britain.

CHALK & CHEESE

In a 1724 travelogue, *Robinson Crusoe* author Daniel Defoe wrote: 'We pass'd Stilton, a town famous for cheese, which is call'd our English Parmesan.' Today, it's no longer served with live mites, and is made with pasteurised milk (there's a breakaway unpasteurised Stichelton cheese). Though named after Stilton, the cheese cannot legally be made there – you'll have to leave the A1 to visit one of the official producers; see www. stiltoncheese.co.uk/ producers

Opposite, from top: St Paul's Cathedral, London; a pork pie, speciality of Melton Mowbray; Alnwick Castle, Northumberland. Previous page: the A1 crosses the River Tyne near East Linton in Scotland

DIRECTIONS

Start // London
End // Edinburgh
Distance // 397 miles (639km)

Getting there // London has six international airports, most of which have flights to Edinburgh. Eurostar trains from Paris, Brussels and elsewhere arrive at St Pancras International, which is next to King's Cross and near Euston – the two main London stations with services to Edinburgh. The A1's official start by St Paul's is within the London congestion charge zone.

When to go // The British weather makes no guarantees, with a rainy drive possible in any month, although the A1 runs near the drier east coast of the country. For a peaceful time on the roads, avoid holiday periods like Easter, the early and late May bank holiday weekends, and the late August bank holiday weekend – and don't leave London on a Friday evening.

Top Marks for Britain's Longest Road

*Opposite, clockwise from top: the abbey
of Melk, seen from the Danube in
Austria; the Petrovaradin Fortress, by
the Danube in Novi Sad, Serbia; the
cobbled back streets of Lille, France*

MORE LIKE THIS
OTHER A1S

A1, FRANCE

The first-billed of France's 140-plus
autoroutes is a tale of two parts. The
Autoroute du Nord as it's nicknamed
strikes boldly north from Paris, but for a
good half of its length, it feels still within
the gravitational pull of the capital. Just
off-road are imposing châteaux such as
Chantilly and Compiègne, and great
forests once used as royal hunting grounds,
remnants of the centuries-long orbit of court
life. As the A1 approaches the River Somme
through open farm country, reminders of
fierce WWI battles become more frequent,
with names such as Bapaume appearing
on road signs. Long before that conflict,
this had been a contested borderland with
the former Spanish- and Austrian-ruled
Netherlands. Cities such as Arras, Douai
and journey's end Lille share much of
their historic architectural look – and love
of beer – with their Belgian neighbours.
One last Parisian outpost to consider: the
branch of the Louvre in Lens.

Start // Paris
End // Lille
Distance // 131 miles (211km)

A1, SERBIA

Running the length of the country, from the
flatlands bordering Hungary to the Preševo
Valley on the frontier of North Macedonia,
the A1 would appear to be Serbia's vital
artery, but its southern trace was completed
as recently as 2019. The appeal of a drive
here lies chiefly in the northern cities it
passes, the southern mountains that its
side-roads wiggle up into, and – despite
the obviousness of the route-numbering
– the sense for many visitors of a road
less travelled. As well as the difference in
landscape between the A1's terminuses,
there's a cultural gradient too, in the
vestiges of vanished empires: Habsburgs in
the north and Ottomans as you go south.
The Serbian capital Belgrade is the biggest-
hitter, but other cities worth stopping in
include Subotica for its Art Nouveau quirks;
Novi Sad, home to the mighty Petrovaradin
Fortress and the Exit music festival; and
Leskovac, whose own Roštiljijada festival is
an ode to grilled meat.

Start // Horgoš
End // Preševo
Distance // 363 miles (584km)

A1, AUSTRIA

The bookends of the 'West Autobahn' need
little introduction: Vienna, city of palaces,
waltzes and coffee-houses, and Salzburg
– birthplace of Mozart and *The Sound
of Music*. But make no haste along this
road, which runs through Austria's historic
heartland. After exiting the Vienna suburbs
through the Wienerwald, the capital's hilly
woodland buffer, the route re-encounters
the Danube under the sprawling, Baroque
hilltop abbey of Melk. At this point it's
really worth doubling back along riverside
roads to discover the Wachau wine region,
but failing that, the autobahn runs on
between the rivers Ybbs and Enns through
the Mostviertel, known for its cider and
perry orchards. The A1 turns away from the
Danube by the culture-packed city of Linz,
to skim the edge of the Salzkammergut,
Austria's superbly scenic lake district. In the
days of the Iron Curtain, this was effectively
a dead-end road – now it's one of Central
Europe's most vital connections.

Start // Vienna
End // Salzburg
Distance // 182 miles (292km)

Dank voor
uw bezoek
Merci de
votre visite
ARTHUR
NICOLAS
COTHUR

ALONG WALES' COASTAL WAY

As Luke Waterson discovered, driving the Coastal Way along Wales' western shoreline involves a tantalising mix of country lanes, prehistoric sites, castle-topped cliffs and sandy beaches.

My start point is St Davids in Pembrokeshire, the southwest tip of Wales, a renowned spiritual spot where a shrine to the country's most prominent holy man, St David, was established in the 12th century. The devout started descending on what became one of Europe's key pilgrimage sites and, fast-forwarding to a 21st-century summer's day, this area is still among the country's most visited destinations, thronging with holidaymakers. Today, unlike most, I have come to Britain's smallest city in order to depart. A 180 mile (290km) road trip is ahead of me and the motor, as they say, is running.

I linger for a moment to stand on Carn Llidi, a rocky hummock with panoramas tumbling back to St Davids and across St George's Channel to Ireland. It also offers the first glimpse of Cardigan Bay, the curve of which I will be following from here until journey's end in Aberdaron on the Llyn Peninsula. This run is officially dubbed 'The Coastal Way', but to me it is the beautiful swathe of seaboard I call home. I have devoted days to foraging Pembrokeshire's seaweed-encrusted shores, dined well in Aberystwyth and roamed Snowdonia's foothills above Barmouth in fair weather and, invariably, foul. But I have never combined all this in one drive.

Coastal Way lesson one: the route doesn't necessarily follow the coast. Tiny turn-off lanes to hidden harbours provide most highlights. One such early stop is Abereiddy's Blue Lagoon, a turquoise-tinted swimming spot created when a former slate quarry was reclaimed by the sea. Another is Porthgain, which exported the slate that Abereiddy quarried and is now a culinary focal point, with The Shed Bistro on the harbourside serving some of this coast's tastiest seafood.

I accelerate a little, wanting to appreciate the bulbous extremity of wild-feeling land that rolls above the main road to Fishguard. This is capped by Strumble Head, the official beginning (or ending) of Cardigan Bay, and always seems far-removed from the excursionist masses, a novelty in peak season. Strumble Head Lighthouse emerges, starkly impressive, crowning a broken island separated by a strait of crashing brine, all overshadowed by one of Pembrokeshire's finest Iron Age hillforts. The headland thrusts so far into the Irish Sea that sightings of migrating seabirds are better than almost anywhere else in Wales. There's no one about except a man slouching by his

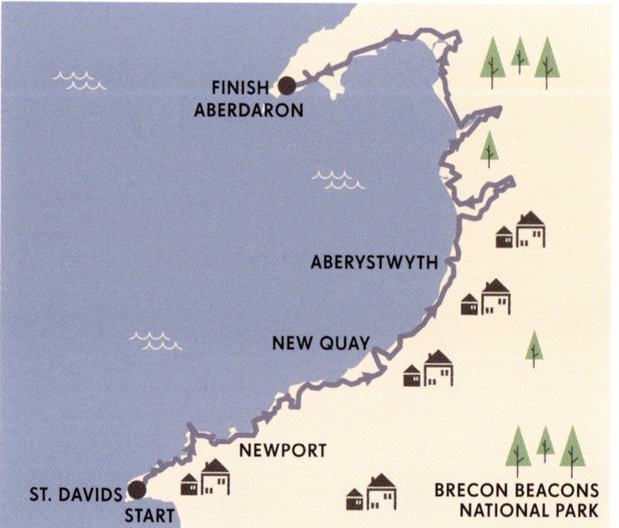

motorhome. 'Better when the mist rolls in, eh?' he says, in reference to the approaching sea fog. 'More Wales-like.' He lets out a sigh. 'Where I'm from in Ireland, a beautiful place like this would be packed. I've seen nobody this last hour, only seals.'

Next, I take what the Welsh might call an *igam ogam* of a road (a long, winding one) around the headland into Fishguard. The coast here saw the last and easily most comic invasion of Britain in 1797, when an Irish-American former adversary of the Brits landed with a motley French crew. Discipline collapsed, the aggressors prioritised getting drunk, and the invasion was quelled — twelve were apprehended by the pitchfork-wielding wife of a Fishguard cobbler.

It seems on the Coastal Way that tourists converge in relatively few places, leaving big expanses in between to the seals, coast-path hikers and capricious weather. Fishguard, despite a ferry connection to Ireland and a colourful historic harbour, has scarcely a holidaymaking soul about. Newport further north though heaves with visitors but Cardigan, where I am staying, is again deserted.

I've just arrived at a pub across the estuary from Cardigan in search of dinner when I smell something fishy. A man has entered with an icebox, opening it in front of the owner, whose

"This run is officially dubbed 'The Coastal Way', but to me it is the beautiful swathe of seaboard I call home"

eyes light up — as do mine. Inside are several muscular sewin, the Welsh sea trout still fished in the River Teifi here using coracles, ungainly tub-shaped boats that fish the water in pairs, a net spread between them. This millennia-old fishing method has protected status and is practised on only three UK rivers by two-dozen-odd people, of whom this fellow, Len, is one. I am in luck. Sewin grace menus only rarely.

'Don't let them serve it with anything but a little butter and salt,' he says, winking.

The county of Ceredigion's portion of Cardigan Bay offers more of what Pembrokeshire's did — fishing villages tucked into folds of cliffs, cavorting seals and dolphins off-shore, lonesome hills littered with ancient monuments — only with even fewer crowds. Wales' best-known bard, Dylan Thomas, penned *Under Milk Wood* after being inspired by time spent in next stop, New

ST DAVID

Patron saint of Wales, leader of men, performer of miracles and the inspiration for one of Europe's most important pilgrimages, St David was born in western Wales around AD 500. Among the most influential figures of Great Britain's early Christianisation, he became renowned as a preacher, eloquent speaker, founder of monasteries and a character of exemplary piety. His shrine lies in St Davids Cathedral, while Henfynyw in Ceredigion has a good claim to being his birthplace.

From left: North Beach in Aberystwyth; the vivid waters of the Blue Lagoon in Abereiddy; dining on Pembrokeshire lobster; Strumble Head Lighthouse. Previous page: the A487 rolls on towards Snowdonia National Park near Dolgellau

Quay. Moving on, candy-coloured Aberystwyth is as animated as ever. Nowhere in Wales better blends seaside kitsch with cultural might. Not for nothing was it considered as a potential capital for Wales before Cardiff got chosen in 1955. Northwards near Borth, it's beach time. One of the country's greatest dune systems beckons at Ynyslas. On the right day you could pass off a selfie here as a convincing snap from a Sahara expedition. I wade out as far as possible into the Dyfi, the estuarine divide between Mid and North Wales. I am hoping to spy signs of the Welsh Atlantis, remnants of petrified forest occasionally exposed by exceptional tides and, according to ancient texts, part of a legendary lost kingdom. Today, though, the waters hold their secrets close.

Snowdonia's black ridges finally come into view, an indication that I am approaching the end of the road. In a café in Criccieth, home to the mightiest castle on the Llyn Peninsula, a man tells me where I can best appreciate views across the route I have just driven. It is Mynydd Rhiw, a rocky explosion of moorland just above the village of Aberdaron. He is right. There it all is. The sickle-like curl of Cardigan Bay, Snowdonia's pointy peaks and, as land slams into sea ahead, the semicolon shape of Bardsey Island, purported burial place of 20,000 saints. Punctuation for another trip, perhaps.

DIRECTIONS

Start // St Davids
End // Aberdaron
Distance // 180 miles (290km)
Getting there // Trains and planes will get you to Cardiff where you can rent a car for the 113 mile (182km) drive to St Davids. Or, train it to Haverfordwest and rent a car there.
When to go // May and September offer the best chance of decent weather with fewer tourists.
Where to stay // Spend a night or two in St Davids before the drive – despite its small size there's lots to detain you, not least the atmospheric cathedral.
What to pack // Swimming and hiking gear for good weather; an umbrella for when it's not. Binoculars for birding.
Further information // www.visitwales.com/inspire-me/wales-way/coastal-way

MORE LIKE THIS
WELSH GEOLOGICAL WONDERS

GOWER PENINSULA, SOUTH WALES

The Gower is synonymous with glorious
beaches, seaside rambles and some of
Wales' best surfing. Britain's first Area of
Outstanding Natural Beauty also has a
dash of cosmopolitanism mixed in, thanks
to its proximity to Swansea, Wales' second
city. A slow drive around the peninsula
– inevitable given the many tractors
and caravans on the roads – allows
appreciation of its relentless beauty. Begin
and end in Swansea, noted for its ties
to Dylan Thomas. Switch from maritime
metropolitan to swanky seaside suburb at
The Mumbles, then hit the Gower proper at
Parkmill, sporting a lovely heritage centre
to welcome you. Next, head around bays
like Three Cliffs, guarded by its castle,
and Oxwich, wonderful for watersports
and Michelin-starred dining. The highlight
is the peninsula's far end, the glorious
2.8 mile (4.5km) curve of Rhossili Bay,
footed by the Worm's Head promontory,
with its impressive rock arch. Loop back to
Swansea via Llanrhidian and Penclawdd.
Start // Swansea
End // Swansea
Distance// 50 miles (80km)

ANGLESEY CIRCULAR, NORTH WALES

Wales' largest island Anglesey emits
ancient history and prodigious geology
like a Welsh dragon breathes smoke. Start
at the exquisite Menai Bridge, the world's
first major suspension bridge, designed
by Thomas Telford and completed in
1826. Head west on back roads to Ynys
Llanddwyn, the tidal island linked with
Wales' patron saint of lovers St Dwynwen.
Continue on to Aberffraw – the ancient
capital of the Kingdom of Gwynedd – and
bountiful sandy strands like Rhosneigr.
Near Holyhead is Anglesey's craggy high
point, Holyhead Mountain, with some
astonishing sea cliffs and stacks. Continue
along the island's oh-so-quiet northern
and eastern stretches towards coastal
charmer Cemaes, with more top-notch cliff
scenery. Then close the circuit via Amlwch
and Moelfre, pausing on a pretty beach
like Lligwy, before finishing with a medieval
flourish at mighty Beaumaris Castle.
Start // Menai Bridge
End // Beaumaris Castle
Distance // 90 miles (145km)

FFOREST FAWR, SOUTHEAST WALES

Roads are scarce in Fforest Fawr – a remote
moorland within Brecon Beacons National
Park – so this trip utilises most of them. Kick
off in Merthyr Tydfil, once one of the world's
key ironwork centres. Climb surrounding hills,
gouged by mining and smelting operations,
onto the road towards Brecon, ogling the
barren, dramatic terrain that rises to Pen y
Fan, the highest point in South Wales. The
road uncoils over the mountain's shoulder,
then swings west via Heol Senni into
Waterfall Country, tumbling from Ystradfellte
to Pontneddfechan. Head north to Dan-yr-
Ogof, claimed to be the UK's largest show
caves; then continue to Llyn y Fan Fach,
a mountain lake majestically wrapped by
crags; then pass ancient hillfort Garn Goch
and the theatrically-perched castle Carreg
Cennen to journey's end, Llandeilo.
Start // Merthyr Tydfil
End // Llandeilo
Distance // 77 miles (124km)

LAPPING THE NÜRBURGRING-NORDSCHLEIFE

Matt Master embarked on a high-speed tour of a German public toll road that doubles as the world's longest, most challenging and most awe-inspiring racetrack.

If the automotive world came up with its own Seven Wonders, the Nürburgring's Nordschleife would undoubtedly figure among them. It's a place steeped in history, both romantic and terrible, a road whose very construction was an extraordinary feat of engineering. The 'Northern Loop' remains hallowed ground for racing drivers and sports car manufacturers alike – the ultimate test of man and machine, of courage and skill, and of wide-eyed, white knuckled tourists.

Situated in the Eifel Mountains of western Germany, the Nürburgring racetrack was built between 1925 and 1927, a dizzying 17.5 mile (28km) ribbon of weaving, climbing and diving asphalt designed to better the best of Europe's contemporary road circuits and purpose-built racetracks. Fearsome speeds were achievable, but a true mastery of such a long and complex course was not easily come by and its heavily wooded straights, cambers and corners soon made the Nürburgring a place as much to be feared as revered.

Although created to showcase German engineering, the Nürburgring was also opened to the general public as a toll road, to drive as that public saw fit. In what feels like a surprising position amid the reticence and censure of modern driving, that status remains to this day. The Nürburgring has evolved into an internationally renowned piece of motoring folklore and a major draw for sports car enthusiasts, who travel long distances to experience the rollercoaster ride of a single flying lap.

The Touristenfahrten, or 'tourist rides', are open days that punctuate a busy race and car manufacturer development calendar throughout the spring, summer and autumn months with access to the 12.9 mile (21km) northern loop of the old circuit, the fabled

Nordschleife. Anyone can simply turn up and pay (from €25 for a single lap to €2200 for a 'Jahreskarte' season pass) before driving through an automated barrier and onto the circuit.

Just such a first drive is an occasion that conjures multiple emotions in this excited, nervous debutante. All of a sudden I am traversing the same sacred loop as pre-war grand prix stars such as Rudolf Caracciola in his Mercedes-Benz Silver Arrow and Bernd Rosemeyer in his vastly powerful Auto Union. This was also the place that separated gods from men in post-war Formula 1, with Juan Manuel Fangio and Stirling Moss bravely going wheel-to-wheel against

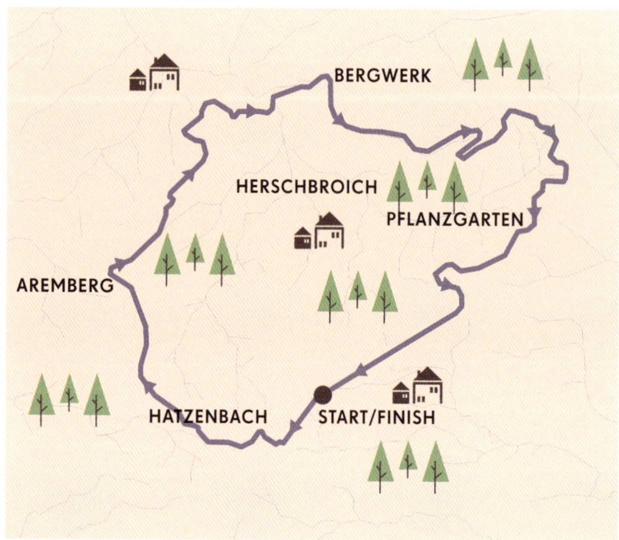

one another, and above all against the circuit itself.

Undeniably, part of the allure of the Nürburgring then and now is an ever-present danger. Over the decades it has been the site of very real tragedy, including former World Champion Niki Lauda's fiery 1976 accident that compelled Formula 1's organisers to abandon the Nordschleife indefinitely. Today it is markedly safer, lined with crash barriers, the worst of its bumps flattened out and its most treacherous corners neutered by sympathetic redesign. But it is nevertheless a place haunted both by macabre history and the spectre of your own fallibility. A place, it seems to me as I steer uncertainly away from the start point, to treat with deference.

The clockwise circuit begins in a line of cars with drivers ranging from complete novice to the committed veteran of the Touristenfahrten. When the barrier lifts, innocuous as a motorway toll, I immediately find myself in the thick of it, heading down towards Tiergarten at the end of the long main straight. And so, with a faster car already glued to my rear bumper, I turn into the tricky S-bend of Hatzenbach, the first of some 73 corners.

Every section of the track ahead has a name and usually a reputation, like Flugplatz ('airfield'), so called for its tradition of launching fast-moving race cars clean into the air. Then there are the fearsomely fast passages of Aremberg and Adenauer Forst, narrow and perilous even for professionals, or the famously tricky Bergwerk, an act of blind faith beneath the shadows of overhanging trees.

Towards the northeast of the loop, approximately 8 miles (13km) in, I finally encounter the infamous and bone-jarring Karussell, a roughly paved and steeply banked hairpin that drivers must 'drop into' for

HIT WITH FEES

Nordschleife newbies should be aware of the cost implications of colliding with the barriers – extra reason to go gently. Contact will cost you €150 for an inspection of the area hit. It's then €10 per metre to remove damaged sections and from €31 per metre to replace it. Should your car need to be recovered, add €500 to your bill. The attendance of a safety car is €82 for every 30 minutes and full circuit closure is €1350 euros.

Clockwise from above: bracing for a Touristenfahrten; the Nordschleife has over a hundred corners; wet conditions are common; Nürburg Castle sits above the circuit. Previous page: a Porsche 911 GT2 RS, ideal for a lap here

© Nürburgring

the fastest line around the bend. An equal test of suspension and dental work, it's fleetingly reminiscent of the banking favoured by pre-war European circuits such as Brooklands in England and Berlin's AVUS. In my modern road car it makes for a noisy and unsettling few seconds before Hohe Acht, the highest point of the circuit.

The names of the Nordschleife's corners are often literal, sometimes significant, occasionally both. Hedwigshöhe is named after Hedwig Creutz, the wife of the local administrator who enabled the construction of the Nürburgring. There is Eiskurve, apparently the corner most likely to freeze, and the sweeping right left of Schwalbenschwanz or 'swallowtail', that leads to Galgenkopf, the gallows hill where public executions were once conducted.

While trying to absorb this history, I find myself facing a series of challenges. Firstly, paying sufficient attention to my rear-view mirror – however adept and confident a driver you are, there's always someone faster, more committed, more determined to pass. And conversely, there's likely to always be someone driving considerably slower ahead, be that a cautious motorbike rider or a coach full of tourists, of which there are many on any given day at the 'Ring. These hazards must be carefully negotiated while still navigating the circuit, assessing speed, braking and track position in a constant, exhilarating and exhausting torrent of information.

My companion and co-driver for this outing, far wiser and more familiar with the perils of the Nordschleife, reassures me I should simply approach it as if driving an unfamiliar country lane. All the better then to marvel at its immensity and its historic significance and, at an appropriate speed, to understand what prompted mid-60s F1 ace Jackie Stewart to dub it 'The Green Hell'. For many drivers, that first lap of the Nordschleife is the start of a lifelong, long-distance love affair. For others, once around is quite enough, an experience neither to be forgotten, nor repeated. The jury here is still out.

"When the barrier lifts, innocuous as a motorway toll, I immediately find myself in the thick of it"

DIRECTIONS

Start/End // The entrance to the Nordschleife lies on the B258 between Nürburg and Meuspath.

Distance // 12.9 miles (21km)

Getting there // The nearest airport is Cologne Bonn.

Car rental // You can rent an extensive range of cars locally in which to tackle the track, including right-hand drive models, with prices from €200 to €2000, depending on value and performance.

When to go // The Nordschleife opens in early March and closes for winter in November. Weather can be seriously unpredictable, ranging from fierce heat to sudden and torrential rain. Fog is also a regular feature – its presence can lead to course closure for hours or even days.

Where to stay // The village of Nürburg has a huge variety of hotels and guesthouses geared around visitors to the circuit.

MORE LIKE THIS
GERMANY FOR PETROLHEADS

THE BUNDESSTRASSE 258

Visitors to the Nürburgring usually arrive by car but a focus on their final destination leads many to overlook the nearby presence of some of Germany's finest driving roads. The Bundesstrasse 258 passes right by the circuit entrance, running from the city of Aachen on the eastern Belgian border southeast to the town of Mayen, just west of Koblenz. This winding and relatively quiet two-lane road crosses the Rhineland, its lush valleys home to many of the region's vineyards and wineries. The central section also dissects the unspoiled and accessible Hautes Fagnes moorlands and Eifel National Park before passing through Nürburg.

Start // Aachen
End // Mayen
Distance // 93 miles (150km)

STUTTGART, GERMANY'S MOTOR CITY

A comprehensive road trip through southwest Germany must include the city of Stuttgart, southeast of the Nürburgring. The physical and cultural centre of the state of Baden-Württemberg, Stuttgart is also home to Mercedes-Benz and Porsche, and key industry suppliers Bosch and Mahle. Karl Benz is thought to have invented the very first car here and both Mercedes-Benz and Porsche have vast, fascinating museums in the city, spanning a century and more of road and race car development. The scenic drives of the nearby Black Forest have been used by technicians and engineers for decades to hone the ride and handling of many of the world's most admired sports cars. The Solitude Circuit, just west of Stuttgart, was the venue for a handful of post-war Grand Prix and is now used for historic racing revivals.

Start // Nürburgring
End // Stuttgart
Distance // 202 miles (325km)

DRIVING ON THE AUTOBAHN

Germany's autobahn (motorway/freeway) system is a political hot potato in a country at once in love with the automobile and also acutely aware of fossil-fuel-powered vehicles' negative impact on the environment. Former Chancellor Angela Merkel repeatedly resisted calls to dispense with the famous stretches where drivers have for decades been allowed to run their cars free from speed restrictions. While a comprehensive national limit now seems inevitable, some 70% of autobahns remain governed only by an advisory limit of 81mph (130kph), and can be driven as fast as your car can carry you – at least in dry weather conditions. Much as with the Nordschleife, an unfettered run on the autobahn is something of a rite of passage for motoring fanatics, but these roads are often narrow and busy with locals experienced at driving substantially faster than you. The A4 from Aachen to Cologne is a famous section – look for the black diagonals on a white roundel that signal the lifting of speed limits, keep one eye on your mirror and have your wits about you.

Start // Aachen
End // Cologne
Distance // 51 miles (82km)

Faszination Technik
Shops
Restaurant
Parkdeck
Mercedes-Benz Center
Classic Kundencenter
VISION

PORSCHE
Coke is it!
MICHELIN
Mobil 1
MICHELIN
Hertz
912
PORSCHE
CHOPARD
GTLM
bott
RECARO
bott
SCHERER
Mobil 1

NORTHERN EUROPE

WEINSBERG

NORWAY'S LOFOTEN ISLANDS

From clear Arctic waters to heart-stopping mountain views, the Lofoten Islands are where nature shows off. Orla Thomas' drive also found tales of fish and folklore on the way.

The tiny wooden huts that cling to the shores of the Lofoten Islands look too flimsy to endure this unforgiving landscape. Towers of granite loom over these insubstantial red and yellow structures scattered along the water's edge, but these modest homes are palatial compared with those of the islands' first inhabitants. Until the first *rorbuer* (fishermen's cottages) were built here in 1120, Lofoten fishermen slept beneath their upturned vessels before flipping them over for a day at sea.

Today's visitors have a rather easier time of it. Arriving late summer at Svolvær Airport, a single runway airstrip on one of the few bits of land that's flat, I set out as apparently the sole driver on Lofoten's only main road, the E10, which connects the islands via a series of bridges and causeways. Deep fjords allow the waters to creep inland – vast, still, lake-like pools, given away only by the rim of seaweed left at high tide. It's an otherworldly landscape with legends to match – each island a new chapter in a storybook spanning centuries.

Page one is Svinøya Rorbuer, one of many places now offering

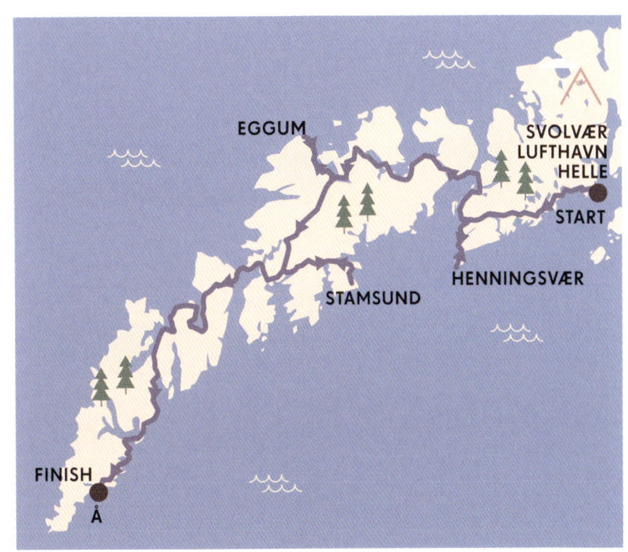

holiday accommodation styled after the traditional fishing huts. Wandering the quayside, I take deep breaths of the clean air. But there's a secondary note to its Arctic freshness – the unmistakable scent of fish. Sat beside the *rorbuer* are immense drying racks, where gutted cod hang in pairs. Stockfish, or dried cod, has historically been Norway's most valuable export commodity – these unalluring creatures made Norway rich, and fishing is still a major industry here.

To sample Lofoten's signature ingredient I head to the wooden-beamed dining room of Børsen Spiseri. Locals call the restaurant, built in 1828, 'the stock exchange', a jokey nickname that refers both to the bench outside – where, historically, town elders gathered to discuss the issues of the day – and its former use as a stockfish house. In common with most menus in these parts, whale is on offer, but I'd rather see the creatures at sea than on my plate – it's not uncommon to spot sperm whales and orcas off the islands' coast.

I plump instead for *lutefisk*. Made from dried stockfish pickled in sodium hydroxide then rehydrated in water, it sounds unappealing, but surely it couldn't be the centrepiece of Norwegian Christmas dinner without redeeming features? The texture is gelatinous but, served with buttery potatoes and crunchy cabbage, it kind of works.

When I leave the restaurant, the dark sky is smattered with stars. I'll have to wait until next season to see the northern lights, once believed here to have been the visible wrath of angry gods.

The next day I swap my rental car for a spot on a RIB in search of trolls – or at least, their lair. Zooming over the water at such an exhilarating speed feels faintly magical, and the narrow entrance to Trollfjord, circled by low-flying sea eagles, does indeed look like it might conceal the home of one of the most fearsome creatures in Norse mythology. Back on dry land, it's thirty minutes by car to Hennigsvær. Occasionally described as 'the Venice of the Lofoten', it's not hard to see why – pale houses overlook the water and there's an art gallery around every corner.

Heading onwards over Gimsøystraumen Bridge, I find more far-flung examples of creativity at Eggum. A sculpted head gazes out to sea at this designated rest-stop on the E10 road, but almost as arresting are the toilets, housed in a futuristic wooden box. Designed by the same team as the Oslo Opera House, they have to be among the world's most stylish loos, but people come here for more than a memorable wee. Behind is a rock amphitheatre thought to be one of the best places in the far north to experience the midnight sun. Midsummer has huge cultural significance in Nordic countries, their reward for enduring long and dark winters.

The islands are among Norway's most exposed territories, so those who live here can't afford to be fair-weather in their commitment to the outdoors. I've heard rumour of a group of women in Stamsund who swim in the sea daily at 7am, whatever the season, so early the next morning I get behind the wheel to try to find them. On the hour, they appear, emerging like phantoms onto the town's deserted high street, with bed hair and towels tucked under their arms. 'Joining us?' asks one, a friendly blonde woman who introduces herself as Euri Ingebrigtsen, a doctor. 'We are four neighbours who swim together. We've been doing it every morning for years.' The water is bone-chilling but will get much colder before the year is out. 'The worst is when it snows,' says Euri. 'That really gets into your skin.' Nevertheless, she is emphatic about the health-giving properties of her daily dip. 'It makes you laugh in the morning – that's important.'

Cold but convinced, I return to the road bright-eyed and am rewarded with views even more inspiring than those I've seen so far. Detouring to the tiny island of Hamnøy, framed by craggy peaks and the Reinefjord, the E10 seems to float on water. I pull up just outside the picturesque village of Reine to get my own version of the shot I've already sent home on postcards. On the final island, Moskenesøy, the southernmost town is – appropriately enough – also the last letter of the Norwegian alphabet: Å. The literal and metaphorical end of the road, it encompasses one of the region's best-preserved fishing villages, now a sort of living museum.

Å has one other notable feature. It sits at the edge of the most dreaded Lofoten legend of all: the Moskenesstraumen Strait. Site of a mighty whirlpool that struck fear into generations of fishermen and inspired Edgar Allan Poe's *A Descent into the Maelstrom*, this is no fictional demon but the result of conflicting tidal currents between two islands. Gazing out across the roaring ocean, I'm relieved my adventure ends here.

VIKING SECRETS

Nutrient-rich and durable, stockfish allowed Vikings to endure much longer voyages than their contemporaries – aiding their conquest of vast swathes of Europe and beyond between the 9th and 11th centuries. Learn more at Borg's Lofotr Vikingmuseum, which has a full-size recreation of the chieftain's house – shaped like an upturned boat – originally found at the site. Costumed guides offer tours, and you can take a short trip on a replica Viking ship.

Opposite from top: cod drying to make stockfish; brightly painted rorbuer (fishermen's cottages) in the village of Hamnoy. Previous page: the Gimsøystraumen Bridge

DIRECTIONS

Start // Svolvær
End // Å
Distance // 125 miles (200km)
Getting there // Svolvær is where you'll find the Lofoten Islands' main airport. Alternatively, you can extend the drive by flying into Harstad/Narvik Airport. Various major car rental companies are represented at both.
When to go // Warmed by the Gulf Stream, Lofoten's climate is much milder than other destinations at the same latitude. Visit between late May and mid-July for the midnight sun and warmest weather, or from September to mid-April for the best chance of seeing the northern lights. January and February are the coldest months, but the mountains look glorious covered in snow.
More info // Check out www.visitnorway.com

Opposite: in Poland's Tatra Mountains,
a man wearing brilliantly-embroidered
Górale costume plays the trombita

MORE LIKE THIS
EXPLORING MORE OF
EUROPE'S FOLKLORE

POLAND'S HIGHLANDS

The Podhale region in the foothills of
Poland's Tatra Mountains is a refuge of
ancient folk traditions. Though relatively
short driving distances are involved, allow
plenty of time for overnight stops and walks
among the forested hills. Begin by getting
acquainted with the glorious views – the
drive from Bustryk to Ząb is especially
scenic. Head next to the resort town of
Zakopane, where you can try *oscypek*
– perhaps the world's most decorative
cheese – and other local dishes, served by
people wearing the ornately-embroidered
costume of the Górale or 'Highlanders'.
Their traditional dwellings inspired the
design of Jaszczurówka Chapel, just outside
town. Swing by pretty, peak-dwarfed
Murzasichle before heading on to Bukowina
Tatrzańska. Every February the village hosts
a Highlander Carnival, celebrating unique
aspects of Górale culture, including singing
and dancing competitions and sleigh-racing.
Start // Bustryk
End // Bukowina Tatrzańska
Distance // 26 miles (41km)

LATVIA'S OLD WAYS

Latvia's long-held folk culture has been
enthusiastically embraced by the next
generation, with traditional dances in capital
Rīga full of young'uns who know the steps.
Begin with a night out at Folkklubs Ala
Pagrabs, a beer-slash-dance hall offering
live music, a friendly atmosphere and lots
of local beers. Next morning, drive out to
the Ethnographic Open-Air Museum of
Latvia, where you can wander among
wooden buildings transplanted from the
countryside while learning about their
history. Turn west and stop by the mystical
boglands of Kemeri National Park – the
Great Kemeri Circle is a good driving route
– and the sleepy town of Kuldiga, home to
a waterfall that looks like a squat version of
Niagara Falls. End in the western village of
Alsunga, a hub for the Suiti people. Fusing
pre-Christian traditions with Catholicism,
their distinctive culture is still much in
evidence today – try to catch a performance
of drone-singing by local women.
Start // Rīga
End // Alsunga
Distance // 130 miles (210km)

THE TALES OF WALES

Get an overview of Wales' distinctive
culture at St Fagans National Museum
of History, just outside capital Cardiff,
which features buildings spanning the
nation's history and demonstrations of
traditional crafts including blanket- and
cider-making. Make a pitstop for Welsh
cakes in Llandeilo before heading through
pretty countryside to Nanteos Mansion.
For centuries home to a wooden cup
claimed to be the Holy Grail, it's now
a posh hotel – the cup is on display at
nearby Aberystwyth's National Library
of Wales. Next, it's on to Beddgelert, a
charming village whose name has become
associated with a folk tale involving Gelert,
the dog of 13th-century Llywelyn the Great,
Prince of Gwynedd. Journey's end is
neighbouring Craflwyn and a walk up to
Dinas Emrys. The rocky hillock was the site
of a legendary battle between two dragons
– the red one was victorious, earning its
place on the Welsh flag.
Start // Cardiff
End // Craflwyn
Distance // 173 miles (278km)

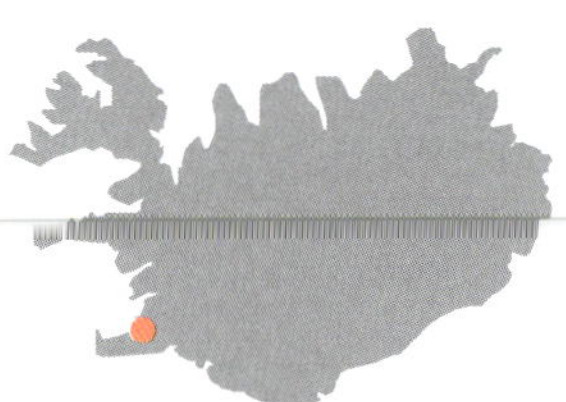

LEGENDARY WEST ICELAND

*Bearing northwest from the Icelandic capital Reykjavík, Alexander Howard plotted
a route steeped in tales of Vikings, explorers, sorcerers, trolls and monsters.*

In the centre of Reykjavík is a remarkable home. Believed to have been built in the year 871 from stone and turf, its foundations (a series of low walls that show the gaps where doorways stood) and the pits where fires once burned are preserved in the capital's Settlement Exhibition. My journey starts here.

Iceland has a rich written history of its settlement, first noted down in the *Landnámabók* (Book of Settlements). Most likely a fusion of oral legend and recorded history, it tells the stories of the nation's earliest settlers. Ingólfr Arnarson, commonly believed to be the first permanent settler of Iceland, left Norway after a blood feud with members of another family. Sighting Iceland's coast, Ingólfr ordered the pillars of his seat thrown overboard – he would settle where the gods chose to bring them to shore. That site would become Reykjavík.

The next day, I drive out of the city, its suburbs giving way to stony fields framed by distant mountains. The road narrows, flanked by pastures. The cloudy sky is a deep Icelandic grey. As my route contorts northwards, winding through the crooks of fjords and bays, it suddenly dips sharply into the earth – the Hvalfjörður Tunnel appears like a magic portal.

Inside the orange glow of the tunnel, I let my mind wander, imagining a very real portal into Iceland's history – down generations of Icelanders and their struggles in the harsh landscape here. When I emerge, West Iceland and a saga are awaiting.

In Borgarnes, I stop at the Settlement Centre, a folk museum that covers the discovery of Iceland and the saga of Egil Skallagrímsson. Born here as a first-generation immigrant, Egil nurtured a warrior-poet persona. He crafted his first poem at the age of three, a boast of his abilities in verse. He also had a penchant for brutality, at one

point killing another boy over a ball game. By the end of his life, he'd become an old man mocked by his servants, yet was still capable of spite – he buried his treasure somewhere outside Borgarnes.

From the museum I head north along Snæfellsnesvegur, a two-lane road through fertile fields populated by the occasional sheep. Signs point the way to farms that still bear the names of early settlers.

Driving west into the Snaefellsnes Peninsula, I arrive at Búðakirkja, the region's famous black church. In 1703, the small community of Búðir was looking for a place to erect a church. A local legend tells how a woman suggested they choose the site by having a blindfolded archer shoot three arrows, one marked

© Eriken | Shutterstock

with a red ribbon. The church would be constructed where the marked arrow landed. That church lasted a hundred years before it was decommissioned in 1816 – the one standing today was reconstructed in 1987.

I continue west toward Arnarstapi, a small fishing village on cliffs overlooking the sea. The area was the setting for one of Iceland's late sagas, *Bárðar saga Snæfellsáss*, which tells the story of Bárðr, a half troll-half human who became the guardian spirit of the region. A short hike reveals stone bridges and basalt columns where colonies of Arctic terns dart through the air. But no trolls.

Near the peninsula's westernmost tip I turn off the main road near Lóndrangar. In the distance, a pillar of volcanic rock shaped like a Viking longship appears. This is where the story of Guðríður Þorbjarnardóttir begins. Born in the area in the 11th century, Guðríður left Iceland, drawn by the tales of Erik the Red, the Viking explorer who founded the first settlement in Greenland. She continued further west to one of the first European settlements in North America, eventually giving birth to Snorri Thorfinnsson, the first European born on the continent. The North American settlement was abandoned and Guðríður returned to Iceland. In later years, she converted to Christianity, eventually going on a pilgrimage to Rome (and possibly

"As my route contorts northwards, winding through the crooks of fjords and bays, it suddenly dips into the earth"

meeting the Pope), before returning to Iceland to live out the rest of her life as a nun. Today, she is also known as Guðríður víðförla, or Guðríður the Far-travelled.

As my drive curves northward around the edge of the Snaefellsnes Peninsula, I pass the lava fields and cones of the region's volcanoes, seeing how this landscape could easily have triggered the imaginations of writers over the centuries – in the dense fog, the gnarled twists of lava rock could be mistaken for a troll. Jules Verne's vivid imagination found inspiration here for his 1864 novel *Journey to the Centre of the Earth* – this is where his heroes found the entrance to the underworld.

In Hellissandur, I stop at the Maritime Museum, a quaint local museum that details the region's intimate relationship with the sea. Heading east, I see Kirkjufell, the arrowhead-shaped mountain made famous in *Game of Thrones* as a landmark north of the Wall.

WHAT'S IN A NAME?

Iceland has a heritage of meticulous record keeping, so many Icelanders can trace their family tree back to settlers from more than a millennium ago. The interconnections here can make dating rather tricky – you never know if that person you spot across the room at a party is actually a blood relation. Luckily, there's an app for that. The Islendinga-App, the 'App of Icelanders', contains the country's genealogical history, and is used to check if that next fling should be flung.

Clockwise from opposite: the distinctively sharp peak of Kirkufell mountain; a monument to Guðríður Þorbjarnardóttir with son Snorri Thorfinnsson, the first child of European descent born in America; a rock arch at Arnarstapi. Previous page: heading through farmland on the Snaefellsnes Peninsula

In Grundarfjörður, I pass a village of colourful buildings wedged between mountains and water, then pass a lava field called Berserkjahraun – a name from a saga in which two Berserker warriors were killed by their master because one fell in love with his daughter.

The story of my trip draws to a close in Stykkishólmur, a fishing village on a northern spur of the peninsula. I rent a kayak to get out on the sea that has paralleled my route so far. Launching into shallow waves, I discover why the town became an important trading post for the region. Protected by Landey Island to the west and a deep fjord to the east, it is perfectly positioned for safe access to the ocean. As puffins splash through the water's surface, I find the rusted hulk of a ship leaning against the shore of a barren island. The wreck is just a few decades old, yet takes its name, *Thorgeir*, from Thorgeir Ljosvetningagodi, a 10th-century chieftain who adopted Christianity while keeping many old pagan traditions alive. His decision saved Iceland from a potentially disastrous religious conflict.

As I paddle back to the harbour, I ponder the span of Icelandic history, stories about the exploration of new lands, and the lasting frisson of a good tale well told.

DIRECTIONS

Start // Reykjavík
End // Stykkishólmur
Distance // 124 miles (199km)
Getting there // Fly into Reykjavík, then choose from one of the city's many car-rental services. Two-wheel drive will suffice.
When to go // July and August for warm(ish) weather and long days for exploration.
Where to stay // On the southern side of the Snæfellsnes Peninsula, the Langaholt Guesthouse and Restaurant makes for the perfect place to overnight. The family-run guesthouse offers views of both the glacier that sits atop Snæfellsjökull volcano and the coast, and the on-site restaurant serves up deliciously fresh, home-cooked Icelandic fare – if you arrive early enough, you'll find the head cook fileting that day's catch for the evening's main course.

Opposite from top: Dante's statue in front of Santa Croce church in Florence, Italy; performing The Tempest at Shakespeare's Globe in London, England

MORE LIKE THIS
LITERARY PILGRIMAGES

NORTHWESTERN ITALY

In 1301 Dante Alighieri was exiled from Florence, the result of politics gone bad. This road trip begins there, in Dante's hometown. Take in its Renaissance streets and elegant *palazzi* before heading out, following the route of the poet's escape. Under threat of death, Dante moved to the Lunigiana region. There, in Massa, you'll find the Castello Malaspina, an 11th-century castle where Dante was first invited to stay. In town, a statue of the poet still stands. From Massa, head north to Verona – for Shakespeare, a city of love; for Dante, another rest stop. Explore the Biblioteca Capitolare, the library where the poet studied ancient texts. Finish off your tour of Dante's enforced trip in Ravenna, the town where he lived out his final days – and where he completed his masterpiece, *The Divine Comedy*.

Start // Florence
End // Ravenna
Distance // 399 miles (642km)

CASTILLA-LA MANCHA, SPAIN

Tilt into Spain's favourite literary legend with this tour of one of the country's most evocative landscapes. Set in 17th century Castilla-La Mancha, *Don Quixote* captures as much of the windmill-strewn landscapes of central Spain as it does the madness of its protagonist. From Toledo and its mix of Christian, Moorish and Jewish architecture, head to Campo de Criptana, where some of La Mancha's traditional windmills still stand. Next, stop at Belmonte, whose turret-topped castle best captures Don Quixote's chivalric imaginings. Finish where the novel (possibly) begins: 'In a village in La Mancha, the name of which I cannot quite recall.' Scholars believe that this place was actually Villanueva de los Infantes, where two bronze statues depict the novel's hero and his beleaguered sidekick, Sancho Panza.

Start // Toledo
End // Villanueva de los Infantes
Distance // 176 miles (284km)

SOUTH & CENTRAL ENGLAND

From the capital to one of the country's most beautiful cities to the birthplace of its most famous playwright, this trip links the heavy literary hitters of south and central England. Begin in London with a performance at Shakespeare's Globe, a reconstruction of the theatre where the Bard's acting company put on their first shows (play Renaissance-era peasant yourself and grab a standing ticket for just £5). Drive west to Bath, known for one of the world's best-preserved Roman bathhouses, as well as streets lined with golden-hued Georgian architecture. Your reading assignment here is Jane Austen's *Northanger Abbey*, which was set among Bath's winter balls and the other social delights of early 19th-century British gentry. Finally head north for a return to England's favourite scribe, with a stop at Shakespeare's birthplace, Stratford-upon-Avon. This is also where – to come full circle – his grave lies, bearing the menacing inscription, 'curst be he yt moves my bones'.

Start // London
End // Stratford-upon-Avon
Distance // 203 miles (327km)

THE WEST COAST OF JUTLAND

*Sara van Geloven drove a campervan along a coastline sculpted by the elements,
from the Wadden Sea to the rugged northernmost tip of Denmark.*

The soft beams of the rising sun stream through the windows of the campervan. It's quiet, the wind that whipped through the marram grass in the night has run its course. The only sound comes from the waves breaking on the deserted beach a stone's throw away. The few other campervans that spent the night in the dunes left at dawn. I pull open the sliding door and step with bare feet onto the cool sand. Here, at the northernmost point of Denmark, I take a deep breath and taste the salt in the air.

Rewind a week, and my partner Jurrien and I are crossing the border from Germany into Denmark to follow the western coast of Jutland all the way up to the top of the peninsula. The roads are mostly flat, perfect for campervan driving, and the sea is ever-present – in the whole of Denmark, the coast is never more than 30 miles (48km) away. The first glimpse of the coast on our road trip, however, includes no sea at all, but rather mudflats stretching to the horizon. We're at the rich wetlands known as the Wadden Sea, a Unesco World Heritage Site, where at low tide a feast for migrating birds is revealed. On the island of Rømø, connected to the mainland by a narrow dike road, guide Signe Vendike of Naturcenter Tønnisgård stands knee-deep in the mud. 'It's great to feel the mud between your toes,' she says. 'It's full of nutrients too, attracting a multitude of animals like the periwinkle.' She wades to a patch of seagrass and points to some sea snails. 'They're a common sight here. They graze on the algae on the grass and, in their turn, get eaten by the millions of birds that migrate here every year. It's like one big seafood banquet.'

On the west side of the island, huge swathes of white sand form one of the widest beaches in Europe, leading to the chilly waters of the North Sea. Cars are allowed and the beach of Lakolk is one

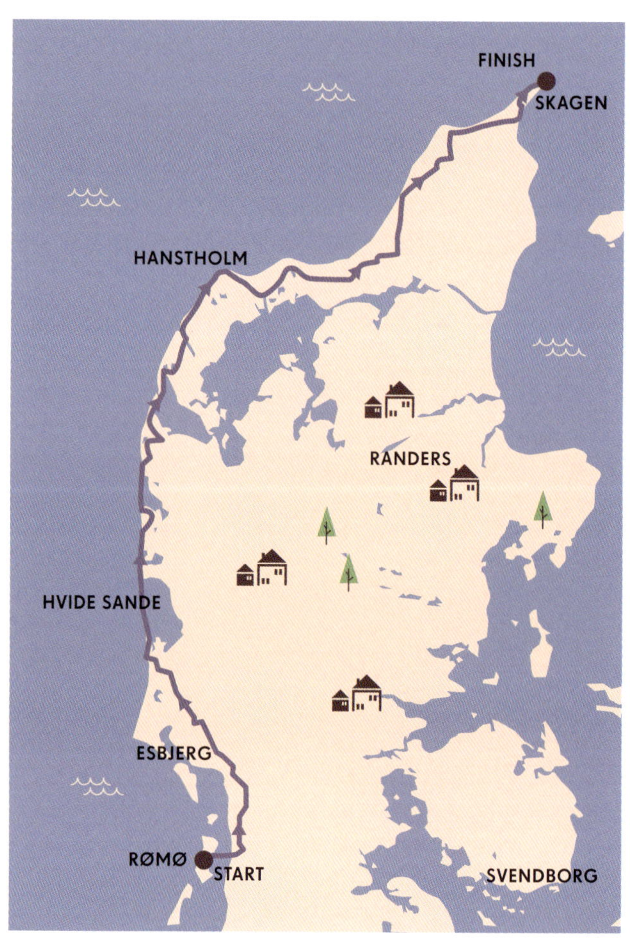

big jumble of colours and sounds: there are kites flapping in the wind; families setting up beach chairs in front of their cars; and a jeep towing a stranded car out of soft sand as the passengers stand cheering to the side. We take care to park the campervan on a stretch of firm sand, before braving a refreshing dip in the sea. It's a joy to be able to get dressed easily in the campervan afterwards and to make lunch in the tiny kitchen. We pull out folding chairs and plop them down, toasting with a pair of cold Radlers from the fridge. I close my eyes as the sun dries the salt on my skin.

Staying on the beach overnight isn't allowed, so at the end of a sun-soaked day we drive off the island and head north. We pass Ribe, the oldest town in Denmark, founded by Vikings, and cross the northern border of the Wadden Sea. It's easy driving – we follow the well-maintained coastal road to a thin strip of land lying between the North Sea on the left and a set of fjords on the right. Dunes hug the tarmac and a village pops up every fifteen minutes or so, often a simple cluster of brightly painted holiday homes, like pieces of Lego strewn across a green baseplate. There are fishmongers churning out fresh seafood too, and plenty of campgrounds. Unlike most of Scandinavia, Denmark doesn't have a freedom to roam law, but there are dedicated areas where campervans can stay overnight in nature – these are easy to seek out with the app Park4Night. We spend that night beside a serene lake, befriending some local fishermen, and the next close to a fjord.

The further north we drive, the wilder the coast becomes. In Thy National Park we hike through a forest of trees twisted into

THE ROLLING LIGHTHOUSE

When it was built, the lighthouse Rubjerg Knude stood 650ft (198m) away from the sea, but due to the merciless onslaught of the elements, the edge of the cliff progressively eroded away. A few years back the lighthouse teetered mere feet from the abyss and the local community decided to act. In 2019, the whole brick tower was put on rails and moved 230ft (70m) inland, where it stands safely. For now.

Clockwise from above: bounty of the fertile terrain around the Wadden Sea; Rubjerg Knude lighthouse at Lønstrup; direct access via campervan. Previous page: breakwaters temper erosion of these fragile shores by the North Sea

strange shapes by the never-relinquishing wind. On the beach of Stenbjerg, fishing boats have been pulled high onto the sand, out of reach of the churning waves. North of Thy, the coastal village of Klitmøller has been dubbed 'Cold Hawaii' and, even on an overcast day, there's a good number of surfers battling the waves. 'I enjoy surfing best when it's really cold,' says Anders Hvass, a local. 'The village is nice and quiet after the summer crowds have gone, there's lots of *hygge* and the waves are more challenging. To get home after a cold surfing session and warm up by the fire, it's the best feeling in the world.'

Past Klitmøller the road turns northeast. Hills start to appear, and the wind picks up even more. At Lønstrup, on a 200ft (61m) high clifftop, I have to squint to keep the sand out of my eyes, as a sea of golden dunes stretches out before me. In a sense this could be mistaken for a desert, were it not for the lighthouse standing right next to me. Rubjerg Knude (the lighthouse's name) was built 100 years ago but has long since gone out of use. It stands set back from the crumbling cliffs, an unfazed watcher of the sea.

Skagen's Grey Lighthouse is even older, but still in operation. When it was built it stood in the centre of the Skagen peninsula, but due to coastal erosion it now borders the turquoise waters of the Kattegat, the strait between Denmark and Sweden. Skagen forms the very northernmost tip of the country and from the top of the lighthouse, I can see the place where the inky waves of the North Sea and the clear waters of the Kattegat meet.

For the final night of our road trip, we park the campervan in the dunes next to the pebble-beach Nordstrand. Tomorrow we'll start to make our way back south, but for now we'll enjoy the rush of the waves in the distance, the beam of the lighthouse that sweeps across the night sky, and the ever-present wind that will rock us to sleep.

> *"Here, at the northernmost point of Denmark, I take a deep breath and taste the salt in the air"*

DIRECTIONS

Start // Rømø
End // Skagen
Distance // 300 miles (480km)
Getting there // Hamburg is the nearest hub, while Copenhagen is also close.
Campervan rental // www.camptoo.com is a sharing platform for campervans. It has a huge offering in the UK and Netherlands especially, for all budgets.
When to go // July and August are busiest but offer the best chance of good weather. The shoulder seasons on either side are quieter and still sunny; winter delivers *hygge* (that Danish sense of cosiness) and sleepy towns.
Tip // If you discover an overnight spot through the app Park4Night, arrive well before sundown to have enough time to find an alternative if the place is already full. Always leave your parking area cleaner than you found it.
Further information // www.visitdenmark.com

Opposite: the Rügen Bridge gives access to the holiday island of Rügen, over the Strelasund from the mainland near Stralsund, Germany

MORE LIKE THIS
COASTAL CAMPERVAN TRIPS

BOHUSLÄN COAST, SWEDEN

This picturesque route takes in Sweden's first national marine park and ends at the Norwegian border. Starting in Gothenburg, sample the many delights of Sweden's second city before heading north along the coast. Just a half-hour drive from Gothenburg awaits a different world: red farm buildings dot green hills and glittering fjords lead to a shoreline from where thousands of small islands fan out. Reserve time for stops in the cute coastal towns for fresh seafood and sauna visits. Highlights include sea kayaking in Grundsund, following in the footsteps of Ingrid Bergman in Fjällbäck, and a boat trip to Väderöarna, the Weather Islands. Finish at Kosterhavets National Park, home to pristine waters, the serene Koster Islands and Sweden's largest seal colony – or continue on across the border into Norway and keep driving.
Start // Gothenburg
End // Kosterhavets National Park
Distance // 142 miles (228km)

WEST COAST, NETHERLANDS

The Dutch are experts at water management and this route takes in some of the most impressive dikes, dams and floodgates in the country. Begin in Middelburg, the medieval capital of Zeeland province, nowadays best-known for its delectable seafood. With plenty of beaches and campgrounds on offer, there's no rush to head north. Drive across the Oosterscheldekering, part of the impressive Delta Works protecting the southwest of the Netherlands from the sea. Make a stop in hip Rotterdam, the country's second city, or drive on to quaint smaller cities like Delft or Gouda. Follow the coastline, forming one long stretch of blissful beach, to seaside towns like Katwijk aan Zee and Bloemendaal. Make a side trip to Amsterdam and cross the IJ River to continue along the coast or take the eastern route following the former Zuiderzee. Then board the ferry in Den Helder for the short crossing to the peaceful island of Texel, your final stop.
Start // Middelburg
End // Texel
Distance // 193 miles (310km)

BALTIC COAST, GERMANY

Home to the biggest port in Germany, Hamburg has been a centre of maritime trade for centuries and nautical influences can be found all over this uber-cool city – a fitting start for a road trip along the Baltic Coast. Head northeast to Lübeck, another icon of the Hanseatic League with a striking medieval Old Town. From here, stick close to the Baltic, heading east for picturesque old harbours, towns with cobbled streets and a strikingly azure sea. Visit the Vorpommersche Boddenlandschaft national park's lagoons before – past the town of Stralsund – crossing the bridge to Rügen. Germany's largest island offers freshly caught seafood, ancient forests and many excellent campgrounds, some close to the beach. Rügen is also home to Germany's smallest national park, Jasmund, with romantic vistas of rugged chalk cliffs that inspired painter Caspar David Friedrich, among many others.
Start // Hamburg
End // Rügen
Distance // 210 miles (337km)

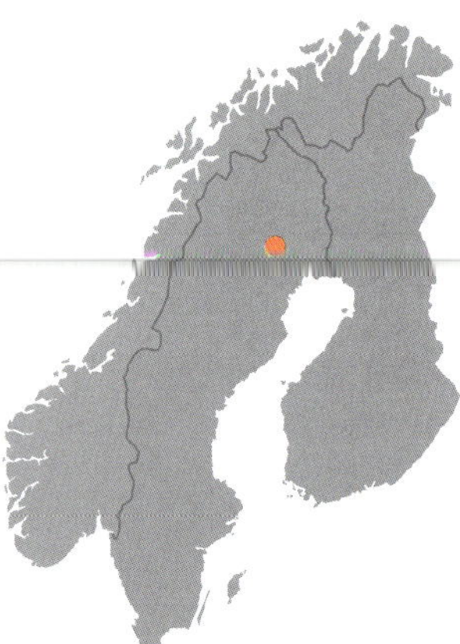

GETTING TO KNOW THE SAMI

Making his way through remote wilderness at the top of Europe, Anthony Ham drove in search of the Sami, the custodians of Scandinavia's Arctic north.

Travelling north into the Scandinavian Arctic takes you deep into the lands of the Sami. For millennia, these ancient people have ranged across Europe's far north, moving with their reindeer with the seasons through Sweden, Norway and Finland. In winter, the roads remain open throughout Sami Scandinavia and the northern lights often dance across the sky during the long nights. Throughout equally lengthy summer days, the roads meander under the midnight sun, as if on their own nomadic course across the spare landscape, through forests of birch and pine and beneath skies of deep Arctic blue.

My journey begins along the E45 in Arvidsjaur, a small town with origins as a Sami marketplace – reason enough to visit on this journey. But Arvidsjaur and its frozen lakes are also where car manufacturers and TV shows like *Top Gear* traditionally come to test drive and show off their cars, seeking excuses to slide across the ice – making it an even more appropriate starting point for this road trip

Forsaking the high-speed thrills of Arvidsjaur, it's a quieter pleasure that always takes hold of me as I journey north towards Jokkmokk. Although the route has yet to cross the Arctic Circle and will only do so just before Jokkmokk, by this stage I have already crossed some unseen frontier of the mind. The traffic thins, temperatures drop, boreal forests unfurl and settlements become smaller, so much so that even Jokkmokk, home to fewer than 3000 souls, is a welcome respite from the growing emptiness of the landscape.

More than any other town in Sweden, Jokkmokk feels Sami. Its excellent Ájtte Museum is one of the finest introductions to Sami life, history and cosmology in the country. Its Sami Winter Market

dates back to 1605. Locals think nothing of wearing their national dress for a trip to the shops. And you'll often hear the Sami language spoken as the lingua franca of commerce and social interactions.

With a taste now for the north and its people, I find myself winding down the windows, regardless of the temperature, as the road weaves between lakes and low hills and forests – and reindeer.

Gällivare, then lakeside Jukkasjärvi (with its ice hotel and charming wooden church) pass by, and my pace quickens as I rush through Kiruna, where the authorities are building a new

town as the old one disappears into the nearby mine, until I reach Abisko.

Wilderness here begins where the town ends, with Abisko National Park pressing close, serving as a reminder that, up here, it is nature that holds sway. Some of Sweden's best hiking, stirring views of the midnight sun and aurora borealis (the northern lights), reindeer led by Sami herders on the way to new pastures – Abisko would be an Arctic cliché were it not spectacularly real.

Continuing the drive means doubling back past Kiruna and Jukkasjärvi before taking new roads as I turn eastwards at Svappavaara, then north at Vittangi. Past Karesuando, Enontekiö, and Leppäjärvi – and suddenly I'm in Norway.

Like the landscapes I've been travelling through south of the border, Arctic Norway is rolling hill country cloaked with forests of pine, bare slopes and rivers, frozen or ice-blue. Not far north of the border, there is no more Sami town in Scandinavia than Kautokeino. Kautokeino is Sami through and through. It is the winter base for the 'reindeer Sami', as opposed to the Sami who live along the coast. Nearly 90 percent of Kautokeino's population speaks some form of Sami as their first language. And it is the sort of place where people wear reindeer skins and

> ## *"In winter, roads remain open throughout Sami Scandinavia and the northern lights often dance across the sky"*

vivid, traditional hand-woven garments, not for the few tourists who pass through but because, well, this is how they've always dressed. It's also a pretty place – a river runs through it, hills surround it – and the joys and caprices of Arctic weather can come together in a single day.

The 79 miles (128km) from Kautokeino to Karasjok will always be one of my favourite sections of this whole journey. It was along this stretch, shadowed by clear rivers gushing down off ice-bound mountains and glaciers, that I first encountered the Sami, and felt that first exhilarating sense of solitude and silence. Other cars are invariably rare. By the roadside, snows remain long into summer. And ahead of me, not for the first time, lies a long, empty road.

At the end of it all, Karasjok inhabits the intersection of river, hill and forest less like a town than a part of the forest itself. If Kautokeino is Sami whether the world cares or not, Karasjok is where the world comes to look through a window onto Sami

ANCIENT PEOPLES

The Sami are Scandinavia's oldest surviving human population: evidence of their presence here dates back more than 3000 years. There are an estimated 80,000 Sami, spread across four countries. The majority, around 50,000, live in Norway, with close to 20,000 in Sweden, about 8000 in Finland and perhaps 2000 in Russia. The Sami refer to their traditional lands as Sápmi or Samiland, and were once known to outsiders as Lapps; Sami is now preferred.

From left: a chilly sleep awaits at Jukkasjärvi's Ice Hotel 365; a red-painted church near Kiruna in Sweden; Sami reindeer-skin bags for sale at a market; a reindeer rests outside a Sami camp. Previous page: the road north of Jokkmokk heads into wilderness

life in its museums, to go dog-sledding and to spend time with Sami makers of knives and jewellery. Rising above it all is the Norwegian Sami Parliament, swathed in mellow Siberian wood, rising amid the pines in the form of a traditional Sami tent.

The road from Karasjok follows the Kárášjokha River, crosses the international border, leaving Norway and snaking down into the beautiful lake country of northern Finland. Like Karasjok, Inari, at journey's end, has its very own Sami parliament building, and a world-class museum dedicated to Sami life. And like the road between Kautokeino and Karasjok, the road from the Norwegian border down to Inari always feels like a traverse of all that's appealing about the Sami north: so many views of pristine snows in the piercing Arctic light; so few towns; and so much silence that I find myself pulling over often to meditate upon the beauty of the land through which I'm passing.

At Inari, the road doesn't so much end as connect with the world beyond. I am always tempted never to take it. I consider my options – perhaps a detour to Lemmenjoki National Park, or maybe go looking for bears further south near Saariselkä. But there's nothing I enjoy more than wandering down to the shores of Inarijärvi, northern Finland's largest lake, to gaze in wonder for one last time at the islands and mountains of Samiland.

DIRECTIONS

Start // Arvidsjaur (Sweden)
End // Inari (Finland)
Distance // 695 miles (1118km)
Number of countries // 3
When to go // This route can be driven year-round, except for during unexpected extremes of weather; remember that it takes really extreme weather for roads to close here, and if you're driving a rental vehicle in winter, it will have snow tyres fitted. There are as many good reasons to drive this route in winter (northern lights, snow-bound scenery) as in summer (midnight sun and long days).
Further information // Lonely Planet's guides to Sweden, Norway, Finland and Scandinavia have detailed coverage of these regions.

MORE LIKE THIS
DRIVES THROUGH
SCANDINAVIAN HISTORY

VARANGERBOTN TO
HAMNINGBERG, NORWAY

The lonely road that follows the shoreline
of Varangerfjord has an austere Arctic
beauty. In and around Varangerbotn are an
engaging Sami museum, a hugely significant
Sami archaeological site at Ceavccageadge,
and Nesseby Church, one of the most
beautifully-sited churches anywhere in the
Arctic. But it's the tundra-like landscapes of
Varangerhalvøya National Park, the colonies
of seabirds and the reindeer herds, the sand
dunes and deserted beaches, the elemental
clouds that form out over Russia in semi-
apocalyptic shapes, that give this wild and
beautiful coast so much presence, and make
it one of Norway's most picturesque drives.
At the end of the road – literally – is tiny,
timber Hamningberg. Remoteness saved
the village from devastation during WWII
(except for one house hit during a Russian
bombing raid) and it was all but abandoned
in the 1960s. The views from here extend
forever out over remote Arctic waters.

Start // **Varangerbotn**
End // **Hamningberg**
Distance // **99 miles (159km)**

UMEÅ TO ROVANIEMI,
SWEDEN & FINLAND

Yet another Scandinavian town with Sami
origins and excellent museums to tell
the story, sub-Arctic Umeå in Sweden
is an appealing lakeside town whose
history dates back to 1622. From Umeå,
the road stays with the Gulf of Bothnia
coast, offering views out across the water.
Close to the halfway point, Luleå was first
chartered just one year before Umeå, in
1621, but its buildings in the charming,
timbered Gammelstad (Old Town) date
back to 1492. Not long after crossing
the border into Finland, the road leaves
the shoreline and tracks northwest to
Rovaniemi, rebuilt in a grid pattern that
evokes a reindeer's antlers after Nazi
bombing destroyed the town in 1944.
Arktikum, a more recent construction, is
one of Scandinavia's best museums –
its coverage of the Sami is particularly
worthwhile. Rovaniemi is the main gateway
town for Finnish Lapland and the Far North.

Start // **Umeå**
End // **Rovaniemi**
Distance // **316 miles (508km)**

KIRKENES TO GRENSE
JAKOBSELV, NORWAY

History (and Russia) looms large over
this corner of Norway. Grense Jakobselv
marks one of the easternmost points
of Western Europe, and the drive here
skirts remote Arctic fjords and runs right
alongside the Russian border on the final
section – only a small stream and stone
border posts separate the two countries
in places and you can even see the onion
domes of Russian Orthodox churches
in some areas. Of more recent vintage
is Grense Jakobselv's forlorn stone
church, King Oscar II's Chapel, which
was built in 1869. The local authorities
constructed the church to deter illegal
Russian fishing boats from crossing into
Norwegian waters – they weren't listening
to the Norwegian authorities, but, so the
argument ran, they might just respect the
border if they saw a church.

Start // **Kirkenes**
End // **Grense Jakobselv**
Distance // **35 miles (56km)**

KYSTRIKSVEIEN, NORWAY'S COASTAL HIGHWAY

The call of Norway's wild north and the chance to drive the country's iconic Coastal Highway drew Anthony Ham to this awe-inspiring and humbling corner of Europe.

In the medieval sagas of old Norway, Steinkjer was a place where journeys began and ended. It was a market town whose inhabitants grew accustomed to travellers – traders bearing exotic goods from the frozen north, pilgrims on their way to Trondheim's cathedral. They heard stories of a wild and untrammelled coastline that tracked into Arctic lands filled with mystery and where nature held sway. Steinkjer was the gateway to another world.

In this, at least, the town has changed little, even if its clean-cut and modern Scandinavian facades suggest little of the drama that lies just beyond the northern horizon. Steinkjer does have a few Viking-era burial mounds, but it remains best known as the southernmost town on the Kystriksveien (Fv17), Norway's Coastal Highway.

The Kystriksveien is a portal between two very different worlds – Norway's central heartland and its Arctic north. It rides the fissured coastline, bucking and weaving along a path that follows the restless contours of a land shaped by cataclysmic natural upheavals during an epic geological past. And it is, quite simply, one of Europe's most beautiful coastal drives.

Leaving Steinkjer, my initial journey meanders without haste. The drive passes through the undulating hill country that defines the terrain where the bulging Norwegian land mass narrows and heads for the north. In these early southern reaches, the Fv17 takes its time in getting going, slowly tracking west and then north in search of the coast that gives this road its name. Suitably for Norway, my first sight of the water is of a fjord that snakes inland, just south of Namsos. The road never again strays far from the coast on its relentless path into the Arctic.

Past Namsos, with its world-renowned museum dedicated to rock music, the Kystriksveien shadows the coast until, 9 miles (15km) before Brønnøysund, the bald rocky outcrop of Torghatten rises improbably from Torget Island, just offshore, like some great, cloaked troll in fossil form. It's an arresting sight, an imposing gatekeeper to what waits for me further up the road.

The Kystriksveien arcs around mountain foothills in great, sweeping curves. It passes the summer cabins that line every Norwegian lake. And it carries me into slightly scruffy Sandnessjøen, whose backdrop still makes it beautiful – the seven summits of the Syv Søstre (Seven Sisters), which range

from 2985ft (910m) to 3517ft (1072m) and offer some of the best hiking anywhere along this trip. Also just offshore is Dønnmannen (2814ft/858m), where a trail leads up to one of those Norwegian precipices so beloved by selfie-loving Instagrammers.

Beyond Sandnessjøen, the Helgeland Bridge sweeps into view, connecting two shorelines beneath mountains that are often flecked with snow well into summer. Onwards I continue, the mountains seemingly higher, the air seemingly purer as the Arctic approaches. Perhaps it's the sight of distant snows. Or the interplay of sky and water and steep rocks that tumble down to the water's edge. Whatever it is, I can feel my excitement grow the further north I go.

After the ferry crossing from Levang to Nesna, the scenery expands again. The road follows the shore of quiet Sjonafjord, passing more stilted cabins painted in oxblood-red. For a moment I feel like I'm returning to civilisation as the road passes through farmlands and the gathering buildings of Utskarpen, near the fjord's innermost reaches. The traffic, such as it is, increases ever so slightly and my pace slows. But the feeling passes as quickly as it came, and the road swings west and leaves town – the traffic lightens and I pick up speed again as I continue around the fjord.

The road hugs the coast, and it's almost as if the Fv17 traces in outline the outermost reaches of the Norwegian mainland: for most of the way, I couldn't get any closer to the shore without getting wet. Beyond Stokkvågen, the Kystriksveien passes the WWII-era fort at Grønsvik, one of more than 350 defences built to fortify Norway's coastline during the Nazi occupation. A little beyond Grønsvik, I pull over to a lookout, turn off the engine and

A MIGHTY MAELSTROM

The Saltstraumen Maelstrom is the largest of its kind on Earth, a tumultuous churning of the waters that occurs in the Saltstraumen Strait four times every 24 hours. As one fjord drains into another, more than 400 million cubic metres of water roil and surge into whirlpools, flowing first one way as the tide comes in, then back the other six hours later. The best views are from the Saltstraumen Bridge. Local tourist offices have tide timings.

Clockwise from above: traditional houses in the city of Mo i Rana; the dramatically framed beach at Storvik; tidal whirlpools at Saltstraumen. Previous page: snowy peaks of Saltfjellet-Svartisen National Park

listen. Silence greets me, and silent awe is indeed the only sensible response to the view – barren islands and skerries too numerous to count rising from the ocean like mainland Norway's echo.

Back at the wheel, there are moments when the road seems to be heading straight for a steep wall of mountains, until, often at the last minute, it disappears into some hidden valley or narrow canyon, emerging into open country on the far side.

On the Kilboghamn-Jektvik ferry, the views call to mind the words of Norway's world-renowned playwright, Henrik Ibsen, who described the mountains of his beloved homeland as 'palace piled upon palace'. The crossing takes an hour. At some point along the way the captain notifies us that we are passing across the Arctic Circle. A silver globe mounted on the shore makes the same point.

A line on the map shouldn't make a difference, but somehow it does. After yet another ferry crossing, this time between Ågskardet and Forøy, with some suddenness, the Svartisen ice cap – Norway's second-largest glacier and part of the high-altitude Saltfjellet-Svartisen National Park – rises above the road to the east. Glacier tongues plunge down off the high plateau towards the shore of Holandsfjorden.

And then, just as I'm coming to terms with the spectacle and perspective-altering drama of Norway's frozen north, I arrive at Storvik, where I find – a beach. It's not just any beach. This one curves around a bay encircled by sheer rock walls. If it weren't for the Arctic temperatures, I could almost be in Hawaii.

From Storvik it's a relatively uneventful final 62 miles (100km) into Bodø – with one exception. At Saltstraumen, ocean tides crash against the fjords and their rocky shore like some giant horizontal waterfall. It's the final act of a stirring, elemental drama that, for the hundreds of miles I've been driving, just happens to have a road running through it.

> *"Kystriksveien is a portal between two very different worlds – Norway's central heartland and its Arctic north"*

DIRECTIONS

Start // Steinkjer
End // Bodø
Distance // 390 miles (630km)
Number of ferry crossings // 6
Getting there // Trondheim and Bodø airports are nearest.
When to go // The road is open year-round, but ice and sudden weather changes can make it treacherous for those not used to driving in the Norwegian winter. Good weather is most likely during the long summer days of July and August – also the busiest months, with plenty of traffic. Mid-May to late June and early September are possibly better options, with generally fine conditions and fewer vehicles.
Further information // For more on the Kystriksveien, go to www.visitnorway.com/places-to-go/northern-norway/kystriksveien. For more on the country's other National Scenic Routes see www.visitnorway.com/plan-your-trip/travel-tips-a-z/norwegian-scenic-routes

Opposite from top: a church at Nesseby, close to Norway's distant northern border with Russia; the Arctic island of Senja

MORE LIKE THIS
INTO NORWAY'S ARCTIC NORTH

ARCTIC HIGHWAY

In any other country, Norway's Arctic Highway would be celebrated for its scenery, and rightly so. But because the Kystriksveien fulfils a similar purpose – connecting central Norway with the far north – the Arctic Highway's traverse of high mountains, fjords and deep inland valleys is often relegated to second choice. If you get the chance, you really should drive both. Known as the E6, the Arctic Highway cuts a spectacular path between the mountains that seal Norway off from Sweden and those that shelter the interior from the coast. There are many highlights: quiet villages; pine forests that cling to steep mountains; and unheralded fjords that are no less beautiful because no one but locals knows their names. Focal points of this journey include the waterfalls of Laksforsen, the east-facing ice wall of Saltfjellet-Svartisen National Park, and a crossing of the Arctic Circle in a suitably wild and snow-filled valley.

Start // Trondheim
End // Fauske
Distance // 404 miles (650km)

SENJA

The Arctic island of Senja is one of Norway's least-known treasures. Norway's second-largest island, it rivals the Lofoten archipelago for sheer, staggering beauty, but relatively few travellers make it out here. Those who do generally arrive in Gryllefjord on the car ferry from Andenes, and the views are quintessentially Norwegian: isolated fishing villages clinging to a steep shore; imposing mountains often capped with snow; and mile upon mile of deserted coastline. Bare, craggy cliffs and the jagged summits of Yttersida provide a backdrop to so many scenes of singular beauty. Sometimes it's fishing villages such as Hamn, Mefjordvær and Husøy that catch the eye. But more often it's the astonishing panoramas, seen from daringly designed viewpoints at Bergsbotn and Tungeneset, that will prompt you to pull to the side of the road and shake your head in wonder.

Start // Gryllefjord
End // Botnhamn
Distance // 63 miles (101km)

ALTA TO KIRKENES

From the Unesco World Heritage-listed rock art of Alta to Kirkenes on the cusp of Russia, this route traverses untouristed Norway's Arctic north. It draws near to Nordkapp, mainland Europe's northernmost point, but this is merely one detour among many. Even by sticking to the road, you'll pass the salmon-fishing grounds of Lakselv, the moose populations of Stabbursdalen National Park and there will be reindeer by the side of (and sometimes across) the road in many places. This is the land of the Sami, Norway's indigenous people, whose soulful presence brings gravitas to Europe's north. In Karasjok in particular, Sami cultural sites fill the village, dog-sledding is a favourite activity and the soaring Sami Parliament building is where Scandinavian architecture, clean-lined and contemporary, meets ancient symbolism. By Varangerbotn and Kirkenes, spare Arctic landscapes take hold, carrying echoes of Russia on ice-bearing winds.

Start // Alta
End // Kirkenes
Distance // 352 miles (566km)

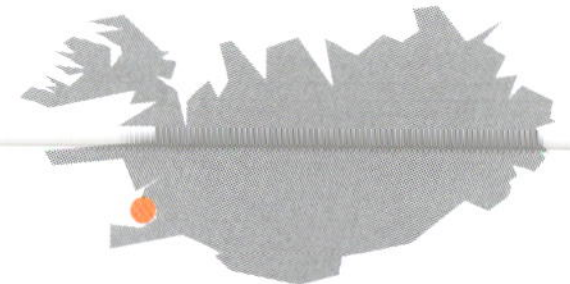

THE MAGIC CIRCLE

Oliver Berry discovered haunting lava fields, wild coastline, powerful waterfalls and majestic ice caps on an elemental journey around Iceland's Ring Road.

t's mid-morning on Iceland's east coast, but it might as well be midnight. Fog cloaks the road, blending land, sea and sky into a spectral grey. Now and then, black peaks materialise from the gloom, and slashes in the cloud reveal sudden glimpses of coastline: rocky cliffs, grassy dunes, wild beaches of black sand. Gulls bank and wheel in the wind.

Wild weather is par for the course on Iceland's Ring Road – or Route 1, as it's designated on highway maps. Circling around the island's coastline for 830 miles (1336km), the Ring Road is an engineering marvel as well as a national emblem, one that has been in service since 1974.

Naturally enough, all distances along Route 1 are measured from Iceland's capital, Reykjavík. Even here, among the art galleries and pubs, hints of Iceland's wilder side are easy to find. Looking north across the bay of Faxaflói, a craggy finger of land extends along the horizon, terminating in the snow-capped summit of Snæfellsjökull, used as the setting for Jules Verne's classic adventure tale, *Journey*

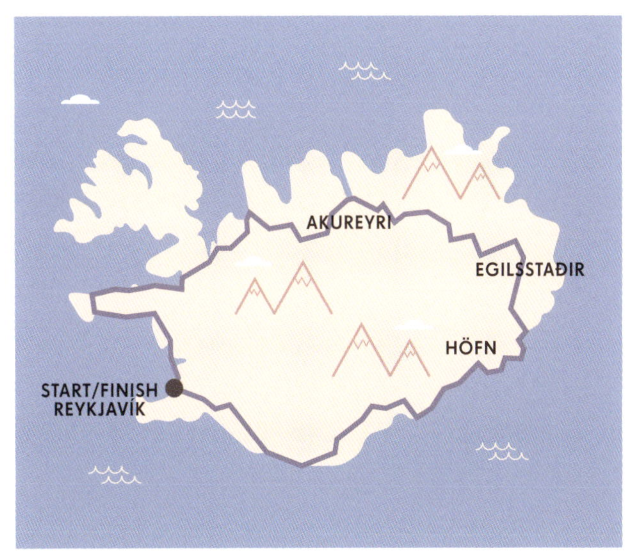

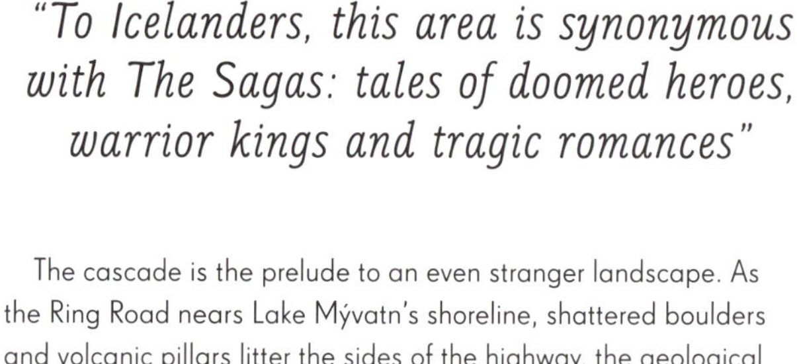

to the Centre of the Earth. The volcano remains a brooding presence as the Ring Road heads north from Reykjavik's suburbs – a reminder that the forces of nature are never far away.

Verne wasn't the first writer to find inspiration among the fjords and valleys of Iceland's west. To Icelanders, this area is synonymous with the Sagas, the tales that are a cornerstone of Icelandic culture. First written down by historians in the 12th and 13th centuries, but rooted in an older tradition of oral storytelling, these tales of family feuds, doomed heroes, warrior kings and tragic romances are part genealogy, part history, part drama.

As the Ring Road swerves inland across the humpbacked hills northwest of Borgarnes, it passes many locations from the Sagas: a farmstead that features in Egil's Saga, a hot spring where the hero of Grettir's Saga soothed his battle-weary bones. While most of the stories are rooted in fact, many have a fantastical streak that stems from Iceland's pantheon of myths and legends: strange tales of trolls, giants and dragons, as well as the island's *huldufólk* (hidden folk) of gnomes, dwarves, fairies and elves.

It's easy to see how Iceland's otherworldly landscape inspired such tales. Sculpted and scarred by thousands of years of geological activity, it often appears not altogether of this world.

Nowhere is this more true than around Lake Mývatn and Krafla, Iceland's most volcanically active area. Here, as the Ring Road drops from the uplands, it loops past Goðafoss (Waterfall of the Gods), a deafening mass of foaming white water that seems to emanate from a ragged crack in the Earth's crust.

"To Icelanders, this area is synonymous with The Sagas: tales of doomed heroes, warrior kings and tragic romances"

The cascade is the prelude to an even stranger landscape. As the Ring Road nears Lake Mývatn's shoreline, shattered boulders and volcanic pillars litter the sides of the highway, the geological remnants of ancient eruptions. Geysers gush and mud pools bubble. Fissures in the earth spew out columns of steam, a reminder that this part of Iceland sits on top of the Mid-Atlantic Ridge, the unstable meeting point of the Eurasian and North American tectonic plates.

As the Ring Road circles around the eastern coast, the landscape becomes wilder and emptier. Isolated villages hunker at the bottom of glacial fjords. Abandoned shepherds' cabins line the roads. Waterfalls cascade down hills, carving canyons through the rock, including the maelstrom of Dettifoss, Europe's most powerful fall.

The east coast has always been isolated, cut off by distance and geography. Prior to the arrival of the Ring Road, many villages were only accessible via mountain passes, which were often snowbound, forcing the delivery of supplies by air or sea. Reaching these villages was a big challenge for the Ring Road's engineers, and required tunnels, embankments and bridges to overcome the topography.

Iceland's most epic playground, the Vatnajökull ice cap, covers 3000 sq miles (7770 sq km) of the country's southeast, making it the

TOLKIEN'S ICELAND

Iceland's legends were an important inspiration for JRR Tolkien, a scholar of Old Norse and the Sagas. Many Tolkien enthusiasts believe Iceland's turf houses, built from peat bricks topped by grass roofs, may have given him the idea for Bilbo Baggins' underground home, Bag End, in *The Hobbit*. They certainly resemble Hobbit houses, but they were actually a pragmatic solution to one of Iceland's enduring problems – a shortage of timber.

From left: pure-bred Icelandic horses; a characteristic red-roofed church; working the annual sheep round-up; Seljalandsfoss waterfall; a statue of explorer Leif Eriksson outside Hallgrímskirkja in Reykjavík. Previous page: Þingvellir National Park

largest volume of ice anywhere in Europe. Driving west from Höfn, a small port in one of Iceland's southeastern fjords, the glacier looms along the skyline, a frozen white sea slicing through a jawbone of dog's-tooth peaks.

As the Ring Road leaves Vatnajökull and cuts west, it enters the flat pastureland of Þingvallavatn, and passes two spectacular waterfalls – Skógafoss, one of Iceland's highest, with a sheer drop of 60m, and Seljalandsfoss, where the spray refracts the sunlight like a prism, conjuring rainbows from thin air. Bit by bit, countryside gives way to civilisation. Towns and villages become more frequent, and greenhouses appear along the roadside. This is also equine country, home to numerous farms that raise Iceland's pure-bred horses.

Further west, and a short detour north from the Ring Road, lies Þingvellir National Park. A place of wild beauty, it was here that the Vikings established the AlÞing, an open-air assembly and Iceland's first parliament. Established in 930 AD, the AlÞing has a legitimate claim as the world's oldest form of democratic government, and holds a deep historical and symbolic significance for Icelanders.

Appropriately enough, the beginning of Iceland's recorded history also marks journey's end for the Ring Road. As it snakes across the magma fields of the Reykjanesfólkvangur nature reserve, it drops down into Reykjavík's suburbs, bathed under streetlights that seem strange after a week of clear skies and starlight. Far ahead across the bay of Faxaflói, the Snæfellsnes ice cap flashes in the evening light, and the Ring Road begins its circular journey north again – a never-ending thread unspooling beneath a silver sky.

DIRECTIONS

Start/End // Reykjavík

Distance // 830 miles (1336km)

Getting there // Iceland has become far more accessible in recent years, with more flights arriving from more destinations. Ferry transport (from northern Denmark) is a good alternative for Europeans wishing to take their own car.

When to drive // June to August is peak season, with higher prices and bookings required way ahead. This is also endless-daylight season, with plenty of activities and festivals to draw you ever onward. May and September are optimal if you prefer fewer crowds and lower prices over cloudless days.

Tip // Don't rush – allocate 10 to 14 days to driving the Ring Road, at a minimum. With just a week to spend in Iceland, concentrate on one or two regions in detail.

*Opposite: luxury cars gather outside
the Casino de Monte-Carlo in Monaco*

MORE LIKE THIS
NATIONAL CIRCUITS

A SIX-SIDED DRIVE, FRANCE

Some countries' shapes are just more
helpful when it comes to visual shorthand:
Italy is a boot, while continental France is
'l'Hexagone' to its citizens. Now, the Tour
de France doesn't demand of its riders that
they visit all six corners of the country in
turn, but this is a drive begging to be done
for those with plenty of time. And map
experience – this is very much a plot-your-
own route, with different interpretations
possible. All that's required is that you stop
at each point of the French hexagon, from
north going clockwise: Bray-Dunes near
Dunkirk on the Belgian border; Lauterbourg
on the Rhine in Alsace; sunny Menton at
the limit of the French Riviera; Cerbère
and Hendaye at the Mediterranean and
Atlantic ends of the mountainous Franco-
Spanish frontier; and Pointe de Corsen at
the wave-lashed tip of Brittany. The latter is
the only one of the corners not shared with
another country.
Start // Bray-Dunes
End // Bray-Dunes
Distance // 2741 miles (4411km)

CIRCUIT DE MONACO, MONACO

The most famous Grand Prix circuit is
notoriously hard to overtake on: the
Monaco street circuit was described by
1980s Formula 1 champion Nelson Piquet
as 'like riding a bicycle around your living
room'. If you're not trying to set a lap
record, however, it's an easy ten-minute
ride through a piece of automobile history,
dating from 1929. The route doesn't cover
the principality's full two-mile length, but it
does show off the sights. From the starting
grid near the main yacht harbour, the track
climbs up towards the Casino de Monte-
Carlo, before descending again – with cars
slowing down for the Grand Hotel (formerly
Loews) Hairpin. Soon after, you pass
through the only tunnel racetrack section
on the Formula 1 calendar and emerge
blinking by the harbourside. Two quick right
turns round La Rascasse and Virage Antony
Noghès complete the lap, whether or not
you see a chequered flag.
Start // Boulevard Albert 1er
End // Boulevard Albert 1er
Distance // 2 miles (3km)

THE LONG WAY ROUND, IRELAND

Ideally undertaken as a two-week break,
this trip explores Ireland's jagged, scenic
and spectacular edges, and there's a case
to be made that its dramatic coastlines
are the very best that the Emerald Isle has
to offer. Travelling out of Dublin towards
the North, and then circuiting the island's
northern, western and southern fringes,
here is a journey of splendid scenery,
mountain ranges, traditional villages
and buzzing urban centres, among them
Belfast, Galway, Sligo and Cork. For an
island-within-an-island circuit, explore
the Arans beyond the desolate beauty of
Connemara, and make the seaside village
of Ardmore your final destination, as it's
one of the southeast's loveliest.
Start // Dublin
End // Ardmore
Distance // 807 miles (1300km)

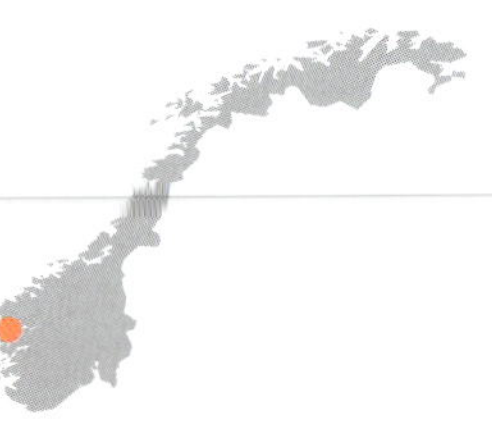

WINDING UP ON NORWAY'S WEST COAST

Norway may not be the cheapest country for a drive, but Peter Thoeming found the upside is you will mostly have its majestic beauty and prize-winning roads to yourself.

Norway means 'narrow way through the straits', rather apt, given the mighty glacial fjords that lacerate its western coast. Admittedly there's not much that's spellbinding as I roll north out of Bergen. The majesty comes later; for now I'm passing the engineering workshops and other small factories serving the oil and gas industry that has made the city rich – again. The charming buildings that surround the harbour are a reminder that Bergen was a successful business centre for many centuries, going back to its days as a Hanseatic port.

I'm riding out in the wonderful, slightly watery, sunshine typical of Norway. As I follow the fjord first east and then north before turning inland again to Voss, the rugged, often vertical countryside begins to work on me, raising thoughts of Vikings and moody gods.

Norway's roads, bridges and tunnels are sparkling examples of their builders' skill and tenacity, but they shrink to scratches on the mile-high cliffs if you look up a little. Whoops! Not enough attention on the road and a long frost break is trying to turn my front wheel

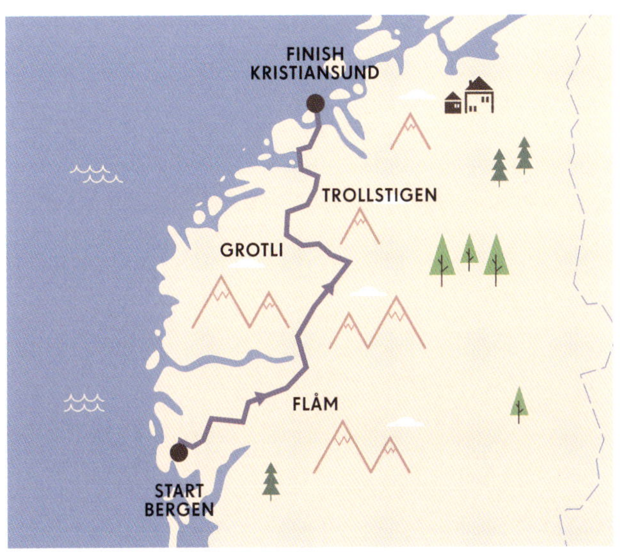

into oncoming traffic. Norway's main roads are excellent, but not all back roads survive the brutal winters unscathed.

I turn north at Voss and then take Stalheimskleiva, the loop of road which runs between two waterfalls and offers 13 hairpins on its mile-long 20-degree climb to the eponymous hotel. It took seven years to build the whole 6 miles (10km) of road, finishing in 1849. The view towards Gudvangen from the hotel is spectacular, with near-vertical cliffs boxing in the narrow green valley bottom.

Not far past Flåm, I face a decision. Carry on straight ahead through the world's longest road tunnel, a 16 mile (28km) marvel, or take the old road across the top? I've ridden through the tunnel before, so the choice is easy. I don't regret it. There are deep snow banks alongside the 30 mile (48km) stretch of narrow, steep and twisting road but its surface is clear and tempts my inner boy racer.

Back at sea level I am speeding along one of the tentacles of Sognefjord. I cross it on a ferry and turn west along its shore before another ferry takes me across to Dragsvik and on to the E39 main road. It's an intoxicating run north and east from here, always either alongside a fjord or crossing a rocky range by hairpins, smooth, long curves and regular blinks of tunnels.

At Grotli I turn west again, and after following the waterside for a while, climb back up to the high, icy country that interrupts the fjords. The drop back down to sea level at Geiranger is a superb stretch of road, which deservedly won a prize at the 1924 World Expo in Paris. Climbing back up from Geiranger is just as impressive. This is Ørnesvingen, the Eagle's Road, and it has a wonderful lookout like a long tongue of concrete at the top.

The high valley before Trollstigen is renowned for its strawberries, and the fields stretch as far as I can see. After a quick visit to Jordbaestova, a café advertising the best strawberry cakes in Norway, I reach the top of the Troll's Ladder. I pull in at the car park and walk to the viewing platform. Piles of stones, balanced on one another, dot the rocks. 'The tourists think the trolls like them,' says a local. 'They don't. Anyway, there are no such things as trolls.' I'm not sure about that. There's one outside the futuristic information centre, with its odd looks combining humour and veiled threat.

The brochure about Trollstigen claims only 11 hairpins for the descent. That may be true in the strictest sense, but it feels like a lot more, as my bike takes me over bridges spanning the white water tumbling the 762 metres to the valley floor, and along short straits with steep drops on one side and more sheer rock on the other. Then it's a short run along Romsdalsfjord and up the peninsula that has Ålesund at its tip. This is a lovely town, best seen from the hill behind its sprawl around the waterways that define it.

There is one more marvel to tackle – the Atlantic Road to the north, on the way to Kristiansund. It's only 5 miles (8km) long, but it squeezes eight bridges into that distance, including the twisting Storseisundet Bridge, which you've probably seen in a car commercial on TV. It's an exhilarating ride, especially when the sea is up, and when I finally reach the long tunnel that will take me to Kristiansund, I'm ready for a beer.

KNOW YOUR LIMITS

Alcoholic drinks are expensive in Norway, so it pays to stock up on duty-free en route. You won't be the only traveller on the ferry with a shopping cart of beer, spirits, wine or magnums of champagne. There is a limit to what you can bring in, so don't be as confident as many locals who believe that no one checks. Find alcohol and tobacco limits at Norwegian Toll Customs (www.toll. no/en/goods/alcohol-and-tobacco/ quotas).

Opposite, clockwise from top: Ornevegen viewpoint over Geirangerfjord; Ålesund; Bergen's shopfronts. Previous pages: the Trollstigen mountain road; Geirangerfjord and the Seven Sisters waterfall

DIRECTIONS

Start // Bergen
End // Kristiansund
Distance // 400 miles (650km), depending on which side roads you take.
Getting there // Take a ferry to Oslo or Kristiansand and ride or drive. Alternatively, take a Hurtigruten ship. These run up the coast frequently and carry both bikes and cars.
When to drive // Between June and August, when Trollstigen is open.
Where to stay // Pre-book hotels or cabins at the many camping grounds.
Visas // Norway is part of the Schengen area. Many Europeans won't need a visa, other nations should check.
Vehicle hire // It can be best to bring your own. It's possible to rent motorcycles and cars (including EVs) but expensive.

*Opposite: the forested Zagorohoria
region of Greece*

MORE LIKE THIS
LESSER-DRIVEN EUROPE

MOLDOVA'S MONASTERY ROUTE

A largely untouristed country, squeezed between Romania and Ukraine, Moldova transports you to its pastoral past beyond the multi-lane mayhem of capital city Chisinau. Headscarved heather vendors stand by the northbound M2, and traffic slows for horses and carts. Take the Ivancea turn-off towards Trebujeni and the scenery transforms from hay bales to ridges of limestone. Encircled by cliffs is Orheiul Vechi, an archaeological complex of cave monasteries. Rejoin the M2 to Orhei for more sacred sites. Turn off to Tipova, a 10th-century cave sanctuary, before continuing to Saharna Monastery, where you can see a treasured relic of the Virgin Mary's footprint. You can hire a car in Chisinau.

Start // Chisinau
End // Saharna
Distance // 100 miles (160km)

CURONIAN SPIT, LITHUANIA

This soothing route rolls from open meadows to the Curonian Spit, a slip of land connecting Lithuania with Russian exclave Kaliningrad. Begin in Šiauliai, site of the Hill of Crosses, where 100,000 crucifixes are amassed as a symbol of Lithuanian identity. Drive west on the E272 until you reach Palanga, the country's merriest seaside town. Then dip south along the Baltic coast to Klaipeda, a port town with a German feel and crammed with waterside taverns. Drive on to a ferry to Smiltyne, then south to Juodkrante, along roads shaded by mighty sand dunes. Pause at Juodkrante's outdoor gallery of pagan sculptures, known as Witches' Hill, then continue to Nida for smoked fish and Baltic beers.

Start // Šiauliai
End // Nida
Distance // 137 miles (220km)

ZAGOROHORIA, GREECE

Mountainous Epirus is largely untouched by the sunshine seekers flocking to Greece. Take the scenic route from Ioannina across Pindos National Park to the Zagorohoria villages of slate and stone, while marvelling at views of the Pindos Mountains. North out of Ioannina, veer east towards the national park. Stop in Dilofo, one of the prettiest of the region's villages. Continue east to Vovousa, and pose by its stone bridge over the Aoös River. At the eastern edge of the national park, roads get smoother (if not straighter). Finish in Grevena, known for weathered churches, forests and tasty mushrooms. Roads are steep and narrow, herds of goats are a distraction and you'll stop for photos by every stone bridge.

Start // Ioannina
End // Grevena
Distance // 100 miles (160km)

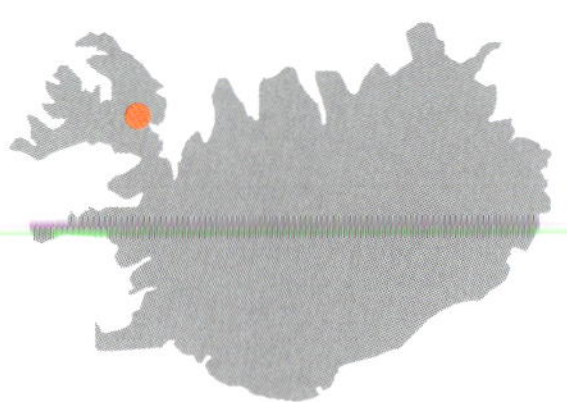

THROUGH THE WILD WESTFJORDS

Ali Wunderman wanted to drive around Iceland's overlooked Westfjords to see if the real and legendary wildlife associated with the region lived up to her expectations.

It's summer in Iceland and the sky isn't giving any indication of what time it is – this far north, the sun is reluctant to set. As I drive into the remote Westfjords region, though, I become grateful for the chance to witness its entirety in sunlight. The scale of the mountains, the depth of the fjords and the proximity of the glittering Arctic waters all load my senses.

The empty, twisting roads are a reminder that, despite Iceland's surge in popularity over the past decade or so, there are corners of the country, the Westfjords being a prime example, that remain relatively undiscovered. The scarcity of other traffic allows me to pull over as I please: to fill my bottle with glacial water flowing freely through volcanic rock; to scoop up a handful of the juicy bilberries that grow wild here; or to admire a pod of pilot whales playing in a narrow fjord they share with just some swans.

My plan is to explore the Westfjords over three days, navigating the fjord-slashed peninsula in search of wildlife. While Iceland is not known for its biodiversity, the creatures that do call the island home are most easily spotted here. Puffins, Arctic foxes and the extremely elusive sea eagle – which only escaped extinction by heading to Iceland's west – are all on my list. But I'm open to creatures of the disputed variety as well – Icelandic culture embraces the supernatural, and though I'm no cryptozoologist, I won't dishonour my host country by refusing to acknowledge an elf or sea monster, should one present itself.

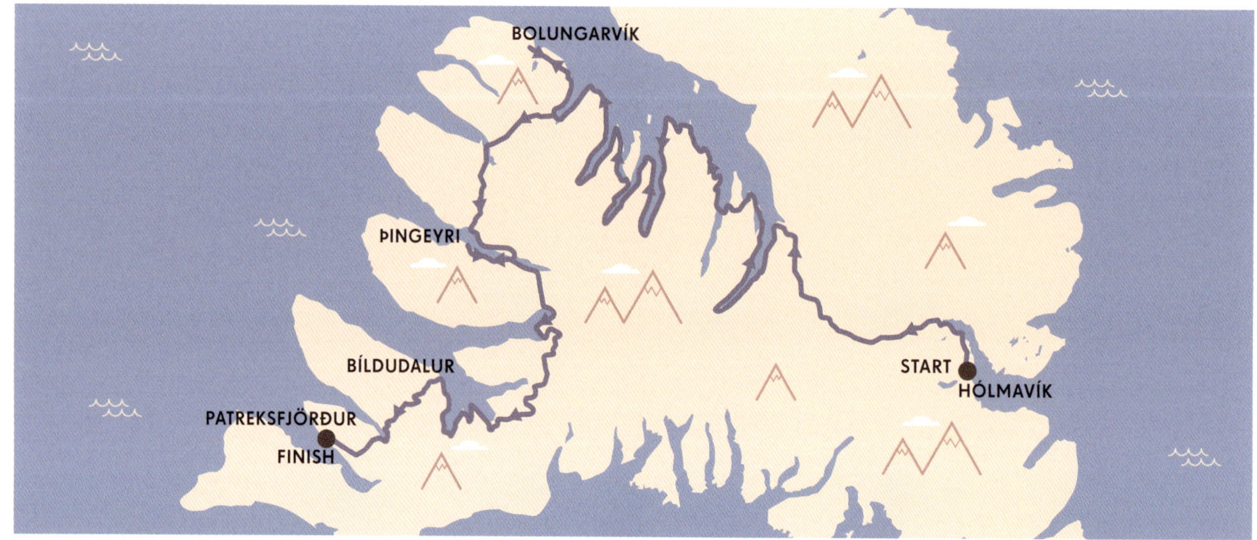

"The scale of the mountains, the depth of the fjords and the proximity of the glittering Arctic waters all load my senses"

The drive will take me through tiny seaside towns, each with a public pool and its own distinct quirks. However, the majority of my time behind the wheel will be through wilderness. The vast emptiness becomes apparent on the route from Reykjavík to Ísafjörður, the largest town in the Westfjords with 2700 residents. When the road splits from Route 1 – Iceland's famous Ring Road – to Route 68 at the Hrútafjörður fjord, Iceland's otherworldliness becomes all-encompassing.

After passing Hólmavík (375 souls), the landscape empties of humans, looking much as it would have when the Vikings first settled here in the 800s. Trees do not grow easily in Iceland, giving the land the look of an immense tundra, even in summer. Arctic grasses poke through ice, eventually making way for mountains with scooped out peaks, known as troll seats by Icelanders. These line the curves of the many fjords between me and my destination. After several hours of following the natural contours of the land, I reach Ísafjörður and my hotel – where I close the blackout curtains, trying to convince my body it's time to sleep.

In the morning I pick up my friend Hákon, an Ísafjörður native who has graciously agreed to accompany me. We begin by heading north to Bolungarvík, a fishing town with a bright orange lighthouse and the Ósvör Maritime Museum, where old turf houses remain for exploration. It's a clear summer's day and Hornstrandir Nature Reserve can be seen far across the fjord. Road tripping to this fabled part of the country isn't possible – a boat to get there and your own legs to get around are the only option – which is too bad since it's the most reliable place in Iceland to spot a wild Arctic fox.

As if to compensate, when we double back towards Ísafjörður I spot a fluffy ball of grey careening through the rocks and grass. We pull to the side and watch as a curious but fearless Arctic fox eyes us up, more focused on finding a meal than evading potential predators. After all, as the only native mammal, they are at the top of the wildlife food chain in Iceland.

We have a lunch of Belgian waffles at an unassuming café called Simbahöllin in Þingeyri, a tiny village (246 people) overlooking the mouth of the Dýrafjörður fjord. Walking around town I come across a shop claiming to specifically repair violins and military tanks, an example of Icelandic humour where the joke teeters on the edge of truth. I like to think people travel from across the world to this small seaside hamlet for all their violin and/or tank repair needs.

The day ends at Dynjandi, the largest waterfall of the Westfjords. The uppermost cascade spreads out like a bride's veil, falling 330ft (100m) before creating six separate waterfalls below, all framed by mossy green banks. Camping is free here, so we set up tents and brace ourselves against the Arctic cold.

Next day, we're back on the road and skirting yet another fjord, this time arriving at the town of Bíldudalur (238 inhabitants) where a road sign warns drivers to watch out for sea monsters – this is where Iceland's equivalent of the Loch Ness Monster has been spotted in the icy waters. Doubtful of spotting one in the wild, I visit the Sea Monster Museum instead, an interactive exhibit that showcases the legends of the local mythical beasts. Stories of wild, terrible creatures play out before my eyes, and I finish my tour relieved that I don't have my own encounter to share.

We detour northwest along the fjord (still no monster sightings) and through dreamlike Lístasafn, a pink-painted open-air museum that was created by Westfjordian artist Samúel Jónsson. Doubling back, we head south past the beached, steel hulk of the *Garðar BA 64* shipwreck and a private collection of US military planes that the owner lets us explore, before reaching the road trip's penultimate destination of Látrabjarg. Here, on the westernmost point of Iceland, are the extraordinary cliffs – over 9 miles (15km) long and 1440ft (440m) high – where millions of seabirds gather: razorbills, guillemots, fulmars, gannets and puffins. We watch the latter stumble to and from the ocean, beaks overflowing with fish for their young, completely disinterested in their human audience.

Our trip ends in Patreksfjörður, a booming village (population 721) with a public pool that overlooks the sea. After the wildness of this journey, we appreciate once again being back among a community of people.

THE WILDER WEST

The Westfjords' wildest peninsula is Hornstrandir, an unpopulated reserve to the north of the region. Tundra dominates the landscape and, thanks to its remoteness and inaccessibility, flora and fauna thrive – you've a good chance of spotting Arctic foxes frolicking among hundreds of different flower species, while the waters swirl with marine life such as whales. Hornstrandir is really only visitable in summer, when boats run from Ísafjörður and companies organise hiking tours.

Opposite from top: the cascades of Dynjandi waterfall (the name translates as 'thunderous'); contrasting, intense colours on the beach at Patreksfjörður. Previous page: an Arctic fox in Hornstrandir Nature Reserve

DIRECTIONS

Start // Holmavík
End // Patreksfjörður
Distance // 360 miles (579km)
Getting there // Keflavík, close to Reykjavík, is the nearest international airport. Internal flights connect to Bíldudalur and Ísafjörður if you don't want to drive from the capital.
When to go // Summer gives the best chance of passable roads, decent weather and long days, but late autumn, before the snow, promises exploration beneath the northern lights.
Further information // Visit Westfjords maintains a well-informed website at www.westfjords.is, as well as an office in Ísafjörður. They are an excellent resource for weather and road conditions, which can change rapidly in the Westfjords.
What to pack // Fleece, raincoat, waterproof walking shoes, thick socks, swimsuit and a towel, binoculars.

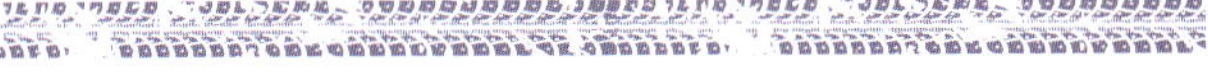

MORE LIKE THIS
WILDLIFE DRIVES

THE STRAIT OF GIBRALTAR &
LOS ALCORNOCALES NATURAL PARK

This trip begins in ancient Jerez, known for
sherry, flamenco and Andalusian horses.
Drive southeast through the Spanish
countryside, past dense collections of
vineyards, and into Los Alcornocales
Natural Park, where fallow deer and elusive
Iberian lynx and European polecats live
among the cork forests. Finally, reach the
Strait of Gibraltar, a narrow channel of
water separating Africa from Europe. It's
one of the sites most visited by migrating
birds as they cross the Mediterranean Sea
every year. Birds of prey such as the griffon
vulture, black kite and honey buzzard are
among 315 total bird species that can be
spotted at this resting area, along with the
likes of bee-eaters and hoopoes to add
vibrant colour to the spectacle. Don't miss
the Rock of Gibraltar, where white storks
can be observed passing overhead from
late summer.

Start // Jerez
End // Gibraltar
Distance // 70 miles (113km)

SCOTLAND'S NORTH &
WEST HIGHLAND ROUTE

Start at the small Highland town of
Ullapool, looking out for the palm-tree-like
cabbage trees that grow here thanks to the
local microclimate. Then hit the coast and
watch for wild seabirds like gannets and the
Atlantic puffin – the topography is similar to
Iceland's Westfjords'. The frigid sea might
just reveal a common dolphin, minke whale
or harbour seal, while the land is home to
other birds like the Scottish crossbill and
western capercaillie, along with red deer,
and – not to be confused with domestic
tabbies – the Scottish wildcat. After the
successful reintroduction of white-tailed
sea eagles, Scotland has become home to
further rewilding efforts, with the once-
native Eurasian beaver and wild boar
now re-established, and lynx potentially
to follow. This drive finishes at tiny but
legendary John O'Groats, with its rainbow
sea-facing buildings and famous 'Journey's
End' signpost.

Start // Ullapool
End // John O'Groats
Distance // 158 miles (254km)

GRAN SASSO E MONTI DELLA LAGA
NATIONAL PARK, ITALY

It's hard to believe anywhere in Italy
could be so untouched by visitors, but
Abruzzo has somehow escaped the
crowds of nearby Rome. The mountainous
Parco Nazionale del Gran Sasso is
predominantly in this central Italian
region, and features jagged mountain
peaks, 2000 plant species and abundant
wildlife, all within one of the largest
protected areas in Europe. Making the
most of this national park will involve
hiking along with road-tripping, a car
being your means to hop between the
trailheads in this widespread area. Rare
animals like the Abruzzo chamois can be
found at altitude here, along with wolves,
golden eagles, brown bears and wild
boar. This is a chance to gain a sense
of what Italy looked like before Roman
civilisation arrived, all without straying too
far from the highlights of the capital city.

Start // Rome
**End // Gran Sasso e Monti della Laga
National Park**
Distance // 104 miles (168km)

EASTERN EUROPE

SLOVAKIA'S STORIED ROUTE 59

Rte 59 weaves together Slovakia's most legendary landscapes. Along this scenic road, Anita Isalska delved into folklore and revolutionary heroics, and met monsters from history and myth.

Rte 59 (the E77) begins with a UFO and culminates at a vampire's lair. It's not your typical itinerary, but this is Slovakia. Villages in this Central European country look plucked from a fairytale, and dark history slumbers beneath the meadows.

Infused with tales of fallen heroes, central Slovakia is a rewarding region to explore by car. Rte 59 winds among some of its most intriguing sights, starting with the town of Banská Bystrica, home to the space-age SNP Museum.

Plotting my route while in the leafy grounds of the museum, it feels as if I am sitting in the shade of the Starship Enterprise. This large dome of concrete and glass is one of the country's most unforgettable brutalist buildings. The SNP Museum within honours the Slovak National Uprising, an anti-fascist rebellion that took place during WWII, and the bloody reprisals that followed. Cradled between the two halves of the dome is a haunting statue that represents the lost, and is illuminated by a coppery shaft of sunlight.

The Slovak National Uprising gathered force right here in Banská Bystrica, but central Slovakia has harboured a spirit of revolution for much longer. Wartime revolutionaries took inspiration from Juraj Jánošík, a 17th-century highwayman who went down in legend for robbing wealthy merchants and sharing his loot with the poor. One partisan group even named themselves after Jánošík. Rte 59 leads me right into the heart of Jánošík's old stomping ground.

The road out of Banská Bystrica heads straight to the mountains, darting between two national parks. Veľká Fatra, to the west of the road, gargles with mineral springs, with spa

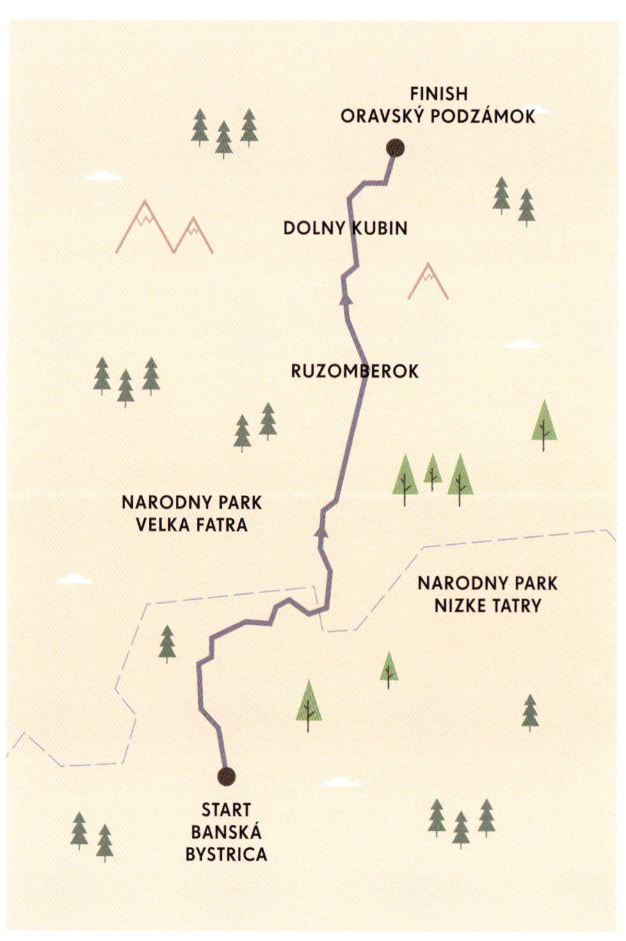

© Marcin Lukaszewicz | Alamy

towns huddled around its western fringe. Spreading east of the road is Slovakia's largest national park, Nizke Tatry (Low Tatras), a 281-sq-mile (728-sq-km) swath of limestone canyons and wind-buffed plains, its valleys furred with maple and beech tree groves. Both parks are thickly forested and dotted with caves: perfect hiding places for a renegade highwayman.

Driving north, my car passes a blur of boxy guesthouses and buttercream-coloured chapels. After an easterly bend, the road is suddenly lined with spruce trees, towering high on both sides. At every bend, mountains whip teasingly into view, only to disappear as I zoom into another corridor of fuzzy greenery. Only the occasional ray of light penetrates, dappling the smooth tarmac in sunshine.

The trees begin to thin out and rockfall litters the road. My car engine whines as the road climbs to reach Vlkolínec, one of Slovakia's most enchanting villages. Here, a congregation of wooden statues startles me into parking my car...

Vlkolínec – which has a population of 19 – is a village of wood-cutters, where wooden statues far outnumber their craftsmen. Hand-carved figures stand guard around the village, most of them illustrating characters from Slovakia's rural past: bread-makers, shepherds, women cradling infants, and the occasional glowering grandmother.

Barely changed since it was founded back in the 14th century, Vlkolínec's 45 houses are painted with jaunty bands of mauve and yellow. Apple trees sway above their dark wooden roofs.

"Clinging to a rocky outctrop, the Gothic towers of Orava Castle rise high above the road – almost like a warning"

Crowning the village is the bell tower of the 1875 Roman Catholic Church of the Annunciation of the Virgin Mary, who gazes out sadly from a stone alcove.

The setting is equally beguiling. Vlkolínec is perched on a hill against a backdrop of the Vel'ká Fatra mountains. Its meadows are flecked with a late bloom of purple marsh orchids and bird's-eye primrose. The valley below is choked by fog. Even the village's name carries mystique: '*vlk*' is the Slovak word for wolf, and I can almost imagine Little Red Riding Hood tottering out of one of the log-lined houses.

Back on Rte 59, I steer past towns that snooze in the shade of mountains. First I pass Ružomberok, once a major trading crossroads, snuggled between three mountain ranges: the Low Tatras, Vel'ká Fatra, and the Choc Mountains. Pressing further north, along roads hemmed by oak trees, I reach another former powerhouse. Dolný Kubín, a medieval quarrying centre, is now resolutely ignored by visitors speeding towards Orava Castle.

Inevitably, this spectacular 14th-century castle is my final destination. For the concluding few kilometres of the road trip, I can see its Gothic towers rising high above the road – almost

SLOVAK SHEEP'S CHEESE

A smoky aroma will tickle your nostrils long before you see a Slovak cheese stall. *Ovci syr* (sheep's cheese) is sold at roadside kiosks. Pungent *bryndza* is a key ingredient in the dumpling dish *bryndzové halušky*. The prettiest cheeses are palm-sized, usually patterned *oštiepky*. *Korbáčiky*, cheesy plaits, and *parenica*, shaped like a snail shell, are moreish snacks. Just beware the lingering cheese odour in your rental car...

From left: beehives in Vlkolínec village; Tatra chamois on a slope in the Low Tatras; Orava Castle; colourful houses of Vlkolínec. Previous page: the Museum of Slovak National Uprising in Banská Bystrica

like a warning. The castle clings to a rocky outcrop above the village of Oravský Podzámok. Thick forest is wrapped around the base of the hill like a cloak.

For a horror movie fan like me, its silhouette is thrillingly familiar. Orava Castle was a filming location for FW Murnau's vampire film *Nosferatu* (1922), a masterpiece of expressionist cinema that is regarded as one of the greatest horror films of all time. The silent movie belongs to an era before vampires became teen heartthrobs that sparkled handsomely under the sun.

Climbing weathered stone staircases, I wander between Orava Castle's grand hallways and chambers. Their walls are decorated with bear skins and coats of arms, and it's all too easy to picture *Nosferatu*'s villain, Count Orlok, scuttling around the fortress. But the castle's horrors aren't confined to the silver screen. Among the successions of aristocrats who moved through these stone walls was Nicolaus Draskovics, a man rumoured to have skinned his servants alive. Also residing here was George Thurzó, the judge who decided the fate of 'blood countess' serial killer Elizabeth Báthory. The infamous Hungarian noblewoman went down in history for murdering hundreds of young women and reportedly bathing in their blood.

These dark legends seem at odds with the glorious serenity of the castle's setting. Peering through embrasures in the castle walls, I can see a tapestry of green meadows rolling towards the High Tatras. But if I've learned anything from this drive, it's that Slovakia's idyllic landscapes conceal its greatest mysteries.

DIRECTIONS

Start // Banská Bystrica
End // Orava Castle
Distance // 56 miles (90km)
Getting there // Slovak capital Bratislava has a convenient airport, 130 miles (210km) west of Banská Bystrica.
When to drive // May to September has the best weather.
Timing // The drive can be done in a day, but it's better to stop halfway. This will allow time for cheese stalls, walks in Vlkolínec, and reaching Orava Castle before closing time.
Where to stay // Ružomberok is a pleasant place to stay the night. Cosy and marvellously friendly Penzión Andrej (www.penzionandrej.sk) is very convenient for drivers.
Tip // The road is cleared of snow in winter and you can ski at Park Snow Donovaly, 17 miles (27km) north of Banská Bystrica, en route.

Opposite: Bran Castle in the
Transylvanian mountains of Romania

MORE LIKE THIS
FOLK CULTURE DRIVES

BRAN PASS, ROMANIA

Careening between fortresses and frozen-in-time villages, Bran Pass is a hair-raising route through Romania's medieval history. Start in the old town of Brasov, where according to legend the Pied Piper of Hamelin emerged in the main square. Drive southwest along Rte 73 to Râsnov, where a maze-like citadel teeters on a high hill, then venture onwards to Bran Castle, whose sharp Gothic towers and forested location have forever linked it with legends of Dracula. Bran, roughly half-way, is packed with romantic places to stay the night; The GuestHouse (www.guesthouse. ro) is a snug but sophisticated choice. The onward drive from Bran to Rucar is as spine-chilling as the folk tales: the road ducks and dives between forlorn country villages, and its hairpin bends overlook the Bucegi Mountains. Drive it between May and October (the Bran–Rucar stretch can be perilous in winter).

Start // Brasov
End // Rucar
Distance // 40 miles (65km)

WOODEN CHURCHES ROUTE, POLAND

Southern Małopolska's churches are Unesco-listed for their unique style and religious art. Locals credit divine intervention with the survival of these all-wooden medieval churches through countless wars. Shaped like dainty wizard's hats, the churches are waystations along an enchanting road trip east of Kraków. Your first stop is Lipnica Murowana, where Gothic St Leonard's Church has stood since the 15th century. Continue east to Binarowa, whose centrepiece is a richly decorated 16th-century church. Dip south to Sekowa's steep-eaved church, which narrowly escaped destruction by fire in WWI, then return north to the main road. A pleasant drive through farming country leads you east to the treasured church of Haczów. It's the largest Gothic-style wooden church in Europe, and a miraculous survivor of Tatar attacks. Finally, trundle into Blizne to see its uniquely decorated log church. For the best weather, set out between May and September.

Start // Kraków
End // Blizne
Distance // 140 miles (225km)

LIVRADOIS-FOREZ, FRANCE

Plunge deep into Livradois-Forez Regional Park via time-honoured folk crafts and cheesemaking. Begin in Vichy, famed for healing thermal waters, and drive south into the verdant hills of Livradois-Forez. Pause in time-trapped Thiers; powered by a thrashing river, artisans have fashioned knives here for over 600 years. Local wisdom insists that when giving a Thiers knife as a gift, the receiver must reciprocate with a coin, to ensure the knife doesn't sever the friendship. Further south, brake in Ambert for creamy blue cheese Fourme d'Ambert, one of France's oldest unchanged cheese recipes. Pull over at La Chaise-Dieu's enigmatic abbey church and finish in Le Puy-en-Velay, where chapels perch on towers of volcanic rock. Stop-offs are part of the fun of this scenic north-south drive: linger in Vichy for spa treatments and allow an overnight stay to fully appreciate Le Puy-en-Velay's green Verveine du Velay liqueur.

Start // Vichy
End // Le Puy-en-Velay
Distance // 100 miles (161km)

CROATIA'S
ADRIATIC HIGHWAY

Alex Crevar celebrates the nearly 400-mile (640km) highway along Croatia's coast, a front-row seat for 1185 islands, an embarrassment of cultural riches and slow-food prowess.

My first brush with Croatia came 20 years ago on the Jadranska Magistrala, or Adriatic Highway, which hugs the country's shoreline from Rijeka, in the north, to the border with Montenegro. It passes nearly 1200 islands, endless vineyards, Unesco sites, national parks and olive groves. But I knew none of this at the time. I was just cruising the sea. On that initial drive, the two-lane ribbon of tarmac – part of the E65 roadway funnelling into the smaller D8 – unfurled beneath my rented, yellow Fiat as I drove between the Dinaric Alps, a string of jagged limestone cliffs teetering above me on one side, and the sea below on the other. Zen-filled open roads, extending to the horizon, would suddenly give way to white-knuckle hairpins and crawling along in first gear as a rainbow of sailboats appeared on the rocky beach below.

In those nascent days as a travel journalist, my sophomoric goal was to choose one of the many secluded villages and hole up in a writer's bungalow. There I would craft something special to stagger my non-existent editors. Salty fishermen sitting in the sun mending nets while puffing cigarettes would be a bonus. Perhaps skiffs would be scattered along a pebble beach, the deep-blue Adriatic slapping at their weathered sterns. I knew I was in the right place when I had to slow to a snail's pace behind a man, rope in hand, coaxing along his donkey loaded with baskets of grapes.

There were fishermen, by the way. And twice each day I joined the procession of villagers filling jugs with fresh spring water that flowed from a pipe sticking out of a rock wall. During those communal moments, I learned of secret beaches, caves,

and where to go for activities I had, until then, not associated with the recently independent country.

Not much has changed, for me, over the past two decades. Every year I use the Adriatic Highway for both business, as a journalist, and for pleasure. However, Croatia is no longer such a secret. But, in many ways, the popularity makes this road of slow discovery even more special.

These days, as time-pressed tourists rush to reach their must-see spots, those with a slower pace in mind, travellers in search of authentic adventure, know different.

© Nino Marcutti | Alamy

"Four Unesco World Heritage Sites crowd the highway, not including the Roman and Hellenic ruins along the route"

'Driving along this highway – or even better, riding on a motorbike – is a great way to experience the diversity of Croatia,' says Veselka Huljic, the general manager of AndAdventure (www.andadventure.com). The Split-based adventure tourism operator offers trips and excursions that include activities such as sea kayaking, hiking and cycling, but specialises in customer-driven, tailor-made tours. 'You can't really get to know the depth of this country until you travel without a schedule,' says Huljic. 'Stop as you please along the coast, take in amazing views of the sea, and hop onto islands to experience culture, the parks, the incredible food and wine. At this speed the country starts to feel like yours.'

Over the years, the Adriatic Highway has become the ultimate insider reference tool for me as I learned about the country's angles and traditions. It would also be a surefire suggestion for the continuous stream of visiting friends and family.

For instance, the highway provides access to five national parks, which each open a window into the character of the coast. Northern Velebit National Park, with sweeping sea views, is a jumping-off spot for long-distance hikers heading into the Velebit mountains, part of the trans-Balkan Via Dinarica trail running from Slovenia to Macedonia. Paklenica National Park, a confluence of sheer canyons, is a famous climbing destination. Krka takes visitors to some of the continent's most beautiful waterfalls. And the island-based Kornati and Mljet National Parks give travellers a sense of the coast's hallmark remoteness.

Four Unesco World Heritage Sites crowd the highway: the Cathedral of St James in Šibenik, the historic town of Trogir, Diocletian's Palace in Split, and Dubrovnik's walled Old Town. Each offers an insight into the timeline of the Adriatic. And this doesn't even include the Roman and Hellenic ruins strewn along the route with such nonchalance that it's common to pass by people milling about atop ancient blocks. The city of Zadar, for example, acts as an open-air museum with the original Roman forum and streets still in daily use.

For those who have heard that Croatia is a gastronomic wonderland, the Jadranska Magistrala is as much a progressive dinner as it is a road trip. The island of Pag in northern Dalmatia is the country's sheep's-cheese capital and specialises in a sort – *paški sir* – that is flavoured by the salty grasses and herbs the animals graze upon. The road then passes through the village of Posedarje, known for its *pršut* (dry-cured ham). Further south, travellers wheel past the Pelješac Peninsula, where drivers-turned-diners pair oysters, pulled directly from the bay moments earlier, with some of the region's best red wine, from a local variety called *plavac mali*.

Two decades ago, the tastes and the images and the notebooks filled with illegible chicken scratch stayed with me long after I pulled off the Adriatic Hwy and returned the yellow Fiat rental. I can't remember if I sold a single magazine story from the trip. I know, for certain, that it was the beginning of my life as a writer. More importantly, the drive changed me forever as a traveller.

REFUELLING

Forget petrol, it is the ingestible liquids on the Adriatic Highway that will rev your engine and rewire your taste buds. All along the drive you'll see roadside stands selling homemade wine, *rakia* (fruit brandy), olive oil and honey. Sure, you can purchase excellent versions of each in a spiffy, labelled, glass vessel. But don't hesitate to sample the rustic versions sold in plastic bottles. They are as fresh and good as any you'll taste on the planet.

Clockwise from left: sheep on Pag island; Croatia's coast road; Prozura locals; looking over Dubrovnik. Previous page: the beautiful Majarska Riviera, north of Dubrovnik

DIRECTIONS

Start // Rijeka
End // Dubrovnik
Distance // 368 miles (593km)
Getting there // Fly in and out of Zagreb, the inland capital, and then drive or take the bus to Rijeka.
When to drive // Avoid the crowds and visit in the shoulder seasons of May to June and September to October.
How to drive // Head north to south, with the setting sun and all of Croatia's 1185 islands to your right.
Where to stay // There is a bevy of hotels and private homestays. The latter are marked with signs and the word 'sobe' (rooms).
Rules of the road // Learn about Croatia's specific laws and where to look for roadside assistance via the Croatian Auto Club (www.hak.hr).

MORE LIKE THIS
WATERY ROUTES

A VENETIAN SOJOURN, ITALY

Pinch yourself, and you might expect to wake from this dream of pink palaces, teal waters and golden domes. Instead, you're in the Veneto, where gondoliers call and water laps at your feet. Scan the coastline and you might spot signs of modern life – beach resorts, malls, traffic. But look closer and you'll catch the waft of fresh espresso from Piazza San Marco's 250-year-old cafés, faded villas on the Brenta Riviera and masterpieces everywhere: Titians in Venice, Palladios in Vicenza and Giottos in Padua. You'll obviously be starting the trip around Venice and Murano by boat, but once on the road you'll be able to access the country retreats of fashionable Venetians in Brenta Riviera, see European architecture change course in Vicenza and prep your camera for Asolo, known as the 'town of 100 vistas' for its panoramic hillside location.

Start // Venice
End // Treviso
Distance // 115 miles (186km)

THE GRACEFUL ITALIAN LAKES

Formed at the end of the ice age, and a popular holiday spot since Roman times, the Italian lakes have an enduring natural beauty. At Lake Maggiore, the palaces of the Borromean Islands lie like a fleet of vessels in the gulf, their grand ballrooms and shell-encrusted grottoes once host to Napoleon, while the siren call of Lake Como draws Hollywood movie stars to its discreet forested slopes. Your drive first clings to Maggiore's shores, from the resort town of Stresa to the dreamy village of Cannobio, before you retrace the pretty 22km to Verbania to board the cross-lake ferry to Laveno. Head on to Lake Como and the elegant town of Como itself, still Europe's most important producer of silk products. After a spectacular drive northeast you'll find it impossible not to be charmed by the waterfront towns of Bellagio, Tremezzo and Varenna, before heading off again down the other 'leg' of Lake Como.

Start // Stresa
End // Bergamo
Distance // 128 miles (206km)

BALTIC SHORES, POLAND

One of the main themes of Poland's historic struggle to define its frontiers has been an often-thwarted yearning for Baltic waves. After both World Wars, Polish armies performed 'Wedding to the Sea' ceremonies to mark recovered sovereignty. There's a poignancy then to a drive along the modern state's full coastline, between the German and Russian borders. Coincidentally, both cut across lagoons on the sea's fringe. Sweeping, sandy beaches cover almost the entire route, beginning in Świnoujście at the western end, and including Wolin and Słowiński national parks. Few roads actually overlook the sea, but you can get just behind the forest-and-dune belt on highways including 102, 215 and 501. Highlights include the old Hanseatic ports of Gdańsk and Kołobrzeg, and seaside resorts such as Sopot with grand hotels of yesteryear. The last stretch, along the Vistula Spit, threads between a wide lagoon and the lapping Baltic.

Start // Świnoujście
End // Krynica Morska
Distance // 292 miles (470km)

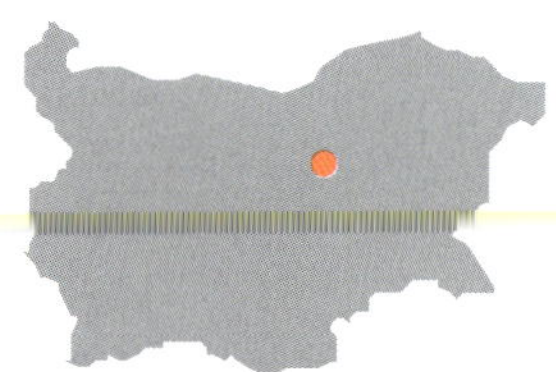

BULGARIA'S FORTRESS ROUTE

Ready to navigate Bulgaria's most thrilling mountain pass? Anita Isalska was, taking this white-knuckle day-drive through the Stara Planina mountains, passing fortresses, ruins and battlefields.

'Rose water is good luck,' insists Radko, as he brandishes a plastic spray bottle. 'I will shower you.'

I'm checking out of Radko's guesthouse, a creaky, wood-beamed den in Veliko Târnovo, but before I hit the road, Radko is summoning the mighty power of rose water to guide my way – whether I like it or not.

He squeezes the trigger, sending fragrant mist directly into my face. I attempt a smile, before discreetly dabbing my eyes with my sleeve.

'The flowers are very powerful, they come from Bulgarian Rose Valley in Kazanlâk,' explains Radko. 'You will drive there.'

Radko turns to his laptop, where he's helping plot out my road trip. The online map suggests a 3hr30 drive, but Radko's assessment is blunt: 'You will drive longer.'

There's more than one way to get from medieval Veliko Târnovo to the ancient city of Plovdiv. The most thrilling route runs southwest, following a serpentine road through the Stara Planina mountains, twisting past hill-top ruins and monuments.

Driving out of Veliko Târnovo, I throw a parting glance towards the town's most famous landmark, Tsarevets Fortress. Wrapped snugly in a bend of the Yantra River, Tsarevets stands as a monument to Bulgaria's Second Empire glory days (12th-14th centuries) – before the country fell under Ottoman rule. My drive will take me to strongholds hidden deeper in Bulgaria's mountainous heart, to secret tombs, forlorn ruins and battle-scarred hillsides.

For the first half hour, I cruise along gentle roads lined with beech trees. I'm slow at reading the Cyrillic alphabet, so I mouth town names on road signs as I pass: So-ko-lo-vo; Sa-la-su-ka; Dry-a-no-vo.

In the latter, a wall of limestone rises out of nowhere. Suddenly my little Fiat is flying through a dark tunnel bored into the rock. On the other side, I emerge in a wilder realm. The road curves and the Stara Planina beckon.

Thirty miles in, I reach the mid-sized town of Gabrovo. Radko had urged me to stop at Gabrovo's House of Humour and Satire museum, so I park and step inside the severe-looking building. After dutifully scrutinising Bulgarian comics and displays on historic gags, while a sole museum attendant scowls in my direction, I start to suspect that the joke is on me.

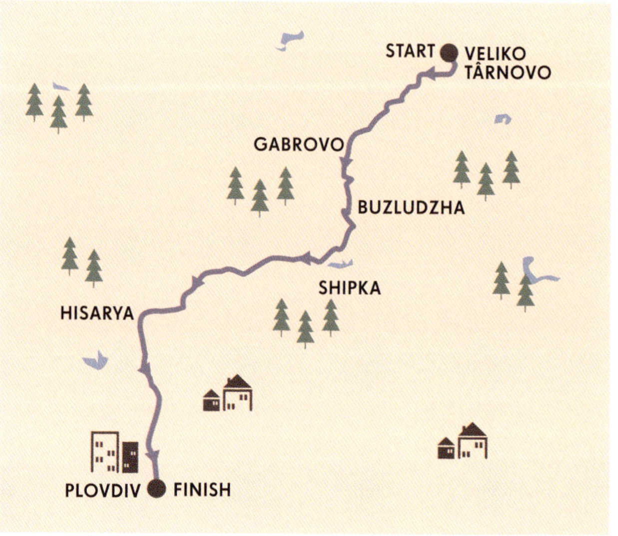

© trabantos | Shutterstock

None the wiser about Bulgarian satire, I buckle up for the next leg of my journey. Almost as soon as I'm out of Gabrovo's suburbs, I'm into a series of unpredictable switchbacks and the engine whines, straining to keep momentum on the ever-steeper incline.

The forest road twists through the mountains and, finally, I emerge to expansive views. Ahead of me spread the Stara Planina foothills, dusky brown in the June sunshine. No sign of human civilisation interrupts my view, until I notice a single castle turret – Bulgaria's Freedom Monument, gazing watchfully from the top of Mt Stoletov (4350ft/1326m).

I pull over and clamber up to the monument. At the top, a tower of granite stands in remembrance of the Battles of Shipka Pass during which more than 7000 Russian troops and Bulgarian volunteers perished in decisive battles against the Ottomans from 1877 to 1878. For locals, the battlefields of this bleak mountain pass stir deep emotions: they're symbols of victory against terrible odds, and the indomitable spirit of everyday Bulgarians.

Back at my car, I steel myself for the most notorious part of the drive, Shipka Pass. The road zigzags wildly, but behind the wheel, I enter a flow state. I steer around tight hairpin bends, barely aware of the groves of spruce trees flying past my window in a blur.

After several intense miles I'm able to ever-so-slightly loosen my grip on the wheel. I stretch my cramping fingers and, one hand at a time, wipe my sweaty palms on my jeans. To my left, silver birch trees are clinging to the mountain's near-vertical flank. To my right unfurls fuzzy green farmland, with Shipka village dead ahead.

I'm ready to sail straight through the village when a flash of colour catches my eye. It's Shipka's Nativity Church. Layered with pink and white and gold, this Russian-style church resembles the most ostentatious of wedding cakes. Rising above the village's otherwise low rooftops, the church is a flabbergasting sight. Complete with five domes and 17 bells that peal from its 174ft (53m) tower, the church was built in 1902 to honour those who died just north in Shipka Pass.

The rise and fall of civilisations – Thracian, Roman, Ottoman – devastated many of Bulgaria's ancient sites, but some treasures remain buried in these hills. This area has been dubbed 'Valley of the Thracian Kings' because of extraordinary excavations hereabouts. Two of them, 4th-century BCE tombs concealed beneath grassy knolls, are instantly noticeable, just south of Shipka's main drag.

Leaving town, I'm tempted to steer east into the Rose Valley, which bursts into bloom at this time of year. But Radko's lucky roses

SCI-FI DETOUR

Sci-Fi-curious drivers can take an hour-long detour along the steep road branching off the E85 between Shipka and Kazanlâk to see what looks like a Bulgarian UFO. A nerve-jangling array of switchbacks leads to Buzludzha, not actually an alien craft but a circular former assembly hall, perched on a 4727ft (1441m) mountain. It's dangerously derelict, so think twice before going inside to see its socialist-era mosaics. Instead, take in the views with a picnic outside.

Clockwise from left: ornate traditional houses near Gabrovo; the Roman theatre of Philippopolis in Plovdiv; harvesting roses. Previous page: glorious views towards Botev Peak in Central Balkan National Park, southwest of Gabrovo

will have to wait. To see the last traces of the day, I must take the meadow-flanked westbound road to Hisarya.

Driving through this ancient city is a treat. The main road follows crumbling Roman walls and pierces straight through a ruined fortress. Plovdiv, just 45 minutes further south, will be my last stop.

In Plovdiv, the common boast is 'Older than Rome, with just as many hills', so after parking up, I make straight for the nearest of those hills, Nebet. The ruins of 1st-century CE Puldin Fortress straggle across the hilltop and locals are balancing on the bastion walls to take selfies in the coppery, late-afternoon light. But I have a more urgent calling than to find my best angle – tired and hungry from the drive, I follow the scent of smoky grilled meat to an open-air restaurant close by.

I have barely settled in my seat when a waiter approaches, handing me a small glass.

'Something special for you,' he says, with a wiggle of his eyebrows. 'Made in Kazanlâk.'

The liqueur is not the usual ice-cold Bulgarian firewater. As I raise it to my lips, a floral scent hits me – this is rose liqueur, heavy and sweet. Wherever the road took me today, Bulgaria's lucky roses still managed to find me.

DIRECTIONS

Start // Veliko Târnovo
End // Plovdiv
Distance // 118 miles (190km)

Getting there // Fly to Sofia or Plovdiv for easy car rental, or take the bus to Veliko Târnovo and hire a driver there.

When to go // Weather from May to June and September to October is ideal for photo ops, with a sweet spot in June when roses bloom. High summer has blazing sunshine and high temperatures. Avoid winter's treacherously icy roads.

Timing // Set out around 9am to time the day perfectly: late-morning rambles at the Freedom Monument; lunch in Shipka; and cruising into Plovdiv late afternoon.

Where to stay // There's abundant accommodation at either end, but stopping in Shipka is a good excuse for mountain hiking; hospitable Shipka It Hotel is a worthy overnight option.

*Opposite, clockwise from top: riverside
Orheiul Vechi monastery, Moldova;
at the Guca Festival, Serbia; bison in
Białowieza National Park, Poland*

MORE LIKE THIS
UNSUNG EASTERN EUROPE

SOUTH TO NORTH IN MOLDOVA

Slice through Moldova, Europe's least-visited country, by driving from capital Chișinău to the church-dotted towns on its northern border with Ukraine. After roaming Chișinău's monuments and having a taste of Moldovan wine, the M2 entices you north. You might be tempted by deeper exploration of wine country – like Cricova's mighty wine cellars – but stay the course and keep going to Orhei. Nearby is ancient Orheiul Vechi, where a riverside monastery and hermit caves have stood for centuries. Pressing on, you'll drive through a string of small towns, including Soroca, locally famous for a 15th-century fortress with four burly watchtowers. Your final destination is 50 miles (80km) further – Ocnița, a sleepy place capped by a glinting gilt-spired Orthodox church.

Start // Chișinău
End // Ocnița
Distance // 147 miles (237km)

EASTERN POLAND'S FOREST TRAIL

Skirting the Poland-Belarus border, this route links farmland and primeval forests, with stop-offs at untouristed villages. Begin in Lublin, an unsung charmer of southeastern Poland, complete with castle, churches and a pretty Old Town. Drive east then north along the 82, parallel to rolling flat farmland en route to the little town of Włodawa. From here, things get more interesting. Heading north, you'll follow the banks of the Bug River, which divides Poland from Belarus, passing whisper-quiet villages as you go. Pause at the Łęg Dębowy Reserve to spot eagles and deer in dense oak forests and allow a little time for Terespol's stately Habsburg history and smattering of ruins. Veering right towards Hajnówka, soon you'll reach an old-growth forest teeming with bison, Białowieża National Park. This Unesco World Heritage Site is a patchwork of swamps, meadows and moss-swathed trees, where Europe's biggest land mammals lumber across the forest floor.

Start // Lublin
End // Białowieża National Park
Distance // 205 miles (330km)

GUCA FESTIVAL, SERBIA

Serbia is one of the most exciting places in the world to hear live music and its throbbing capital, Belgrade, is a great place to start, with all kinds of venues and clubs. But the event that really gets music travellers' pulses racing is the Guca brass band festival, held every year in the small town of Guca in central Serbia. This free festival – yes, that's several days of music, folk dancing and celebration at no cost – happens every August and culminates in a battle of the brass bands where a jury chooses the finest blowers from across the country. The drive from Belgrade to Guca is spectacular and, if all the brass partying becomes too much, you can head into the surrounding countryside where forests and lakes abound.

Start // Belgrade
End // Guca
Distance // 98 miles (158km)

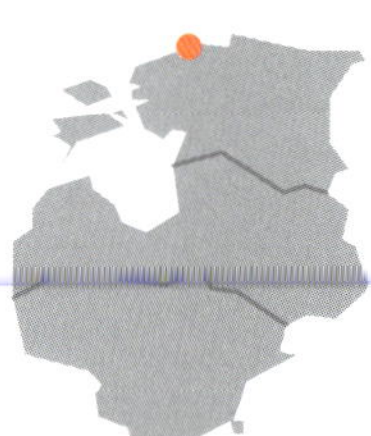

ROVING THE BALTIC: ESTONIA TO LITHUANIA

Brandon Presser drove through the crossroads of several mighty European powers: the Baltic countries twist their own brand of Northern culture with a history steeped in millennia.

At a dinner in Riga over a decade ago, as I pushed around a slab of grey pork and side of boiled potatoes, I learned that the Latvian language – one of the oldest tongues still spoken on the planet – had no word for 'mountain'. The term *kalns*, or hill, serves as the best substitute, as there are no true mountains in the entire region – no borrowed term has been added to the local lexicon. And there's really no need for one: from cobbled alleys of coastal Tallinn to the desolate recesses of the Curonian Spit, the entirety of the Baltic shield is blanketed by an undulating current of towering pine.

The green carpet – unbothered by the brutal winter weather – seems uniform from the car window year after year, no matter how many times I return to visit. But a turn onto a lonely side road reveals thousands of years of fascinating geopolitical history.

Sure, Tallinn, Riga and Vilnius, the triad of Baltic capitals, each stir their own brew of old-meets-new, but it's the countryside – the veritable battlefields of both ancient and modern empires – that narrates a more nuanced history of subjugation and glory.

Latvia's largest national park, the Gauja, follows its namesake river as it snakes between tribal war mounds and medieval castle ruins; I do the same. Subtle bumps in the terrain mark the strongholds of the tribes that waged war in the region over 2000 years ago – archaeologists have uncovered old stones from other parts of the planet lending credence to the notion that the area was an epicentre of global trade.

A rich medieval history comes to life at the rosy-red tower of Turaida Castle and at the ashen stone spires of Cesis castle. In Sigulda, I spot my first Soviet relic – a cluster of tenements and a strange ribbon of concrete. In the cities, the austerity of the

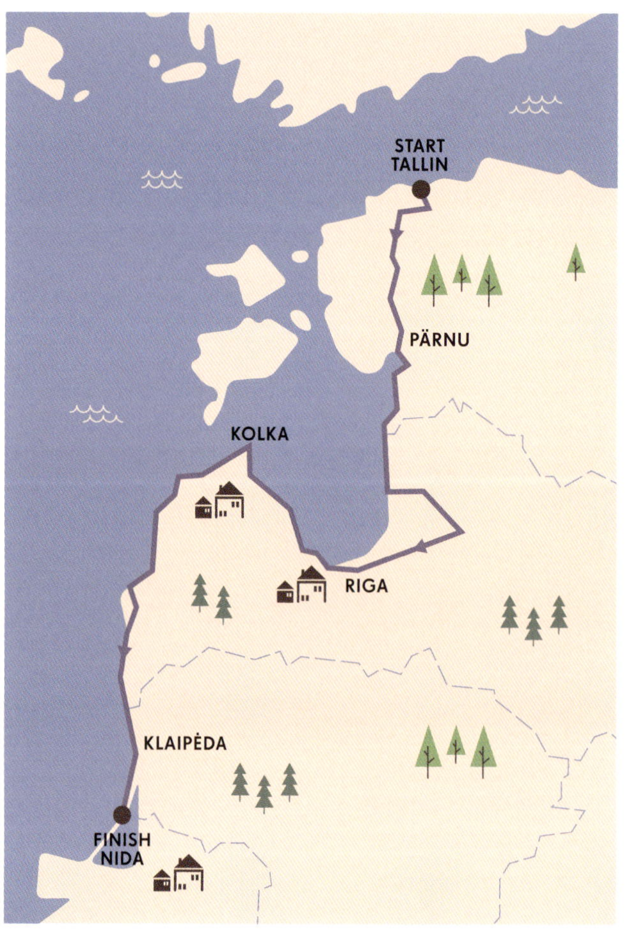

© Evgeny Shmulev | Alamy

architecture seems like an unassuming patch of the urban quilt, but in the forest, surrounded by swatches of deep greens, the structures are shockingly dour.

It was in Sigulda that the Soviet bobsled team trained for international championships, like the Olympics. The facility was abandoned after the fall of the USSR, and today local business owners offer introductory spins on the track with various sleighs.

Following a stomach-churning ride down the concrete corkscrew, I meet up with a friend-of-a-friend who has invited me to his *pirts* (sauna). Like the Finnish, Estonians and Latvians have an elaborate and enthusiastic sauna culture, but without any of the modesty assigned to the ritual by other Western nations.

After a hardy shake of hands, my friend-of-a-friend strips to his birthday suit and lies upwards on the thin birch planks of his pond-side sauna. I follow and an older woman, the sauna master, immediately enters the chamber holding bushels of dried twigs and flowers. What follows is a choreographed dance – almost in nature – as she swishes her branches through the air to raise the humidity then beats us with garlands to open our pores. The branch-beating session lasts some 15 minutes, after which I'm grabbed by the arm and tossed in the chilly lakelet out the door. Lather, rinse, repeat with a splash of vodka and some cured meats, and by the end of the afternoon I feel fully indoctrinated into the Baltic way of life and ready to continue my journey.

The trees continue to march on like noble warriors, save the odd clearing marking a cool, dark lake in the near distance, until suddenly the crash of the frigid Baltic Sea breaks their stride. The

LITGATNE BUNKER

In Latvia's pine forests lies one of the most compelling artifacts from the Soviet Era, lending the land's dystopian history some context. Discovered early this century in the basement of a convalescence home, the nuclear shelter was to protect the highest officials of the Union. And no item has been changed since the 1980s: propaganda scrawled on the walls, levers in the control room, and one single bed – for the senior commandant.

Clockwise from above: Tallinn's colourful facades; blue skies over a Baltic beach; the skyline of Tallinn from Toompea Hill. Previous page: Turaida Castle above the Gauja River

seaside enclave of Jurmala softens the transition between worlds with its cottage architecture and art nouveau flourishes. In the summer months the beach teems with day-tripping Rigans, but out of season the veneer fades on the holiday town, and the so-called sanitariums lie bare along the coast like beached cruise liners.

Latvia's coastline swerves up to a point at Kolka where the Baltic Sea meets the Bay of Riga. A line, where the purple seas lap over the clearer waters of the bay, can be seen from the haunting sea stacks formed by faraway timber. The area was strictly off limits to civilians during the Soviet occupation, and therefore feels lost in time, save the odd concrete wartime watchtower along the shore.

The Cape of Kolka is the indigenous territory of the Livs, or Livonians, one of the ancient regional tribes that guarded their land claims with the legendary ferocity of the Vikings. Today, only a handful of ethnic Livs remain – fewer than a dozen are native speakers – their sea-blue eyes catch your attention as they tend to the small cottages and fish-smoking shacks along the shore.

The solitude of the cape crescendos with activity as I pass through seaside towns. In laid-back Pavilosta locals are zipped to the neck in neoprene, battling the Baltic waves on their kiteboards. Further on, grungy Liepaja provides interesting contrast, with its roaring nightclubs built in old port-side warehouses.

Then the road quite literally comes to an end on the Lithuanian side of the border, and suddenly the Baltic's trademark pines are gone – replaced with a landscape so severe that it feels almost Soviet in nature: a desert. Small vacation villages with adorable chalet-style architecture have popped up where the sand meets the sea, but the vast expanse of dunes, seemingly ripped from the depths of the Sahara, always make me wonder what's more surprising: the lack of Baltic vocabulary for 'mountain' or the fact that locals have seven words for 'desert'?

"The area near Kolka was strictly off limits to civilians during the Soviet occupation and feels lost in time"

DIRECTIONS

Start // Tallinn, Estonia
End // Nida, Lithuania
Distance // 589 miles (948km)
When to drive // June is the optimal month for travel, when the three Baltic nations embrace their pagan roots with celebrations held around the summer solstice; July, August and September remain delightfully busy along the coast as well.
Where to eat // Tallinn offers plenty of hipster hangouts: start with Must Puudel (the Black Poodle); in Riga try upmarket Vincents, which pioneered the down-to-earth food movement that supplanted pork and potatoes and put Latvia on the culinary map.
What to take // Much of the terrain between towns is undeveloped tracts of land, which lends itself well to some blissful camping experiences – pack all the accoutrements for a summertime tenting adventure.

Opposite: Palermo's Norman cathedral, dating to 1185 and converted to a mosque by the Saracens in the 9th century CE

MORE LIKE THIS
HISTORIC COASTLINES

MODERN ART MEANDER, FRANCE

There's a particular kind of magic that happens when you connect with a work of art in the place it was created, and Provence is where many 20th-century artists found their greatest source of inspiration. Cross this photogenic, good-time region and discover its vivid, creative history along the route, not only in the region's stellar art museums, but also the bays, beaches, fields, hilltop eyries, bars and bustling boulevards where the modern masters lived, worked and partied. Bathed in the south of France's glorious ever-inspirational light, and taking in some stretches of gorgeous coast road, appreciate what stimulated Cocteau in Menton, Chagall and Matisse in Nice, Picasso in Antibes, Cezanne in Aix-en-Provence and Van Gogh in Arles. Permanent galleries and museums dedicated to these artists, and many more besides, are found in the fine towns and cities lining this beautiful drive.

Start // Menton
End // St-Rémy de Provence
Distance // 211 miles (340km)

ALNWICK TO LINDISFARNE, ENGLAND

This picturesque route drinks in Northumberland's panoramic coastline, one of Britain's best-kept secrets. Drive from the pretty market town of Alnwick, north up the A1 and across to the Holy Island. Before setting out from Alnwick, visit Barter Books. Sited in an old Victorian railway station, Barter is one of the largest second-hand book stores in Europe and a veritable wonderland. Its café also serves the best fruit cake in England, bar none. En route to Lindisfarne, the views to the passenger's side are a bucolic delight of rolling hills and moorland and on the driver's side serve up the dramatic spread of the North Sea. There are also three of the UK's best-preserved castles to visit: Alnwick, made famous by the *Harry Potter* films; Bamburgh; and Lindisfarne, which is hauntingly evocative. Lindisfarne is only accessible by car at low tide, so check the tide times before departing *and* making the return journey. It's worth noting also that Lindisfarne Priory is closed from November through January.

Start // Alnwick Castle
End // Lindisfarne Priory
Distance // 35 miles (56km)

WONDERS OF ANCIENT SICILY

A Mediterranean crossroads for 25 centuries, Sicily is heir to an unparalleled cultural legacy, from the temples of Magna Graecia to Norman churches made kaleidoscopic by Byzantine and Arab craftsmen. This trip takes you from exotic, palm-fanned Palermo to the baroque splendours of Syracuse, once the largest city in the ancient world, and lava-black Catania. On the way, you'll also experience Sicily's startlingly diverse landscape, including bucolic farmland, smouldering volcanoes and long stretches of aquamarine coastline. Fifty miles (80km) along the A29 from your start at Palermo, Segesta's huge Greek temple is a magical site, while further around the winding, undulating coast road you'll arrive at the ruins of ancient Akagras at Agrigento. Awaiting you at the conclusion of this panoramic trip is the perfect horseshoe-shaped Greek theatre at Taormina, suspended between sea and sky, with glorious views to brooding Mt Etna through the broken columns.

Start // Palermo
End // Taormina
Distance // 368 miles (592km)

© Gurgen Bakhshetyan | Shutterstock

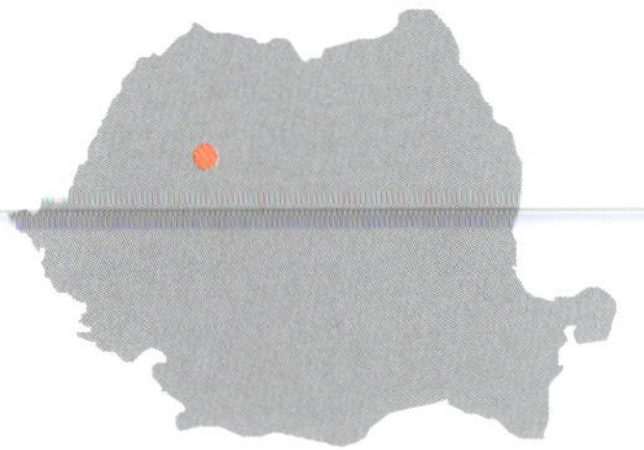

A TOUR OF TRANSYLVANIA

Wanting to go beyond Transylvania's 'vampire tourism', Garth Cartwright took a drive that revealed a diverse Romanian region in the shadow of the Carpathian Mountains.

Back in 1897, Bram Stoker's *Dracula* put Transylvania on the map, and since then the region has been synonymous with vampires and the blood-sucking count. Yet this huge stretch of Romania includes much else to discover, from historic cities, towns and villages to mountains, lakes and rivers.

Transylvania begins in the west at Romania's border with Hungary and ranges as far north as Ukraine and east to Moldavia. Historically multicultural, with Romanians, Hungarians, Saxons, Roma and other small ethnic groups living alongside one another, it has often been fought over. Romania asserted ownership after WWI and Hungary took control during WWII, but Romania was definitively awarded the region under the 1947 Treaty of Paris.

Ruled by pro-Nazi fascists during WWII, who murdered almost all members of the nation's Jewish communities, and then by communists, Romanians experienced much bleakness in the 20th century. And yet Transylvania emerged from the worst of the carnage with so much that had characterised it for centuries still intact.

In a place of so many opportunities, the challenge is deciding where to start. I will be driving the route with Mona, a German friend, and we choose to meet in Târgu Mureş, a small, welcoming and characterful city in central Transylvania, with fin de siècle Austro-Hungarian palaces and a blend of different communities.

The following morning we head out for Sighet in Maramureş, Transylvania's northernmost area, and as we drive up the highway the region's charms became more evident, turning ever more rural, all rolling hills, small farmsteads and picturesque villages. In late summer we sense a life dictated by the seasons, with families tossing freshly-cut grass into cupcake-shaped formations which, once dry, will provide fodder for cattle through the winter. Men with long scythes over their shoulders walk the roads and paths, while those building the hay cones use long rakes to gather the grass and pitchforks to toss it high. It is a strikingly archaic scene which wouldn't look out of place in a Dracula movie.

The next day we make a short drive west to Săpânţa, a small town right on the border with Ukraine. We stroll through the Merry Cemetery, its graves decorated with blackly comic painted markers that reveal the cause of death of those buried here. The rest of the afternoon is spent visiting villages that hint at how European peasant life once was, and walking through more idyllic countryside.

The third day finds us driving east along the edge of vast Maramescu National Park, the road rising and falling through dense forests. Roadside stalls sell delicious local honey, salami and fresh produce. We stay the night in Piatra Neamț, a compact, handsome city that is a pleasure to explore, then head southwest the next morning to Sighișoara, a 14th-century walled Saxon town. Within those walls the pedestrianised centre contains a remarkable series of centuries-old towers. The town's history also includes a claim to fame as the former home of Vlad Dracul – the cruel warlord whose name Stoker borrowed for his novel's antagonist. Mona is fascinated by the Saxon contribution to Transylvania, recalling that when she was at school, a girl from Romania arrived in her class who spoke old German with a strange accent. Turns out that the communist dictator Nicolae Ceaușescu exchanged Transylvania's Saxons with Germany for hard currency during his rule, and few remain today.

We rise early the next morning and drive directly south to tackle the Transfăgărășan Highway, dubbed by locals as 'Ceaușescu's Folly'. Although I'd visited Transylvania several times before, I'd never driven the Transfăgărășan. My interest had been piqued by a claim made on the TV show *Top Gear* that this is 'the best road in the world'. I took the bait, and so up – and up and up – we go. Rising to an altitude of 6699ft (2042m), the road zigzags across the southern Carpathians, its route determined by the paranoid Ceaușescu who saw it as a defensive military road in case the Soviets invaded Romania (as they had Hungary and Czechoslovakia). The fact that extreme weather closes this highway from late October to early June apparently wasn't taken into consideration.

The surrounding landscape is bleak, even in summer. At the top is a car park packed with stalls selling pastries, boiled corn, cheese the size of cannonballs and a multitude of smoked meats. Romanians now choose to ride the Transfăgărășan as a holiday activity – peering down we can see large tour buses awkwardly picking their way up the mountain side. We want to drive on, leaving Transylvania and the buses behind, but being low on gas and seeing an empty, petrol-station-free landscape ahead, we decide we have to retrace our route – and find ourselves stuck in a mountain traffic jam. Crawling our way down, we pick up two Polish hitchhikers. They are happy we are heading to Sibiu, and only say of their time camping in these mountains: 'It was enough. Now for the city.'

Another Saxon beauty, Sibiu is a small place with a lively atmosphere. Here we dine well on grilled meats accompanied by dark beer and *palinka* (a fruit brandy). A folk festival is underway, with locals wearing embroidered outfits and dancing the *hora* – a circular dance where everyone holds hands. Meanwhile, a Roma trio whips up magic on the violin, accordion and cimbalom. The music of Transylvania's marginalised minority is a highlight of this mysterious, tantalising, pleasingly vampire-free region, unusual in Europe for its preservation of such traditional experiences.

WAVING A LIFT

Extra care is needed when driving in Transylvania: horses and carts share the roads with cars, and locals often drive at some speed. With poor public transport and generally low wages, hitchhiking remains a common mode of getting about in rural Romania (a hand waved downwards, rather than a thumb stuck out, is the symbol). While caution should always be exercised, lifts are always appreciated and are a good way to engage with locals.

Opposite: roast pork and potatoes, often served with palinka (plum brandy); farmland in Maramures. Previous page: an aerial view captures the many twists of the Transfagarasan Highway.

DIRECTIONS

Start // Târgu Mureș
End // Sibiu
Distance // 660 miles (1063km)
Getting there // Transylvania has several airports – including Cluj-Napoca, Târgu Mureș and Brașov – with regular connections to West European cities. Daily trains from Bucharest and Budapest stop at several regional stations. Romanian airports have car rental – but at many you'll have to return the car to where it was rented to avoid a hefty fee.
When to go // Late March to early November will find most roads open – except the Transfăgărășan Highway – and plenty of activities on offer.

Tip // English is widely spoken in tourist areas and big cities, less in villages and towns. Romanian is a Latin language so a working knowledge of French, Italian or Spanish can help.

*Opposite from top: Fort Lovrijenac
in Dubrovnik, Croatia; dancing the
flamenco on the Plaza de Espana
in Seville, Spain*

MORE LIKE THIS
FOLLOW THE MUSIC

BELGRADE TO OHRID,
SERBIA & NORTH MACEDONIA

This road trip takes you down the spine
of the former Yugoslavia. From start point
Belgrade, Serbia's capital, to the finish in
Ohrid, a lakeside city in North Macedonia,
you can hear traditional Balkan music all
the way. Belgrade is a large, busy place
with brutalist buildings and a vibrant
club scene. Leaving here you drift south,
stopping for lunch in Niš, a dusty but
engaging city that is the gateway to the
southern Balkans and home to a statue
of the late Šaban Bajramović, a legend
amongst Roma musicians. A night in
Skopje, North Macedonia's capital, allows
for exploration of its rock, jazz and folk
music scenes. The journey to Ohrid winds
through hills and ends at one of Europe's
most delightful small cities where, in
summer, you can attend jazz festivals and
hear folk music in restaurants.

Start // Belgrade
End // Ohrid
Distance // 388 miles (624km)

SPLIT TO SARAJEVO,
CROATIA & BOSNIA

From the port of Split to Bosnian capital
Sarajevo, drive a route that allows both
for reflection on the violent dissolution of
Yugoslavia and immersion in the music
of the region. Split is a lively small city
with Roman ruins. In summer, acts from
rock bands to turbo folk stars ply their
trade here. The coast road south is one of
Europe's most attractive drives, winding
around bleached cliffs, through fishing
villages and across a small section of
Bosnia and Herzegovina to Dubrovnik,
the walled Venetian city that is now often
crowded with tourists – and some fine local
buskers entertaining them. Head inland
and soon you cross the border into Bosnia
and Herzegovina again, chugging up
mountain roads towards beautiful, battered
Sarajevo, the epicentre of *sevdah* music,
folk songs that are the sound of Bosnia's
soul. There's also rock, jazz and dance
music to enjoy in this energetic capital.

Start // Split
End // Sarajevo
Distance // 290 miles (466km)

SEVILLE TO MÁLAGA

This drive could be called 'the flamenco trail'
as it hits several of the centres for flamenco
in Andalucía. Seville is a striking regional
capital, alive with flamenco bars and wide
boulevards. Heading south, the road leads
directly to Jerez de la Frontera, a busy
city that has developed greatly in recent
decades yet proudly claims to be where
flamenco singing began. Further south you
hit the port of Cádiz, raw, full of character
and one of Europe's oldest continuously
inhabited cities. It was also once home to
the late Camarón de la Isla, considered the
greatest flamenco singer of all time. From
here, drive inland through Los Alcornocales
National Park and then east to the seaside
city of Málaga, where you'll find flamenco
and much else to enjoy, including a museum
dedicated to native son, Pablo Picasso.

Start // Seville
End // Malaga
Distance // 221 miles (355km)

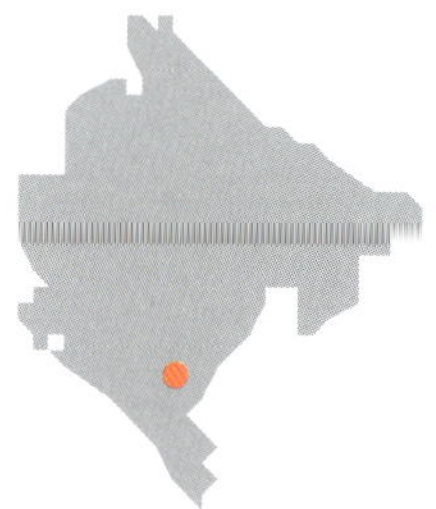

MONTENEGRO'S CANYONS AND COASTLINE

Touring Montenegro's contrasting terrains, Christina Webb followed hairpin bends into canyons by ancient monasteries in the north and cruised above the shimmering Adriatic in the south.

One day I'm trudging through a knee-deep blanket of undisturbed snow in a dense spruce forest. On another I'm gazing out at an azure pool against a backdrop of mountains descending seamlessly into the water, the sun warming my shoulders.

It's hard to resist the lure of Montenegro's sparkling southeastern shores, but the shroud of mystery surrounding the nation's unsung north and the promise of contrasts has piqued my curiosity. So, instead of following the coastal route from the capital, Podgorica, I take the E80 the opposite way, up to Kolašin.

For May it's unusually warm here. Traffic is scarce, but caution is still required – with no national highways to follow, the only option is to tackle the country's narrow, winding old roads. The start is ambitious. My route has gained notoriety for its precarious passes. I'm thrown onto the challenging roads that carve through the Morača Valley, with the sky kissing the rocky walls alongside and turquoise water rushing through a 1312ft-deep (400m) canyon below. I stare meekly over a sheer drop – of the sort that will come to typify my journey – and marvel at how small my rental car feels.

As the roads widen and I catch my breath again, Morača Monastery emerges into view. An imposing and well-preserved Serbian Orthodox masterpiece, it comprises two fresco-filled churches that have decorated the valley of the Morača River for eight centuries. Livestock amble through the courtyard as I join a handful of visitors to step inside and gaze at the murals.

After a lunch of local trout in a rustic restaurant by a watermill, I reach the mountain resort of Kolašin – at this time, with summer approaching, a ghost town. With ski season well past, I feel like the only tourist for miles. My first evening on the road is spent warming my hands over a fire pit, accompanied by the distant rustle of trees and chirp of wildlife, before I hit the hay in an unusual hand-crafted chamber – one of a succession of mushroom-shaped buildings that line the hilltops, built single-handedly by a resident of the town.

Next morning, I set off early towards Biogradska Gora National Park, one of the few remaining virgin forests in southeastern Europe. The precious absence of human manipulation of this environment is clear on my short hike around pristine Lake Biograd.

I head northwest towards Durmitor National Park, the road becoming progressively more dramatic with every bend, hitting a

peak with the impressive Tara River Canyon – at 4265ft (1300m) to its base, the deepest in all of Europe. I lurch on through the mountains into the heart of Durmitor, taking a pit stop to admire the view from Đurđevića Tara Bridge, arched high above the choppy Tara River. I look on, content to be a mere observer, as various thrill-seekers strap themselves in ahead of rafting the gorge.

Swinging right, I continue on the still-winding main road to Žabljak. With not a lot going on even in high season, this calm small town is just the place to rest after a day of driving. The landscape brings with it a smattering of snow in the low fields and a full blanket over the mountains skirting the horizon.

The following day my footsteps crunch through the wintry floor of a forest of pines, as I meander towards the Black Lake. With no fellow humans or signs around to help point the way, the lake's sudden appearance through an opening in a glade catches me by surprise, the inky surface of its glacial waters both brooding and deeply reflective. Feral dogs roam Durmitor National Park, and I am joined by an unexpected, yet charming, crew of them. We trundle contentedly along a deserted 2 mile (3.2km) track that weaves on through the forest, reaching my base for the night as the light starts to dwindle.

"I drive challenging valley roads, with the sky kissing rocky walls alongside and turquoise water rushing through a deep canyon below"

Leaving the north behind, I turn south towards Montenegro's Central region in pursuit of the famed Ostrog Monastery. My urge to visit means an additional hour behind the wheel, but the twists and turns to get here make for a fun driving challenge. As the road opens up and I glimpse a blindingly white monastery on the cliffs, I know the detour was entirely justified. Located at 2953ft (900m), the gravity-defying construction is as arrestingly beautiful as it is somehow miraculous. Built as a refuge from the Ottoman Empire, the monastery became an important site for pilgrims of predominantly Serbian Orthodox faith, but also for Catholics and Muslims. I'm surrounded by more people here than I have seen in days. I step inside cave chapels and admire golden frescoes adorning the rocks within – they vie for attention with the views of a brilliant, expansive sky from the terraces.

BAY VILLAGES

While it's easy to lose yourself in Kotor town, the bay's villages tempt with scenic views and striking architecture. Hike tranquil Stoliv's olive groves enjoying stirring panoramas of Kotor's Old Town or drive out 7 miles (12km) to Venetian-style Perast. The village is home to over a dozen churches in a cohesive Baroque design and a speckling of small islands, including the arrestingly picturesque, church-clad Our Lady of the Rocks.

From left: Perast on the Bay of Kotor; rafting on the Tara River; at the Ostrog Monastery; a statue in Podgorica. Previous page: serene Lake Biograd in Biogradska Gora National Park

Back behind the wheel I continue south, reaching Kotor Municipality in a little over an hour. I merge onto the coastal route, swinging round a sharp bend to see a flash of deep blue from the sea. As I pull up to peer over the glimmering Bay of Kotor, undulating villages can also be seen perched beyond. My route now descends to track alongside the bay, and I have the sense that it's just me alone with the water.

Arriving in Kotor, I take my bearings in the resplendent Old Town. I climb 1300-plus steps to the top of fortifications in the shade of the early morning, and sample seafood delicacies on sunny terraces. Although I plan to spend the next few days resting here, for the moment I'm eager to get back in the driver's seat and dedicate the afternoon to exploring further.

I embark on an exhilarating finale, tackling a famed course of hairpin bends – 25 of them lead up from the bay towards Mount Lovćen. Each dizzying turn is marked with a sign-posted number and a deep sigh of relief from me. As I gain elevation, the rewards are delivered in the form of unbeatable panorama after panorama. The clouds start to creep closer, so I turn back to chase the views before they disappear entirely – these mountainous Montenegrin vistas have become a little addictive.

DIRECTIONS

Start // Podgorica
End // Kotor
Distance // 250 miles (400km)
Getting there // Fly into Montenegro's capital city, Podgorica, where rental cars are available.
When to go // June to September is peak season in the south; November to March is high season for skiing in the north. Consider driving in May and October to avoid crowds; it's warm enough to both soak up the sun in the Bay of Kotor and find the main roads in the north free from snow.
Tip // Northern Montenegro is still a relatively novel region for non-skiing visitors, so expect to see few tourists and hotel closures if visiting in the warmer months. This means it's a good idea to book car rental from the capital and your accommodation in the north before your trip.

MORE LIKE THIS
MOUNTAINS TO WATER

NAVIGATING THE FJORDS, NORWAY

Located just thirty minutes from Bergen, Osterøy, Europe's largest inland island, gives a swift but satisfying introduction to Norway's fjords. Take the singular gateway to the island, the E16 over Osterøy Bridge, enjoying 360-degree views of deep blue waters and sheer cliffs. Traditional island life endures here despite proximity to Bergen's cosmopolitan charms – Osterøy's fondness for craftsmanship and ancient customs can still be seen in relics of moss-clad stone settlements and the island's proudly displayed open-air museum. Head northwest after the bridge to visit the 17th-century Hamre Church on the grassy slopes of Osterøy's west coast, erected where fjords from each cardinal point meet, or turn east after the bridge and drive to Bruvikvegen at the foot of Bruviknipa Mountain, where a 1.5 mile (2.5km) hike to its sheer rock face gives impressive views of the Sørfjorden Valley.

Start // Bergen
End // Osterøy
Distance // 44 miles (70km) including either detour to Hamre Church or Bruviknipa Mountain.

BALKAN CITY-HOPPING

This drive is bookended by the experiences of sipping Balkan-style coffee in the alcoves of cobbled Sarajevo, listening to the morning call to prayer, and dining al fresco in Dubrovnik, with the sun setting in the background. From Sarajevo, head into Bosnia and Herzegovina's mountain valleys and over the narrow Neretva River at the rafting sweet spot of Konjic. Cruise alongside emerald-green Lake Jablaničko, set against the highlands of Mount Prenj. The route rolls on to Bosnia's most photographed sight: Mostar Bridge. Gasp at locals leaping into the water below. Continuing south across the border you arrive at Vjetrenica and Croatia's largest cave network, believed to stretch all the way to the Adriatic. Then meet the sea as you descend onto the Adriatic Highway, loop the bay of Mali Zaton and smile as magnificent Dubrovnik comes into view.

Start // Sarajevo
End // Dubrovnik
Distance // 164 miles (264km)

NORTH MACEDONIA
FROM NORTH TO SOUTH

Start in North Macedonia's capital Skopje before driving west to Tetovo for a visit to its Painted Mosque. Head southwest, skipping the main highway in favour of the older R1206 road that snakes through sublime Mavrovo National Park. Park up and walk to the banks of Lake Mavrovo to look for St Nicholas, an abandoned church famously submerged in its depths. Expect this sight to be at its most remarkable at the end of a hot summer, when the lake has been known to dry up. Back on the road, swing by one of the most atmospheric monasteries in North Macedonia, Saint Jovan Bigorski, and the Duf Falls, near the village of Rostuša. Drive along the crystalline Radika River and Lake Debar, to arrive at last on the shores of glorious Lake Ohrid. Named the 'Jerusalem of the Balkans', the city of Ohrid once had 365 churches.

Start // Skopje
End // Ohrid
Distance // 128 miles (206km)

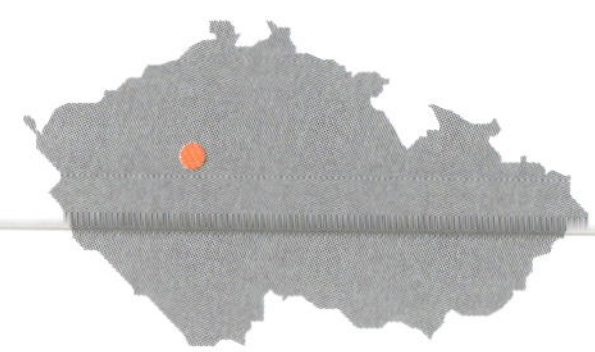

A BOHEMIAN BEER LOOP

Some of Europe's most storied beers attracted Brett Atkinson to Bohemia in the Czech Republic,
with a charismatic blend of historic and spa towns making the drive all the more appealing.

'm in Prague. To begin this drive and head west into central Bohemia, the efficient way to leave the Czech capital would be through the Strahov Tunnel, travelling for 1.25 miles (2km) beneath football stadiums, shopping centres and suburbia. My preferred exit route, though, is slower and significantly more labyrinthine – and presents a cinematic showcase of the best of the 'City of 100 Spires'.

Crossing the Vlatva River on the Mánes Bridge, to my left is the elegant pedestrians-only profile of Charles Bridge, in front the towers of St Vitus Cathedral crown Prague Castle's sprawling city-within-a-city, and on the western horizon the Petřín Tower channels a compact version of the Eiffel Tower. Despite so much to look at, I stay focused on sticking to the right and let Prague's fleet of red-and-white trams trundle safely down the middle of the road. After driving through the leafy Chotovy Gardens, another quieter tree-lined detour leads me through the park framing the northern edge of Prague Castle, then I link to the main road west at Patočkova.

From Prague to the spa town of Karlovy Vary it's a journey of around 78 miles (125km), travelling through farmland and rural villages. Pastel-coloured Art Nouveau hotels and apartments line the Teplá River, and I pause to stroll along Karlovy Vary's narrow valley, past graceful colonnades to thermal springs that have attracted visitors for decades. Preferred local form is to sip Karlovy Vary's therapeutic, mineral-rich waters with a side order of crisp, sweet wafers known as *oplatky*, but I'm looking forward to a different spa experience – with a different beverage.

Continuing from Karlovy Vary, I drive south to Chodová Planá, where I'm immediately drawn to a sign espousing 'Beer Wellness

Land' outside the town's 19th-century family-owned brewery. The zesty aroma of Czech hops fills the air, and I'm soon trying the brewery's signature beer spa activity – a combination of relaxing in a warm bath of beer infused with fresh hop flowers while sipping on a tall glass of Czech lager. Factor in the experience of being wrapped in warm towels for a natural sauna in granite tunnels dating from the 12th century, and 'Beer Wellness Land' is the kind of place I'd happily move to.

To the southeast, local *pivo* (beer) is also the focus at my next stop in Plzeň, known as Pilsen in German and the 1842 birthplace of the easy-drinking pilsner beer style now enjoyed around the

world. After exploring Náměstí Republiky, the city's sprawling main square, I cross the Radbuza River to the Pilsner Urquell Brewery and continue my Czech beer pilgrimage. Joining a tour, I learn about the history of one of Europe's most famous breweries, before enjoying a taste of fresh *pivo nefiltrované* (unfiltered beer) in Pilsner Urquell's historic fermentation cellars. Packed with a citrusy punch, it makes ordering another glass at Plzeň's Na Parkánu pub an easy decision for later in the evening.

Continuing southeast the following morning, rural backroads lead to Český Krumlov. My early start from Plzeň is rewarded by being able to explore one of Europe's best-preserved medieval towns, before the influx of day-trip visitors arrives from Prague. Topped with an imposing castle and centred on an elegant main square framed by Renaissance and Baroque facades, Český Krumlov is a superb place to wander. My meanderings across pedestrian bridges around the twists and turns of the Vltava River lead me to the historic Eggenberg brewery. On a previous visit, this was my disembarkation point after canoeing down the river – today I'm perfectly happy to just enjoy a cold beer in the southern Bohemian sunshine.

Driving north from Český Krumlov, it's a short journey to České Budějovice, crossing the Vlatva a couple more times, through a rolling landscape of hills and more historic towns. En route, the forests of the Blanský Les protected region are popular for spring and summer hiking, but my focus is on Bohemia's other famous beer town. České Budějovice is known as Budweis in German, and the city's famous amber liquid provided inspiration for the

CRAFT BEER

Balancing its long brewing heritage, the Czech Republic is also home to a new breed of craft brewers more influenced by contemporary beer styles, including pale ales and IPAs. Visit the Craft Beer Spot or ALE! Bar in Prague to discover what's new from brewers including Sibeeria, Pivovar Chroust and Pivovar Clock. Regional brewpubs to explore on this journey include Pivovar Raven and the Brewhemian Beer Bistro in Plzeň, and Pivovar Solnice in České Budějovice.

Clockwise from above: enjoying a glass of cold pilsner-style beer; the spooky chandelier in Sedlec Ossuary, Kutná Hora; the medieval town of Ceský Krumlov. Previous page: Prague's pedestrian-only Charles Bridge

American beer Budweiser (in truth, the locally-brewed Budvar is far superior to the anodyne flavours of US-style 'Bud'). I readily sign up for another brewery tour before dinner at the popular Budvarka beer hall. It's always good to have a theme for a road trip, and this journey's hoppy focus – with overnight stops for sampling – is hitting the spot.

North from České Budějovice, my interest switches back to history in the intriguing town of Tábor. Founded by the militant followers of Jan Hus, a 14th-century religious reformer, the Hussites who first established the town were passionate non-conformists, giving rise to the word 'bohemian' in modern parlance. Radiating randomly in zigzag fashion from Tábor's main square, the fortress town's web of streets, lanes and alleys was designed to make it difficult to attack. It confuses modern-day invaders, too – on a couple of occasions I'm forced to ask for guidance from 21st-century Bohemians in negotiating their historic maze and relocating my rented Škoda Fabia.

Continuing north from Tábor, the town's compact footprint contrasts with my final destination, Kutná Hora, before the return leg to Prague. Made rich through silver mining, this place was once a legitimate competitor to Prague as the financial heart and soul of Bohemia. The magnificent 14th-century Gothic Cathedral of St Barbara dominates the now-sleepy town and hints at what might have been. I visit Kutná Hora's other essential sight, the Sedlec Ossuary, where the bones of more than 40,000 people have been used to craft a remarkable homage to both life and death, including an especially spooky chandelier made entirely of human bones. Simultaneously poignant and macabre, this is a bewitching location to draw my Bohemian road trip almost to a close – just the one last push westwards to Prague remains.

> *"I'm soon relaxing in a warm bath of beer infused with fresh hop flowers while sipping on a tall glass of Czech lager"*

DIRECTIONS

Start // Prague
End // Prague
Distance // 429 miles (690km)
Getting there // Prague's Václav Havel Airport has frequent flights from many European and other international destinations. Key rail connections include Berlin, Munich, Budapest and Vienna.
When to go // June and September are the best months for good weather and to avoid the peak of summer tourism.
Further information // www.visitczechrepublic.com has lots of information in English.
Best castle to visit // Konopiště, en route from Tábor to Kutná Hora, is a huge castle and former home of Archduke Franz Ferdinand (of assassination and WWI fame).
Tip // Be aware of the alcohol content of the beers you're tasting, along with local driving regulations. Factor in overnight stays for sampling – or have a designated driver.

*Opposite: draining steins in a beer
garden during Munich's Oktoberfest*

MORE LIKE THIS
EUROPEAN BEER ROUTES

GERMAN BEER LOOP

Beer has been brewed in Germany for
three millennia. It's a major part of the
country's culture, with many regional styles.
Begin with a delicate straw-coloured *kölsch*
in the shadow of Cologne Cathedral
before heading southeast to Bamberg,
home of interesting *rauchbiers* made with
smoked malt. South, near the border with
Austria, Munich is famous for its golden
helles lagers and the annual Oktoberfest
beer festival, while to the north, in the
former East Germany, the traditional
beer style of Leipzig is *gose*, a tart beer
flavoured with salt and coriander. Nearby,
Berlin is famous for Berliner Weisse beers,
refreshingly low in alcohol, and often
spiked with berry syrup. To the southwest,
via Hanover and Saxony, Düsseldorf is the
heartland of copper-coloured *altbiers* – the
name translates to 'old beer', as this is one
of Germany's most historic brews.
Start // Cologne
End // Düsseldorf
Distance // 1130 miles (1818km)

SOUTHEAST IRELAND SUDS EXPLORER

Guinness in Dublin and Murphy's in
Cork are two of Ireland's most renowned
breweries, and linking these heavyweights
is this itinerary visiting up and coming
craft breweries in between. After touring
Guinness' historic St James's Gate brewery,
continue south for a hoppy Wildfire red
ale from Wicklow Wolf Brewery, before
making the 20-minute drive along the
Irish Sea to the Wicklow Brewery. Sunday
roast for lunch is always a good time to
visit the brewery's Mickey Finn's pub.
Continue through a patchwork of farmland
to YellowBelly Beer in County Wexford.
YellowBelly's seasonal brews include
unusual sours and farmhouse ales, while
the Gallow's Hill barley wine, found west at
the Dungarvan Brewing Company, is ideal
in cooler months. Complete a hop-fuelled
Irish journey with a pint of Murphy's stout at
the Shandon Arms in Cork.
Start // Dublin
End // Cork
Distance // 236 miles (380km)

TRAPPIST BEERS OF BELGIUM

Explore Belgium while tasting beers
from Trappist breweries, where monks
have been creating flavourful beers for
centuries before the contemporary focus
on craft beer. Begin northeast of Antwerp
at Café Trappisten, where Westmalle
beers are matched with cheeses also
made by monks from the adjacent
Westmalle Abbey. Heading south through
Brussels, beers from the Rochefort Brewery
are partnered at local cafés with venison
from the nearby Ardennes region. It's then
a 50 mile (80km) drive further south to
Orval for their bottle-conditioned beer,
a favourite of many craft brewers around
the world. To the northwest, a quick spin
of the wheels through France brings you
to Scourmont Abbey, the base for Chimay.
At the Poteaupré Inn at the Espace
Chimay visitor centre, try the Chimay 150,
originally brewed in 2012 to celebrate the
brewery's 150-year anniversary. From here,
it's then a two-hour drive north to Vleteren,
to end the trip with some excellent beers
from Westvleteren.
Start // Westmalle
End // Vleteren
Distance // 347 miles (558km)

INDEX

A

A1, Austria 208
A1, France 208
A1, Serbia 208
A7, Spain 106
A89, France 106
Albania
 Underrated Albania 22–25
Algarve, Portugal 190
Alnwick to Lindisfarne, England 296
Alta to Kirkenes, Norway 252
Andorra
 Port de Cabús 14–17
Anglesey, North Wales 214
Annecy, France 82
Apennines of Abruzzo, Italy 154
Appenzell to St Moritz, Switzerland 88
Arctic Highway, Norway 252
Argyll, Scotland 172
Asturias, Spain 38
Austria
 A1, The 208
 Lake Constance via Four Nations 130
 Ötztal Glacier Road 14
 Grossglockner Hochalpenstrasse 180–183
autobahn, Germany 220

B

B6318 Military Road, England & Scotland 76
Baltic Coast, Germany 240
Baltic Shores, Poland 284
Bath, England 114–117
Belfast, Northern Ireland 120–123, 258
Belgium
 Spa-Francorchamps 68
 Trappist Beers 314
 Wallonia 50
Belgrade, Serbia 302
Bernina Pass, Switzerland 136
Bertha Benz Memorial Route, Germany 76
Black Forest, Germany 202
Bohuslän Coast, Sweden 240
Bordeaux Wine Country, France 142
Bosnia & Hercegovina
 Balkan City-Hopping 308
 Split to Sarajevo 302
Bran Pass, Romania 278
Brenta Dolomites, Italy 154
Brittany, France 32
Bulgaria
 Fortress Route 286–289
 Narrow-Gauge Railway to Bansko 202
Bundesstrasse 258, Germany 220

C

Camino del Cid, Spain 76
campervan & camping road trips
 Across Orkney in an EV Campervan,
  Scotland 126–129
 Baltic Coast, Germany 240
 Bohuslän Coast, Sweden 240
 Moors to Dales, Yorkshire, England 130
 West Coast, Netherlands 240
 West Coast of Jutland, Denmark 236–239
Carpathians, Ukraine 290
Castilla-La Mancha, Spain 234
Catalonia, Spain 46–49
Chianti Road, Italy 178
Circuit de Monaco, Monaco 258
coastal road trips
 Across Orkney in an EV Campervan,
  Scotland 126–129
 Across the Top of Scotland 168–171
 Algarve, Portugal 190
 Alnwick to Lindisfarne, England 296
 Along Wales' Coastal Way 210–213
 Anglesey Circular, North Wales 214
 Archipelago Trail, Finland 100
 Argyll's Secret Coast, Scotland 172
 Around the Heel of Italy 52–55
 Baltic Shores, Poland 284
 Belfast Loop, Northern Ireland 120–123
 Brittany, France 32
 Circuit of Istria, Croatia 26
 Cornish Fishing Ports, England 100
 Costa Brava, Spain 44
 Croatia's Adriatic Highway 280–283
 Cruising the Coastal Camino, Spain 34–37
 Cruising Western Crete 58–61
 Curonian Spit, Lithuania 264
 Fort William to Mallaig, Scotland 172
 Gargano Peninsula, Italy 56
 Gower Peninsula, South Wales 214
 High Coast of Sweden 190
 Hvar, Croatia 44
 Isle of Arran, Scotland 160
 Isle of Wight, England 160
 Kefallonia, Greece 62
 Kirkenes to Grense Jakobselv, Norway 246
 Kystriksveien, Norway 248–251
 Legendary West Iceland 230–233
 Ligurian Coast, Italy 190
 Lipari Loop, Italy 112
 Long Way Round, Ireland 258
 Magic Circle, Iceland 254–257
 Menorca, Spain 50
 Milos, Greece 62
 Modern Art Meander, France 296
 Mountain Roads of Mallorca 10–13
 Naples & the Amalfi Coast, Italy 40–43
 Navigating the Fjords, Norway 308
 Naxos, Greece 62
 North Noast Gozo, Malta 112
 Norway's Lofoten Islands 224–227
 Norway's West Coast 260–263
 On the Front Lines in Belgium
  & France 192–195
 Outer Hebrides from Barra to Lewis,
  Scotland 172
 Peloponnese, Greece 44

Portugal's Atlantic Coast 186–189
 Roving the Baltic: Estonia to
  Lithuania 292–295
 Sardinia, North to South 28–31
 Senja, Norway 252
 Shetland, Scotland 160
 Snæfellsnes Peninsula, Iceland 32
 Southwest Coast, France 100
 Split to Sarajevo, Croatia & Bosnia 302
 Tinos, Greece 32
 Treasures of Catalonia, Spain 46–49
 Trieste to Piran, Italy & Slovenia 26
 Umeå to Rovaniemi, Sweden & Finland 246
 Varangerbotn to Hamningberg,
  Norway 246
 West Coast of Jutland, Denmark 236–239
 Wild Atlantic Way, Ireland 96–99
 Wild Westfjords, Iceland 266–269
 Wonders of Ancient Sicily 296
Corfu, Greece 112
Cornwall, England 100
Corsica, France 108–111
Costa Brava, Spain 44
Crete, Greece 58–61
Croatia
 Adriatic Highway 280–283
 Balkan City-Hopping 308
 Circuit of Istria 26
 Hvar 44
 Split to Sarajevo 302
cultural road trips
 Alnwick to Lindisfarne, England 296
 Alta to Kirkenes, Norway 252
 Around the Heel of Italy 52–55
 Balkan City-Hopping 308
 Belgrade to Ohrid, Serbia &
  North Macedonia 302
 Bohemian Beer Loop, Czech Republic 310–313
 Bordeaux Wine Country, France 142
 Bran Pass, Romania 278
 Brittany, France 32
 Castilla-La Mancha, Spain 234
 Circuit of Istria, Croatia 26
 Croatia's Adriatic Highway 280–283
 Cruising Western Crete 58–61
 Deutsche Märchenstrasse, Germany 94
 Dordogne River Valley, France 56
 Getting to Know the Sami, Sweden, Norway
  & Finland 242–245
 Latvia's Old Ways 228
 Legendary West Iceland 230–233
 Livradois-Forez, France 278
 Magic Circle, Iceland 254–257
 Menorca, Spain 50
 Modern Art Meander, France 296
 Northwestern Italy 234
 Norway's Lofoten Islands 224–227
 Piedmont, Italy 50
 Poland's Highlands 228
 Romancing the Road, Germany 90–93
 Roving the Baltic: Estonia to
  Lithuania 292–295
 Seville to Málaga, Spain 302
 Slovakia's Storied Route 59 274–277

Snæfellsnes Peninsula, Iceland 32
Southbound in Germany's East 162–165
South & Central England 234
Split to Sarajevo, Croatia & Bosnia 302
Tales of Wales 228
Tinos, Greece 32
Top Marks for Britain's Longest Road,
        England & Scotland 204–207
Tour of Transylvania, Romania 298–301
Treasures of Catalonia, Spain 46–49
Upper Lusatian House Road, Germany 166
Venetian Sojourn, Italy 284
Venice to Rimini, Italy 26
Wallonia, Belgium 50
Wooden Churches Route, Poland 278
Curonian Spit, Lithuania 264
Czech Republic
    Bohemian Beer Loop 310–313

D

Danube Bend, Hungary 124
Denmark
    West Coast of Jutland 236–239
Deutsche Burgenstrasse, Germany 94
Deutsche Märchenstrasse, Germany 94
Dolomites, Italy 150–153
Dordogne River Valley, France 56, 142
Douro Valley, Portugal 178
Dublin, Ireland 124

E

Edinburgh, Scotland 207
electric vehicles *see* sustainable road trips
Emilia-Romagna, Italy 16–19
England
    Alnwick to Lindisfarne 296
    B6318 Military Road 76
    Cornish Fishing Ports 100
    Hardknott & Wrynose Pass 148
    Isle of Wight 160
    Moors to Dales, Yorkshire 130
    Oxford to Bath via the Cotswolds 114–117
    Snake Pass 148
    South & Central England 234
    Top Marks for Britain's Longest
        Road 204–207
Estonia
    Roving the Baltic 292–295

F

Finland
    Archipelago Trail 100
    Finnish Lakeland 82
    Getting to Know the Sami 242–245
    Umeå to Rovaniemi 246
food & drink road trips
    Asturias, Spain 38
    Bohemian Beer Loop,
        Czech Republic 310–313
    Bordeaux Wine Country, France 142
    Chianti Road, Italy 178
    Cruising the Coastal Camino, Spain 34–37
    Culinary Circuit of Emilia-Romagna,
        Italy 16–19
    Douro Valley, Portugal 178
    Galicia, Spain 38
    German Beer Loop 314
    La Rioja, Spain 38
    Lavaux Vineyards, Switzerland 178
    Loire Valley Châteaux, France 138–141
    Milan & the Rice Region, Italy 20
    Portugal's National Route 2 102–105
    Rome to Naples, Italy 20
    Route des Vins d'Alsace, France 174–177
    Southeast Ireland Suds Explorer 314
    Southwest Coast, France 100
    Tasty Tour of Tuscany, Italy 20
    Trappist Beers of Belgium 314
Fort William, Scotland 172
France
    A1, The 208
    A89, The 106
    Annecy 82
    Bordeaux Wine Country 142
    Brittany 32
    Cathar Castles, Languedoc-Roussillon 142
    Corsican Grand Tour 108–111
    Dordogne River Valley 56
    Hilltop Villages of Provence 118
    Livradois-Forez 278
    Loire Valley Châteaux 138–141
    Luz Ardiden 14
    Modern Art Meander 296
    Mont Ventoux 184
    Route des Vins d'Alsace 174–177
    Route de Turini 68
    Route Napoléon 72–75
    Six-Sided Drive, France 258
    Southwest Coast 100
    Vallée de la Dordogne 142
Furka Pass, Switzerland 132–135

G

Galicia, Spain 38
Gallipoli, Turkey 196
Gargano Peninsula, Italy 56
Geneva to Neuchâtel, Switzerland 88
Geneva to Zermatt, Switzerland 201–204
Germany
    Baltic Coast 240
    Beer Loop 314
    Bertha Benz Memorial Route 76
    Bundesstrasse 258 220
    Deutsche Burgenstrasse 94
    Deutsche Märchenstrasse 94
    Driving on the Autobahn 220
    Fairy-Tale Drive in the Black Forest 202
    German Avenues Route 166
    Lake Constance via Four Nations 130
    Nürburgring-Nordschleife 216–219
    Oberjoch Pass 184

Romancing the Road 90–93
Southbound in Germany's East 162–165
Strasse der Romanik 94
Stuttgart, Germany's Motor City 220
Thuringian Forest Nature Park 166
Upper Lusatian House Road 166
Glasgow, Scotland 78–81
Gower Peninsula, Wales 214
Gozo, Malta 112
Gran Sasso e Monti della Laga National
        Park, Italy 270
Great St Bernard Pass, Switzerland 136
Greece
    Cruising Western Crete 58–61
    Kefallonia 62
    Milos 62
    Mount Pantokrator Circuit, Corfu 112
    Naxos 62
    Peloponnese 44
    Tinos 32
    Zagorohoria 264

H

Hardknott & Wrynose Pass, England 148
historical road trips
    Across Orkney in an EV Campervan,
        Scotland 126–129
    Alnwick to Lindisfarne, England 296
    B6318 Military Road,
        England & Scotland 76
    Bertha Benz Memorial Route,
        Germany 76
    Bulgaria's Fortress Route 286–289
    Camino del Cid, Spain 76
    Cathar Castles, Languedoc-Roussillon,
        France 142
    Costa Brava, Spain 44
    Cruising Western Crete 58–61
    Deutsche Burgenstrasse, Germany 94
    Driving Interest in Underrated
        Albania 22–25
    Gallipoli Campaign, Turkey 196
    Hilltop Villages of Provence,
        France 118
    Hill Towns of Central Sicily, Italy 56
    Hvar, Croatia 44
    Kirkenes to Grense Jakobselv, Norway 246
    Loire Valley Châteaux, France 138–141
    Medieval Spain 118
    Memories of Terror, Poland 196
    Moldova's Monastery Route 264
    Naples & the Amalfi Coast, Italy 40–43
    Naxos, Greece 62
    On the Front Lines in Belgium
        & France 192–195
    Oxford to Bath via the Cotswolds,
        England 114–117
    Peloponnese, Greece 44
    Route Napoléon, France 72–75
    Roving the Baltic: Estonia to
        Lithuania 292–295
    Sardinia, North to South, Italy 28–31

Slovakia's Storied Route 59 274–277
South to North in Moldova 290
Split to Sarajevo, Croatia & Bosnia 302
Strasse der Romanik, Germany 94
Tour of Transylvania, Romania 298–301
Tuscan Hill Towns, Italy 118
Umeå to Rovaniemi, Sweden & Finland 246
Vallée de la Dordogne, the Lot & Dordogne,
    France 142
Varangerbotn to Hamningberg, Norway 246
War & Peace in Russia 196
Wonders of Ancient Sicily 296
Wooden Churches Route, Poland 278
Hungary
    Round the Danube Bend 124
Hvar, Croatia 44

I

Iceland
    Legendary West Iceland 230–233
    Magic Circle, The 254–257
    Snæfellsnes Peninsula 32
    Through the Wild Westfjords 266–269
Ireland
    Dublin 124
    Long Way Round, The 258
    Southeast Suds Explorer 314
    Windswept Wild Atlantic Way, The 96–99
Isle of Arran, Scotland 160
Isle of Man TT Course 156–159
Isle of Wight, England 160
Istria Circuit, Croatia 26
Italy
    Apennines of Abruzzo 154
    Around the Heel of Italy 52–55
    Brenta Dolomites 154
    Chianti Road 178
    Culinary Circuit of Emilia-Romagna 16–19
    Gargano Peninsula 56
    Graceful Italian Lakes 284
    Gran Sasso e Monti della Laga
        National Park 270
    Hill Towns of Central Sicily 56
    In Pursuit of the Targa Florio, Sicily 64–67
    Ligurian Coast 190
    Lipari Loop 112
    Milan & the Rice Region 20
    Mille Miglia, Italy 68
    Naples & the Amalfi Coast 40–43
    Northwestern Italy 234
    Passo di Gavia 154
    Piedmont 50
    Rolling Through the Dolomites 150–153
    Rome to Naples 20
    Sardinia, North to South 28–31
    Stelvio Pass 184
    Tasty Tour of Tuscany 20
    Trieste to Piran 26
    Tuscan Hill Towns 118
    Venetian Sojourn 284
    Venice to Rimini 26
    Wonders of Ancient Sicily 296

J
Julier Pass, Switzerland 136
Jutland, Denmark 236–239

K
Kefallonia, Greece 62
Kirkenes to Grense Jakobselv, Norway 246
Kystriksveien, Norway 248–251

L
lakeside road trips
    Annecy, France 82
    E-Grand Tour of Switzerland 84–87
    Finnish Lakeland 82
    Geneva to Neuchâtel, Switzerland 88
    Graceful Italian Lakes 284
    Joining the Lochs from Glasgow,
        Scotland 78–81
    Lake Constance via Four Nations 130
    Lake Ohrid to Lake Prespa,
        North Macedonia 82
    Torridon to Diabaig, Scotland 148
Latvia's Old Ways 228
Lavaux, Switzerland 178
Ligurian Coast, Italy 190
Lipari, Italy 112
Lithuania
    Curonian Spit 264
    Roving the Baltic 292–295
Livradois-Forez, France 278
Loire Valley, France 138–141
London, England 204
Luz Ardiden, France 14–69

M
Magic Circle, Iceland 254–257
Mallorca, Spain 10–13
Malta
    North Coast Gozo 112
Maas to 'Mountains', Netherlands 124
Menorca, Spain 50
Milan & the Rice Region, Italy 20
Mille Miglia, Italy 68
Milos, Greece 62
Moldova
    Monastery Route 264
    South to North 290
Monaco
    Circuit de Monaco 258
Montenegro
    Montenegro's Canyons &
        Coastline 304–307
motorsports circuits see racing-circuit road trips
mountain road trips
    Apennines of Abruzzo, Italy 154
    Appenzell to St Moritz, Switzerland 88
    Bernina Pass, Switzerland 136
    Brenta Dolomites, Italy 154
    Bulgaria's Fortress Route 286–289

City to Carpathians Route, Ukraine 290
    Furka Pass, Switzerland 132–135
    Great St Bernard Pass, Switzerland 136
    Grossglockner Hochalpenstrasse,
        Austria 180–183
    Hardknott & Wrynose Pass, England 148
    Hill Towns of Central Sicily, Italy 56
    In Pursuit of the Targa Florio, Sicily 64–67
    Julier Pass, Switzerland 136
    Lapping the Nürburgring-Nordschleife,
        Germany 216–219
    Lugano to Zermatt, Switzerland 88
    Luz Ardiden, France 14
    Mont Ventoux, France 184
    Mount Pantokrator Circuit, Corfu 112
    Mountain Roads of Mallorca 10–13
    North–South Route, Switzerland 106
    Oberjoch Pass, Germany 184
    Ötztal Glacier Road, Austria 14
    Passo di Gavia, Italy 154
    Piedmont, Italy 50
    Poland's Highlands 228
    Port de Cabús, Andorra & Spain 14
    Rolling Through the Dolomites, Italy 150–153
    Route de Turini, France 68
    Route Napoléon, France 72–75
    Sardinia, North to South 28–31
    Shore to Summit from Geneva to Zermatt,
        Switzerland 201–204
    Stelvio Pass, Italy 184
    Treasures of Catalonia, Spain 46–49
    Underrated Albania 22–25
Myrdal, Norway 202

N
Naples & the Amalfi Coast, Italy 40–43
Naxos, Greece 62
Netherlands
    From Maas to 'Mountains' 124
    West Coast, The 240
Northern Ireland
    A Day on the Belfast Loop 120–123
North Macedonia
    Belgrade to Ohrid 302
    Lake Ohrid to Lake Prespa 82
    North to South 308
Norway
    Alta to Kirkenes 252
    Arctic Highway 252
    Getting to Know the Sami 242–245
    Kirkenes to Grense Jakobselv 246
    Kystriksveien, Norway's Coastal
        Highway 248–251
    Lofoten Islands 224–227
    Navigating the Fjords 308
    Norway's North 130
    Road & Rail to Myrdal 202
    Senja 252
    Varangerbotn to Hamningberg 246
    Winding Up on the West Coast 260–263
Nürburgring-Nordschleife, Germany 216–219

O

Oberjoch Pass, Germany 184
Orkney, Scotland 126–129
Ötztal Glacier Road, Austria 14
Oxford, England 114–117

P

Paris, France 208
Peloponnese, Greece 44
Piedmont, Italy 50
Poland
　　Baltic Shores 284
　　Eastern Poland's Forest Trail 290
　　Highlands, The 228
　　Memories of Terror 196
　　Wooden Churches Route 278
Port de Cabús, Spain 14
Portugal
　　Algarve 190
　　Atlantic Coast 186–189
　　Douro Valley 178
　　National Route 2 102–105
Provence, France 118

R

racing-circuit road trips
　　Around the Isle of Man TT Course 156–159
　　Circuit de Monaco, Monaco 258
　　In Pursuit of the Targa Florio, Sicily 64–67
　　Lapping the Nürburgring-Nordschleife,
　　　　Germany 216–219
　　Mille Miglia, Italy 68
　　Route de Turini, France 68
　　Spa-Francorchamps, Belgium 68
Romania
　　Bran Pass 278
　　Tour of Transylvania 298
Romantic Road, Germany 90–93
Rome to Naples, Italy 20
Route des Vins d'Alsace, France 174–177
Route de Turini, France 68
Route Napoléon, France 72–75
Rovaniemi, Finland 246
Russia
　　War & Peace 196

S

Sarajevo, Bosnia & Hercegovina 302
Sardinia, Italy 28–31
Scotland
　　Across Orkney in an EV
　　　　Campervan 126–129
　　Across the Top of Scotland 168–171
　　Argyll's Secret Coast 172
　　B6318 Military Road 76
　　Britain's Longest Road 204–207
　　Fort William to Mallaig 172
　　Isle of Arran 160

Joining the Lochs from Glasgow 78–81
North & West Highland Route 270
Outer Hebrides, from Barra to Lewis 172
Shetland 160
Torridon to Diabaig 148
Senja, Norway 252
Serbia
　　A1, The 208
　　Belgrade to Ohrid 302
　　Guča Festival, 290
Seville to Málaga 302
Shetland, Scotland 160
Sicily, Italy 56
Slovakia
　　Route 59 274–277
Slovenia
　　Trieste to Piran 26
Snæfellsnes Peninsula, Iceland 32
Snake Pass, England 148
Spa-Francorchamps, Belgium 68
Spain
　　A7, the 106
　　Asturias 38
　　Camino del Cid 76
　　Castilla-La Mancha 234
　　Costa Brava 44
　　Cruising the Coastal Camino 34–37
　　Galicia 38
　　La Rioja 38
　　Medieval Spain 118
　　Menorca 50
　　Mountain Roads of Mallorca 10–13
　　Port de Cabús 14
　　Seville to Málaga 302
　　Strait of Gibraltar & Los Alcornocales
　　　　Natural Park 270
　　Treasures of Catalonia 46
Split, Croatia 302
Stelvio Pass, Italy 184
Strasse der Romanik, Germany 94
Stuttgart, Germany 220
sustainable road trips
　　Across Orkney in an EV Campervan,
　　　　Scotland 126–129
　　E-Grand Tour of Switzerland 84–87
　　Lake Constance via Four Nations 130
　　Moors to Dales, Yorkshire, England 130
　　Norway's North 130
Sweden
　　Bohuslän Coast 240
　　Getting to Know the Sami 242–245
　　High Coast 190
　　Umeå to Rovaniemi 246
Switzerland
　　Appenzell to St Moritz 88
　　Bernina Pass 136
　　E-Grand Tour of Switzerland 84–87
　　Furka Pass 132–135
　　Geneva to Neuchâtel 88
　　Great St Bernard Pass 136
　　Julier Pass, Switzerland 136
　　Lake Constance via Four Nations 130

Lavaux Vineyards 178
Lugano to Zermatt 88
North–South Route 106
Shore to Summit from Geneva
　　to Zermatt 201–204

T

Targa Florio, Sicily 64–67
Thuringian Forest Nature Park, Germany 166
Tinos, Greece 32
Tirana, Albania 24
Transylvania, Romania 298–301
Trieste, Italy 26
Turkey
　　Gallipoli Campaign 196
Tuscany, Italy 20, 118

U

Umeå, Sweden 246
Upper Lusatian House Road, Germany 166

V

Vale of Ewyas, Wales 144–147
Vallée de la Dordogne, France 56, 142
Varangerbotn to Hamningberg, Norway 246
Veneto, Italy 284
Venice to Rimini, Italy 26
Vienna, Austria 208

W

Wales
　　Anglesey Circular 214
　　Coastal Way 210–213
　　Fforest Fawr 214
　　Gower Peninsula 214
　　Tales of Wales, The 228
　　Vale of Ewyas 144–147
Wallonia, Belgium 50
Westfjords, Iceland 266–269
Wild Atlantic Way, Ireland 96–99
wildlife road trips
　　Alta to Kirkenes, Norway 252
　　Eastern Poland's Forest Trail 290
　　Gran Sasso e Monti della Laga National
　　　　Park, Italy 270
　　Scotland's North & West Highland Route 270
　　Strait of Gibraltar & Los Alcornocales
　　　　Natural Park, Spain 270
　　Through the Wild Westfjords,
　　　　Iceland 266–269
　　Thuringian Forest Nature Park, Germany 166
wine *see* food & drink road trips

Z

Zagorohoria, Greece 264

Epic Road Trips of Europe
August 2022
Published by Lonely Planet Global Limited
CRN554153
www.lonelyplanet.com
10 9 8 7 6

Printed in Malaysia
ISBN 978 1 8386 9509 5
Text & maps © Lonely Planet 2022
Photos © as indicated 2022

General Manager, Publishing Piers Pickard
Associate Publisher Robin Barton
Commissioning Editor Peter Grunert
Designer Jo Dovey
Picture Research Ceri James
Editor Clifton Wilkinson
Index Polly Thomas
Print Production Nigel Longuet

Lonely Planet Global Limited
Digital Depot, Roe Lane (off Thomas St),
Digital Hub, Dublin 8,
D08 TCV4
Ireland
(EU authorised representative)

STAY IN TOUCH lonelyplanet.com/contact

Authors Ann Abel; Brett Atkinson; Alexis Averbuck; Oliver Berry; Garth Cartwright; Henry Catchpole; Alex Crevar; Rory Goulding; Anthony Ham; Alexander Howard; Anita Isalska; Gabrielle Jaffe; Vardhan Kondvikar; Stephen Lioy; Matt Master; Craig McLachlan; Etain O'Carroll; Richard Porter; Brandon Presser; Andrea Schulte-Peevers; Oliver Smith; Phoebe Smith; Regis St. Louis; Peter Thoeming; Orla Thomas; Glenn van der Knijff; Sara van Geloven; Kerry Walker; Luke Waterson; Christina Webb; Adam Weymouth; Tony Wheeler; Nicola Williams; Ali Wunderman.

Cover illustration by Ross Murray (www.rossmurray.com).